## DATE DUE

DEUTSCHES

ARCHAEOLOGISCHES INSTITUT

ERNEST NASH

# PICTORIAL DICTIONARY OF ANCIENT ROME

VOLUME II

FREDERICK A. PRAEGER, *Publisher*

NEW YORK

BOOKS THAT MATTER
Published in the United States of America in 1962 by
Frederick A. Praeger, Inc., Publisher, 64 University Place, New York 3, N. Y.
Copyright by Verlag Ernst Wasmuth Tübingen
All rights reserved
Library of Congress Catalog Card Number: 61–11329
The blocks are made by Graphische Kunstanstalten Meisenbach, Riffarth & Co, Berlin (302),
Carl Ruck, Stuttgart (302) and Künstle, Tübingen (60)
Printing and binding by Ensslin-Druck Reutlingen
Printed in Germany

# ABBREVIATIONS

## A. Bibliography

AA     Archäologischer Anzeiger, Beiblatt zum Jahrbuch des Deutschen Archäologischen Instituts, Berlin 1889 –

AC     Archeologia Classica, Roma 1949 –

ActaArch     Acta Archaeologica, Kopenhagen 1930 –

ActaInstSueciae     Acta Instituti Romani Regni Sueciae, Lund 1932 –

P. Adinolfi     P. Adinolfi, Roma nell'Età di mezzo, Roma 1881

AJA     American Journal of Archaeology, Concord, N. H. 1885 –

AJP     American Journal of Philology, Baltimore 1880 –

W. Altmann, Rundbauten     W. Altmann, Die italischen Rundbauten, Berlin 1906

W. Amelung, VatCat     W. Amelung – G. Lippold, Die Sculpturen des Vaticanischen Museums, Berlin 1903–1956

Ant     Antiquarium, descrizione delle collezioni dell'Antiquarium Comunale a cura del Governatorato di Roma, 1929

AntC     L'Antiquité Classique, Bruxelles 1932 –

Archaeology     Archaeology, a magazine dealing with the antiquity of the world, Brattleboro, Vermont 1948 –

ArchStor     Archivio Storico, Artistico, Archeologico e Letterario della città e provincia di Roma, Roma I–V, 1875–1883

ArchStorPat     Archivio della Deputazione Romana di Storia Patria, Roma 1878 –

Th. Ashby, Aqueducts     Th. Ashby, The aqueducts of Ancient Rome, Oxford 1935

Th. Ashby, Top 1581     A topographical study in Rome in 1581; a series of views by E. Du Pérac, ed. by Th. Ashby for the Roxburghe Club, London 1916

Athenaeum, NS     Athenaeum, studi periodici di letteratura e storia dell'antichità, nuova serie, Pavia 1923 –

AttiAccNapoli     Atti della Reale Accademia di Archeologia, Lettere e Belle Arti di Napoli, Napoli I–XXV 1865–1908; nuova serie, I–XV, 1910–1936

Atti...CStR     Atti del... Congresso Nazionale di Studi Romani
1. Roma 1929
2. Roma 1931
3. Roma 1935
4. Roma 1938
5. Roma 1939–45

AttiScStor     Atti del Congresso Internazionale di Scienze Storiche, V, Sezione IV, Roma 1904

Atti...StorArch     Atti del I Congresso Nazionale di Storia dell'Architettura, Firenze 1938
Atti del III Convegno Nazionale di Storia dell'Architettura, Roma 1940

BACrist     Bullettino di Archeologia Cristiana, Roma 1863–1894

BArte     Bollettino d'Arte del Ministero della Pubblica Istruzione, Roma 1907 –

A. Bartoli, Disegni     A. Bartoli, I monumenti antichi di Roma nei disegni degli Uffizi di Firenze, Roma 1914–22

BCom     Bullettino della Commissione Archeologica Comunale di Roma, Roma 1872 –

M. Bernhart, Münzkunde     M. Bernhart, Handbuch zur Münzkunde der römischen Kaiserzeit, Halle 1926

M. E. Blake I     M. E. Blake, Ancient Roman Construction in Italy from the prehistoric period to Augustus, Washington, D. C. 1947

M. E. Blake II     M. E. Blake, Roman Construction in Italy from Tiberius through the Flavians, Washington, D. C. 1959

P. H. von Blanckenhagen, FlArch     P. H. von Blanckenhagen, Flavische Architektur und ihre Dekoration untersucht am Nervaforum, Berlin 1940

H. Bloch, Bolli     H. Bloch, I bolli laterizi e la storia edilizia romana, Roma 1947

BMC, Emp     H. Mattingly, Coins of the Roman Empire in the British Museum, London 1923–1950

BMC, Rep     H. A. Grueber, Coins of the Roman Republic in the British Museum, I–III, London 1910

BollIstArch     Bollettino del Reale Istituto di Archeologia e Storia dell'Arte, Roma 1922–1943

L. Borsari, Top     L. Borsari, Topografia di Roma Antica, Milano 1897

C. E. Boyd, Libraries     C. E. Boyd, Public libraries in Ancient Rome, Chicago 1915

D. F. Brown, AN     D. F. Brown, Architectura Numismatica, part I, the temples of Rome (manuscript dissertation, New York University), New York 1941

D. F. Brown, Temples     D. F. Brown, Temples of Rome as coin types (Numismatic notes and monographs N. 90), New York 1940

BSR     Papers of the British School at Rome, London 1902 –

BullInst     Bullettino dell'Istituto di Corrispondenza Archeologica, Roma 1829–1885

M. Cagiano, AM     M. Cagiano de Azevedo, Le Antichità di Villa Medici, Roma 1951

| | |
|---|---|
| F. Cancellieri, Mercato | F. Cancellieri, Il mercato, il lago dell'Acqua Vergine ed il Palazzo Panfiliano nel Circo Agonale detto volgarmente Piazza Navona, Roma 1811 |
| Capitolium | Capitolium, rassegna mensile di attività del governatorato di Roma, Roma 1925 – |
| F. Castagnoli, CM | F. Castagnoli, Il Campo Marzio nell'antichità, in MemLinc, serie 8, vol. I, fasc. 4, Roma 1947 |
| ClJ | The Classical Journal (Classical Association of the Middle West and South, Classical Association of New England), Chicago 1905 – |
| ClPhil | Classical Philology, Chicago 1906 – |
| CodTop | R. Valentini – G. Zucchetti, Codice Topografico della città di Roma, Roma 1940–1953 |
| A. M. Colini, Celio | A. M. Colini, Storia e topografia del Celio nell'antichità, MemPontAcc VII, Roma 1944 |
| CR | The Classical Review, London 1887 – |
| CRAI | Comptes rendus des séances de l'Académie des Inscriptions et Belles Lettres, Paris 1857 – |
| Crd'A | La Critica d'Arte, Rivista bimestrale di arti figurative, Firenze 1935–1951 |
| L. Crema, ArchRom | L. Crema, L'Architettura Romana, Enciclopedia Classica, Sezione III, Vol. XII, Torino 1959 |
| C. D. Curtis, Arches | C. D. Curtis, Roman Monumental Arches, Supplementary Papers of the American School of Classical Studies in Rome, Vol. II, 1908 |
| De Gregori | G. De Gregori, Biblioteche dell'antichità, Accademie e Biblioteche d'Italia, XI, 1937, pp. 9–24 |
| R. Delbrück, HB | R. Delbrück, Hellenistische Bauten in Latium, Strassburg I, 1907, II, 1912 |
| E. De Ruggiero | E. De Ruggiero, Il Foro Romano, Roma-Arpino 1913 |
| DissPontAcc | Dissertazioni della Pontificia Accademia Romana di Archeologia, ser. 1, I–XV, Roma 1821–1880; ser. 2, 1–XV, Roma 1881–1923 |
| DizEpigr | E. De Ruggiero, Dizionario Epigrafico di Antichità Romane, Roma 1895 – |
| Doxa | Doxa, rassegna critica di antichità classica I–IV, Roma 1948–1951 |
| Ecclesia | Ecclesia, rivista mensile a cura dell'ufficio informazioni, Città del Vaticano 1942 – |
| EncArtAnt | Enciclopedia dell'Arte Antica Classica e Orientale, Roma 1958 – |
| EphEpigr | Ephemeris Epigraphica, Corporis Inscriptionum Latinarum Supplementum, Bd. I–IX, Berlin 1872–1913 |
| Epigraphica | Epigraphica, rivista italiana di epigrafia, Milano 1939–1948 |
| Eranos | Eranos, Acta Philologica Suecana, Upsala – Gothenburg 1896 – |
| A. Erman, Ob | A. Erman, Römische Obelisken, Abhandlungen der Preuss. Ak. der Wissenschaften, phil.-hist. Klasse, 1917, N. 4 |
| EsplVat | B. M. Apollonj-Ghetti, A. Ferrua, E. Josi, E. Kirschbaum, Esplorazioni sotto la confessione di San Pietro in Vaticano, Città del Vaticano 1951 |
| T. Frank, Buildings | T. Frank, Roman buildings of the Republic, Rome 1924 |
| FUR | G. Carettoni, A. M. Colini, L. Cozza, G. Gatti, La pianta marmorea di Roma antica, Forma Urbis Romae, Roma 1960 |
| V. E. Gasdìa, Casa | V. E. Gasdìa, La casa pagano-cristiana del Celio, Roma 1937 |
| O. Gilbert, Rom | O. Gilbert, Geschichte und Topographie der Stadt Rom im Altertum, Leipzig I, 1883, II, 1885, III, 1890 |
| C. Gioffredi, Tribunali | C. Gioffredi, I tribunali del Foro, Studia et Documenta Historiae et Juris, IX, 2, 1943, pp. 3–58 |
| Gnomon | Gnomon, Kritische Zeitschrift für die gesamte klassische Altertumswissenschaft, Berlin, München 1925 – |
| Heemskerck | Ch. Hülsen – H. Egger, Die römischen Skizzenbücher von Marten van Heemskerck, I und II, Berlin 1913–1916 |
| W. Helbig, Führer | W. Helbig, Führer durch die öffentlichen Sammlungen klassischer Altertümer in Rom, 3. Aufl. von W. Amelung, E. Reisch, F. Weege, Leipzig 1912–13 |
| Hermes | Hermes, Zeitschrift für Klassische Philologie, Berlin-Wiesbaden 1866 – |
| Hesperia | Hesperia, Journal of the American School of Classical Studies at Athens, 1932 – |
| P. Hommel, Giebel | P. Hommel, Studien zu den römischen Figurengiebeln der Kaiserzeit, Berlin 1954 |
| Hülsen-Carter | Ch. Hülsen, The Roman Forum, translated by J. B. Carter (2), Rome 1909 |
| Ch. Hülsen, Chiese | Ch. Hülsen, Le Chiese di Roma nel Medio Evo, Firenze 1927 |
| Ch. Hülsen, FR | Ch. Hülsen, Das Forum Romanum (2), Rom 1905 |
| Ch. Hülsen, Sangallo | Ch. Hülsen, Il libro di Giuliano da Sangallo, Codice Vaticano Barberiniano Latino 4424 I testo, II tavole, Lipsia 1910 |
| JdI | Jahrbuch des Deutschen Archäologischen Instituts, Berlin 1886 – |
| JHS | Journal of Hellenic Studies, London 1880 – |
| H. St. Jones, Cons | A Catalogue of the Ancient Sculptures preserved in the Municipal Collections of Rome. The Sculptures of the Palazzo dei Conservatori ed. by H. Stuart Jones. Oxford 1926 |
| H. Jordan, Top I, 1, 2 | H. Jordan, Topographie der Stadt Rom im Altertum Bd. I, 1 und 2, Berlin 1878, 1885 |
| H. Jordan, Top I, 3 | H. Jordan, Topographie der Stadt Rom im Altertum Bd. I, 3 bearbeitet von Ch. Hülsen, Berlin 1907 |
| H. Jordan, Top II | H. Jordan, Topographie der Stadt Rom im Altertum Bd. II, Berlin 1871 |
| JRS | The Journal of Roman Studies, London 1911– |
| E. Junyent, Titolo | E. Junyent, Il titolo di San Clemente in Roma, Roma 1932 |
| J. P. Kirsch, Titelkirchen | J. P. Kirsch, Die römischen Titelkirchen im Altertum, Paderborn 1918 |
| R. Krautheimer, Corp | R. Krautheimer, Corpus Basilicarum Christianarum Romae, I, Città del Vaticano 1937–1954 |
| D. Krencker, Kaiserthermen | D. Krencker – E. Krüger, Die Trierer Kaiserthermen, Augsburg 1929 |
| R. Lanciani, Frontino | R. Lanciani, Topografia di Roma Antica. I Commentarii di Frontino intorno le acque e gli acquedotti, silloge epigrafica aquaria. Roma 1880 (estratto degli Atti della R. |

|  |  |
|---|---|
|  | Accademia dei Lincei, ser. III, memorie della classe di scienze morali, storiche e filologiche, IV, 1879/80, pp. 215–616) |
| R. Lanciani, FUR | R. Lanciani, Forma Urbis Romae. Consilio et Auctoritate Regiae Academiae Lincaeorum, Mediolanum 1893–1901 |
| R. Lanciani, Ruins | R. Lanciani, The Ruins and Excavations of Ancient Rome, Boston and New York 1897 |
| R. Lanciani, Storia | R. Lanciani, Storia degli Scavi di Roma I–IV, Roma 1902–1912 |
| J. Le Gall, Tibre | J. Le Gall, Le Tibre, fleuve de Rome, dans l'antiquité, Paris 1953 |
| A. Lindsström | A. Lindsström, Kring Obeliskerna i Rom, Stockholm 1931 |
| G. Lugli, Centro | G. Lugli, Roma Antica, Il Centro Monumentale, Roma 1946 |
| G. Lugli, Mon I–III | G. Lugli, I monumenti antichi di Roma e suburbio, I–III, Roma 1930–1938 |
| G. Lugli, Mon IV | G. Lugli, I monumenti antichi di Roma e suburbio, supplemento, Roma 1940 |
| G. Lugli, MonMin | G. Lugli, Monumenti Minori del Foro Romano, Roma 1947 |
| G. Lugli, Roma Aet | G. Lugli, „Roma Aeterna" e il suo culto sulla Velia, Accademia Naz. dei Lincei, problemi attuali di scienza e di cultura, quaderno 11, Roma 1949 |
| G. Lugli, Tecnica | G. Lugli, La Tecnica Edilizia Romana, Roma 1957 |
| V. Lundström | V. Lundström, Undersokningar i Roms Topografi, Göteborg 1929 |
| L'Urbe | L'Urbe, Rivista Romana di Storia, Arte, Lettere, Costumanze, Roma 1936–43, 1947 – |
| H. Lyngby, ForBoarium | H. Lyngby, Beiträge zur Topographie des Forum-Boarium-Gebietes in Rom, Lund 1954 |
| MAARome | Memoirs of the American Academy in Rome, Rome 1917 – |
| MALinc | Monumenti Antichi pubblicati per cura del l'Accademia Nazionale dei Lincei, Milano e Roma 1890 |
| O. Marucchi, Ob | O. Marucchi, Gli obelischi egiziani di Roma (2), Roma 1898 |
| Matz-Duhn | F. Matz – F. von Duhn, Antike Bildwerke in Rom mit Ausschluß der größeren Sammlungen, Leipzig 1881–1882 |
| Mededeelingen Rome | Mededeelingen van het Nederlandsch Historisch Instituut te Rome, 's – Gravenhage 1921 – |
| Mél | Mélanges d'Archéologie et d'Histoire de l'École Française de Rome, Rome 1881 – |
| MemLinc | Memorie, classe di scienze morali, storiche e filologiche dell'Accademia Nazionale dei Lincei, Roma, ser. 6, 1925–1939; ser. 7, 1941–1944; ser. 8, 1947 – |
| MemPontAcc | Atti della Pontificia Accademia Romana di Archeologia, Memorie, Roma 1924 – |
| M. Mercati, Ob | M. Mercati, Degli Obelischi di Roma, Roma 1589 |
| J. H. Middleton | J. H. Middleton, The Remains of Ancient Rome, London 1892 |
| D. Mustilli | D. Mustilli, Il Museo Mussolini, Roma 1938 |
| Nardini – Nibby | Roma Antica di Famiano Nardini, ed. quarta Romana di Antonio Nibby, Roma 1818–1820 |
| NBACrist | Nuovo Bullettino di Archeologia Cristiana, Roma 1895–1922 |
| A. Nibby, RomAnt | A. Nibby, Roma nell'anno 1838, Parte I Antica, Roma 1838; Parte II Antica, Roma 1839 |
| NSc | Notizie degli scavi di Antichità, comunicate alla Accademia Nazionale dei Lincei, Roma 1876 – |
| ÖJh | Jahreshefte des Österreichischen Archäologischen Instituts, Wien 1898 – |
| B. d'Overbeke | Les restes de l'ancienne Rome, recherchez avec soin, mesurez, dessinez sur les lieux et gravez par feu Bonaventure d'Overbeke, sous les pontificats d'Innocent XI, d'Alexandre VIII et d'Innocent XII, Amsterdam 1709 |
| P-A | S. B. Platner – Th. Ashby, A Topographical Dictionary of Ancient Rome, London 1929 |
| Palladio | Palladio, Rivista di Storia dell'Architettura, Roma 1937–1943; N. S. 1951 – |
| A. Palladio, Terme | Le Terme dei Romani disegnate da Andrea Palladio e ripubblicate con la giunta di alcune osservazioni da Ottavio Bertotti Scamozzi, Vicenza 1797 |
| R. Paribeni, MusNaz | R. Paribeni, Le Terme di Diocleziano e il Museo Nazionale Romano (2), Roma 1932 |
| R. Paribeni, OP | R. Paribeni, Optimus Princeps, Messina 1926, 1927 |
| C. Pietrangeli, Scavi | C. Pietrangeli, Scavi e Scoperte di antichità sotto il pontificato di Pio VI (2), Roma 1958 |
| Platner-Bunsen, Beschreibung | E. Platner, C. Bunsen, E. Gerhard, W. Röstell, L. Urlichs, Beschreibung der Stadt Rom, Stuttgart und Tübingen 1829–1842 |
| A. Prandi, Cel | A. Prandi, Il complesso monumentale della Basilica Celimontana dei SS. Giovanni e Paolo, Roma 1953 |
| RA | Revue Archéologique, Paris 1844 – |
| RACrist | Rivista di Archeologia Cristiana, Roma 1924 – |
| RE | Pauly-Wissowa, Realencyclopädie der classischen Altertumswissenschaft, Stuttgart 1894 – |
| F. Reber, Ruinen | F. Reber, Die Ruinen Roms (2), Leipzig 1879 |
| RendAccNapoli | Rendiconti dell'Accademia di Archeologia, Lettere e Belle Arti Napoli, Nuova Seria XVI, 1936 – |
| RendLinc | Rendiconti dell'Accademia Nazionale dei Lincei, Roma ser. 6, 1925–1939, ser. 7, 1939–1943, ser. 8, 1946 – |
| RendPontAcc | Rendiconti della Pontificia Accademia Romana di Archeologia, Roma 1923 – |
| RhM | Rheinisches Museum für Philologie, 3. Folge, Frankfurt a. M. 1842 – |
| C. Ricci, VdI | C. Ricci, A. M. Colini, V. Mariani, Via dell'Impero (Itinerari dei Musei e Monumenti d'Italia No. 24), Roma 1931 |
| I. A. Richmond, Wall | I. A. Richmond, The City Wall of Imperial Rome, Oxford 1930 |
| O. Richter, Beiträge | O. Richter, Beiträge zur Römischen Topographie, I–IV, Berlin 1903–1910 |
| RINum | Rivista Italiana di Numismatica, Milano 1888 – |
| RivFil | Rivista di filologia e d'istruzione classica, Torino 1872 – |

| | |
|---|---|
| G. T. Rivoira, RomArch | G. T. Rivoira, Roman Architecture, transl. from the Italian by G. McN Rushforth, Oxford 1925 |
| RM | Mitteilungen des Deutschen Archäologischen Instituts, Römische Abteilung, 1886 – |
| Roma | Roma, Rivista di studi e di vita romana, Roma 1923–1944 |
| Röm Gebälke I | F. Toebelmann, Römische Gebälke, hrsg. von E. Fiechter und Ch. Hülsen, I. Teil, Heidelberg 1923 |
| Röm Gebälke II | H. Kähler, Römische Gebälke, II. Teil, Lief. 1: Die Gebälke des Konstantinsbogens, Heidelberg 1953 |
| RömQuart | Römische Quartalschrift für christliche Altertumskunde und für Kirchengeschichte, Rom und Freiburg 1887 – |
| P. Rosa, Relazione | P. Rosa, Relazione sulle scoperte archeologiche della città e provincia di Roma negli anni 1871–72, Roma 1873 |
| W. H. Roscher | W. H. Roscher, Ausführliches Lexikon der griechischen und römischen Mythologie, Leipzig 1884–1937 |
| L. Rossini, Archi | L. Rossini, Gli Archi di Trionfo degli Antichi Romani, Roma 1835 |
| G. Säflund, Mura | G. Säflund, Le Mura di Roma Repubblicana Upsala 1932 (ActaInstSueciae I) |
| M. Santangelo, Quirinale | M. Santangelo, Il Quirinale nell'antichità classica, MemPontAcc V, 2, 1941 |
| I. Scott Ryberg, Rites | I. Scott Ryberg, Rites of the State Religion in Roman Art, MAARome XXII, 1955 |
| F. W. Shipley, Agrippa | F. W. Shipley, Agrippa's building activities |
| StRom | in Rome, St. Louis 1933 (Washington University Studies, new ser., language and literature, No. 4) Studi Romani, rivista di archeologia e storia, Roma I, 1913, II, 1914, III, 1922 |
| E. Strong, SR | E. Strong, La Scultura Romana da Augusto a Costantino, Firenze 1923–1926 |
| S. Stucchi, Mon | S. Stucchi, I monumenti della parte meridionale del Foro Romano, Roma 1958 |
| Studi Romani | Studi Romani, rivista bimestrale dell'Istituto di Studi Romani, Roma 1953 – |
| H. Thédenat, FR | H. Thédenat, Le Forum Romain et les Forums Impériaux (6), Paris 1923 |
| E. B. Van Deman, Aqueducts | E. B. Van Deman, The building of the Roman aqueducts, Washington 1934 |
| M. J. Vermaseren, Corpus | M. J. Vermaseren, Corpus Inscriptionum et Monumentorum Religionis Mithriacae, Hagae Comitis I, 1956; II, 1960 |
| WarbJourn | Journal of the Warburg and Courtauld Institutes, London 1937 – |
| M. Wegner, Ornamente | M. Wegner, Ornamente kaiserzeitlicher Bauten Roms, Soffitten, Köln 1957 |
| E. Welin, SFR | E. Welin, Studien zur Topographie des Forum Romanum, Lund 1953 |
| F. Wirth | F. Wirth, Römische Wandmalerei vom Untergang Pompejis bis ans Ende des dritten Jahrhunderts, Berlin 1934 |
| G. Zoega | G. Zoega, De origine et usu obeliscorum, Roma 1797 |
| G. Zorzi, Palladio | G. Zorzi, I Disegni delle Antichità di Andrea Palladio, Venezia 1959 |

## B. Pictorial Sources

| | |
|---|---|
| Alinari | Fratelli Alinari S. A., Via Due Macelli 100, Roma |
| Anderson | Foto Anderson, Via del Babuino 98, Roma |
| Arch Vat | Archivio Fotografico Vaticano, Monumenti Musei e Gallerie Pontificie, Città del Vaticano |
| Ashby | British School at Rome, Via Antonio Gramsci 61, Roma |
| Brogi | Fratelli Alinari S. A., Via Due Macelli 100, Roma |
| Brunner | Brunner & Co., Via 27 Maggio 20, Como |
| Foro | Soprintendenza Palatino e Foro Romano, Via di S. Maria Nova 53, Roma |
| Fot | Fototeca di Architettura e Topografia dell'Italia Antica, Via Angelo Masina 5, Roma |
| GFN | Gabinetto Fotografico Nazionale, Via in Miranda 5, Roma |
| Inst Neg | Istituto Archeologico Germanico (Deutsches Archäologisches Institut, Römische Abteilung), Via Sardegna 79, Roma |
| Ist Rest | Istituto Centrale del Restauro, Piazza S. Francesco da Paola 9, Roma |
| MCR | Museo della Civiltà Romana, Archivio Fotografico, Palazzo Braschi, Piazza di S. Pantaleone, Roma |
| Mus Cap | Direzione dei Musei Comunali, Via della Tribuna di Campitelli 33, Roma |
| Mus Napoli | Soprintendenza alle Antichità della Campania, Via Museo 18, Napoli |
| Parker | British School at Rome, Via Antonio Gramsci 61, Roma |
| Pont Com | Pontificia Commissione di Archeologia Sacra, Via Napoleone III, 1, Roma |
| Prandi | Prof. Adriano Prandi, Piazza del Grillo 5, Roma |
| Rip X | Comune di Roma, Ripartizione X, Via della Tribuna di Campitelli 33, Roma |
| Sopr Lazio | Soprintendenza ai Monumenti del Lazio, Archivio Fotografico, Monumento a Vittorio Emanuele II, Via Aracoeli, Roma |

LACUS IUTURNAE. The sacred precinct of Iuturna, which lies immediately south-east of the three upright columns of the Temple of Castor, was excavated early in 1900. The complex consisted of the Lacus itself, an aedicula for the statue of the goddess, and other rooms, which, from the early part of the 4th century, were used by the STATIO AQUARUM, or headquarters of the Rome water service. According to legend, the Dioscuri watered their horses at the spring of Iuturna after they had brought news of the victory at Lake Regillus, in 496 B.C. Their statues were found in the basin, badly broken. They probably stood on the north side of the Lacus, in a small sanctuary which is recognizable on a fragment of the Severan marble plan.

R. LANCIANI, Storia II, p. 202; E. PETERSEN, RM XV, 1900, pp. 338–344; G. BONI, NSc, 1900, pp. 291–295; 1901, pp. 41–144; id., AttiScStor, pp. 530–539; V. FEDERICI, NSc, 1900, pp. 571–573; TH. ASHBY, CR XV, 1901, pp. 139–141; L. DEUBNER, Neue Jahrbücher f. d. klass. Altertum IX, 1902, pp. 370–388; D. VAGLIERI, BCom XXVIII, 1900, pp. 67–74, 285–295; XXXI, 1903, pp. 166–198; CH. HÜLSEN, RM XVII, 1902, pp. 67–71; XX, 1905, p. 81 f.; id., Klio II, 1902, pp. 233–235; id., FR, pp. 144–150; E. DE RUGGIERO, pp. 236–243; H. THÉDENAT, FR, pp. 120 f., 279–281; E. B. VAN DEMAN, JRS XII, 1922, pp. 5, 21; E. STRONG, SR, p. 233; P–A, pp. 311–313; R. ARTIOLI, Atti 3 CStR I, pp. 378–388; G. LUGLI, Centro, p. 183 f.; id., Tecnica I, pp. 25, 413; M. E. BLAKE I, p. 255; II, p. 26; V. ORAZI, Capitolium XXX, 1955, pp. 117–121; A. DAVICO, BArte XL, 1955, p. 346 f.; E. NASH, AC XI, 1959, pp. 227–231.

675 The Lacus Iuturnae seen from the Temple of Castor.                                                    Fot 91

676  The interior of the basin. The walls are opus reticulatum faced with marble.                    Fot 92

677 Marble altar with reliefs, which was found in the Lacus: Helena as Selene, goddess of light.      Fot 4331

678 Side of the altar, Iuppiter.      Fot 4332

679 The Dioscuri on the opposite side of the altar from the Helena relief.      Fot 4330

680 Leda, on the opposite side from Iuppiter.      Fot 4333

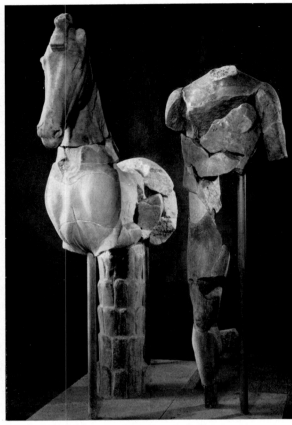

681, 682  The statues of the Dioscuri, found in the Lacus, now in the Antiquarium of the Forum Romanum.
GFN E 32247, 32249

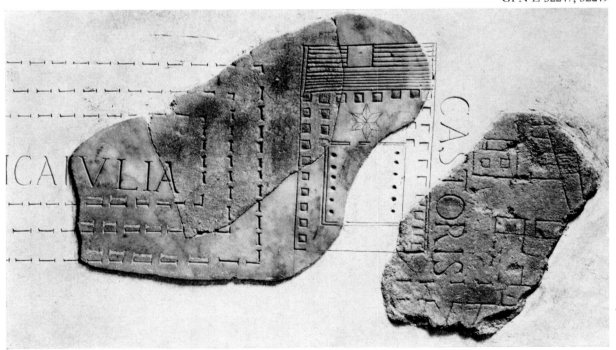

683  Fragment of the Forma Urbis (FUR, Tav. XXI, 18 a) showing a structure bordering on the site of the Lacus Iuturnae
with two square bases, probably a shrine for the statues of the Dioscuri.                                        Fot 3044

684 Palmette frieze which decorated the grand hall, where the statue of Aesculapius stands, east of the Lacus (s. Statio
    Aquarum II, 1185).                                                                                      Fot 3655

685 The Aedicula Iuturnae before its restoration.                           Fot 262

686  The Aedicula restored in 1953/1955.

687  The marble wellhead (puteal) with an inscription of M. Barbatius Pollio, who was Quaestor in 41 B. C.; later, as
      aedilis curulis, he restored the Lacus and the Aedicula.                                          Fot 4681

688  The altar in front of the puteal of Barbatius Pollio, with a relief showing Iuturna taking leave of her brother Turnus,
     King of the Rutuli.

Fot 4683

LACUS SERVILIUS. The fountain in the south-west part of the Forum, known as the Lacus Servilius, became famous at the time of Sulla, for it was there that the dictator exhibited the heads of the Senators he had ordered to be executed. Agrippa decorated the fountain with the statue of a Hydra. According to Festus (290), it was situated "in principio vici Iugari continens Basilicae Iuliae". At this point, where the vicus Iugarius meets the Sacra Via there is, between the steps of the Basilica Iulia and the buttress of the vicus Iugarius, a cavity which could have contained a fountain of modest dimensions (6.70 × 2.50 m.). The water was supplied by a conduit which branched off the Aqua Marcia behind the Temple of Saturn, on its way from the Quirinal to supply the Capitol. It was drained off into a channel which ran under the steps of the Basilica Iulia and into the Cloaca Maxima.

H. JORDAN, Top I, 2, p. 390; R. LANCIANI, BullInst, 1871, p. 241 f.; id., Ruins, pp. 274, 275, 278; H. THÉDENAT, FR, pp. 153, 175; TH. ASHBY, CR XVI, 1902, p. 94; E. B. VAN DEMAN, JRS XII, 1922, p. 25 f.; T. FRANK, Buildings, p. 75 f.; P–A, p. 314; F. W. SHIPLEY, Agrippa, p. 83 f.; A. M. COLINI, BCom LXVIII, 1940, p. 228; id., BullMusImp XIII (BCom LXX), 1942, p. 163 f.; G. LUGLI, Centro, p. 96; M. E. BLAKE I, p. 144; E. NASH, AC XI, 1959, pp. 231–233.

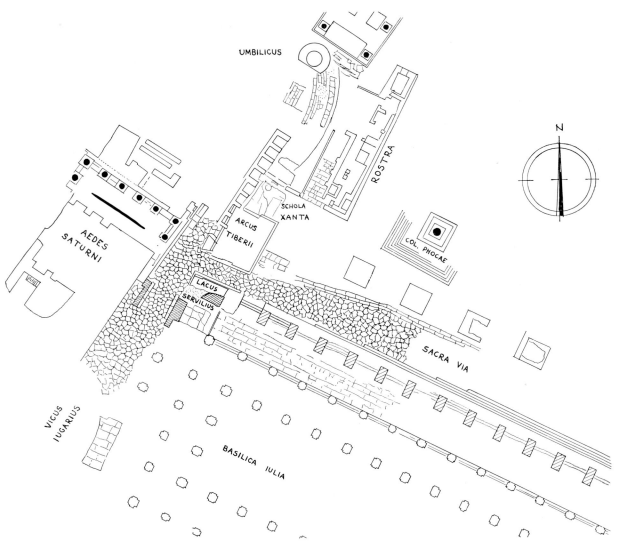

689 Site-plan of the Lacus Servilius at the entry of the vicus Iugarius into the Forum.

690 Cavity between the final pier of the Basilica Iulia (centre foreground) and the buttress of the vicus Iugarius which
   is built of square tufa blocks.

Fot 204

691 The cavity of the Lacus Ser-
    vilius at the junction of the
    vicus Iugarius and the Sacra
    Via; the drain is on the left
    under the steps.        Fot 82

692 Opening of the drain which ran under the steps of the Basilica Iulia into the Cloaca Maxima.        Fot 78

LAPIS NIGER. In January 1899, a square of black marble paving was discovered between the Comitium and the Forum, which Festus (177) and other Roman writers refer to as the Lapis Niger, or the TOMB OF ROMULUS. In May of the same year, a group of archaic monuments was found beneath it, consisting of a foursided stele with inscriptions (CIL VI, 36840), the stump of a conical column, and the foundations of a sacellum, with tufa bases in front of it which may have supported the statues of recumbent lions. Even in antiquity the meaning of these monuments was unknown. The so-called tomb was attributed not only to Romulus, but also to his foster father, Faustulus, or to Hostus Hostilius, the father of King Tullus. The excavations were resumed in 1955 and have confirmed that there is no tomb under the Lapis Niger.

G. BONI, NSc, 1899, pp. 151–158; G. F. GAMURRINI, ib., pp. 159–169; L. SAVIGNONI, NSc, 1900, pp. 143–146; D. COMPARETTI, Atene e Roma II, 1899, pp. 145–164; TH. ASHBY, CR XIII, 1899, p. 232 f.; XV, 1901, p. 85 f.; XIX, 1905, p. 77; CH. HÜLSEN, RM XVII, 1902, pp. 22–31; XX, 1905, pp. 40–46; id., FR, pp. 96–103; L. A. MILANI, RendLinc 5, IX, 1900, pp. 289–303; CIL I², 2, pp. 367–369; D. VAGLIERI, BCom XXXI, 1903, pp. 102–123; F. STUDNICZKA, ÖJh VI, 1903, pp. 129–155; E. PETERSEN, Comitium, Rostra, Grab des Romulus, 1904; G. PINZA, Il comizio romano nella età repubblicana, 1905, pp. 53–56; M. WARREN, AJP XXVIII, 1907, pp. 249–272, 373–400; O. RICHTER, Beiträge IV, pp. 5–10; E. DE RUGGIERO, pp. 215–229; H. THÉDENAT, FR, pp. 77–83, 242–245 (Bibl: p. 77 f.); E. B. VAN DEMAN, JRS XII, 1922, pp. 7, 23–25; T. FRANK, Buildings, p. 61 f.; P–A, pp. 482–484 (Bibl: p. 484); J. STROUX, Philologus LXXXVI, 1931, pp. 460–491; F. LEIFER-E. GOLD- MANN, Klio, Beiheft XXVII, 1932; L. A. HOLLAND, AJA XXXVII, 1933, pp. 549–553; E. NORDEN, Aus altrömischen Priesterbüchern, 1939, pp. 258–260; F. RIBEZZO, Atti 3 CStR I, pp. 325–341; P. DUCATI, Come nacque Roma, 1939, pp. 199–202, 210–214; P. G. GOIDÀNICH, Atti 4 CStR IV, pp. 107–112; id., MemLinc 7, III, 1943, pp. 317–501; E. GJERSTAD, ActaInstSueciae V, 1941, pp. 97–158; G. LUGLI, Centro, pp. 115–125 (Bibl: p. 125 f); id., MonMin, pp. 18–27 (Bibl: p. 1); id., Tecnica I, p. 248; M. E. BLAKE I, pp. 129, 146, 153; A. DEGRASSI, Doxa II, 1949, pp. 59–61; id., Inscriptiones lat. liberae rei publicae I, 1957, pp. 4–6; G. DUMÉZIL, Revue des Études Lat. XXXVI, 1958, pp. 109–111; G. A.–A. C. BLANC, AC X, 1958, pp. 41–49; G. MARCHETTI-LONGHI, AC XI, 1959, pp. 50–69; G. CARETTONI, JRS L, 1960, p. 195 f.; F. CASTAGNOLI, BCom LXXVII, 1959/60, p. 9 f.

693 The Lapis Niger, an air photograph of 1900.                                  Fot 6408

694  The group of archaic monuments beneath the Lapis Niger; left, the tufa bases of the sacellum.                Fot 51

695 The inscribed stele, dating from the end of the period of the Kings, second half of the 6th century B. C.; south and west sides.  Alinari 47007

696 The inscribed stele, north side.  Anderson 3512

697 The inscribed stele, east side.      Anderson 3192

Ludus Magnus. The Ludus Magnus was the principal training school for gladiators; it was known from the Regionary Catalogue and from inscriptions, as well as from fragments of the Severan marble plan, even before 1937, when part of the building was discovered between Via Labicana and Via di S. Giovanni in Laterano, about 60 m. east of the Colosseum. In the centre of a portico, an eliptical practice ring with two entrances, in the long and cross axes respectively, was surrounded by a narrow belt of low seats, arranged in tiers. The portico was enclosed in the multi-storeyed, rectangular building of the barracks.

R. Lanciani, Ruins, p. 386 f.; H. Jordan, Top I, 3, p. 298 f.; P-A, p. 320; V. Lundström, pp. 24–28; A. M. Colini, BCom LXVI, 1938, p. 246 f.; LXVII, 1939, p. 191; id., RendPontAcc XIV, 1939, pp. 61–66; id., Palladio III, 1939, p. 37 f.; id., Celio, p. 60 f.; H. Fuhrmann, AA 1940, pp. 452–455; M. Pallottino.

Roma XIX, 1941, p. 365 f.; G. Lugli, Centro, p, 347 f.; id., Tecnica I, p. 599; M. E. Blake II, p. 110; L. Crema, ArchRom, p. 298; FUR, p. 65, Tav. XVII. A. M. Colini – L. Cozza, Il Ludus Magnus, 1962 (Bibl: p. IX).

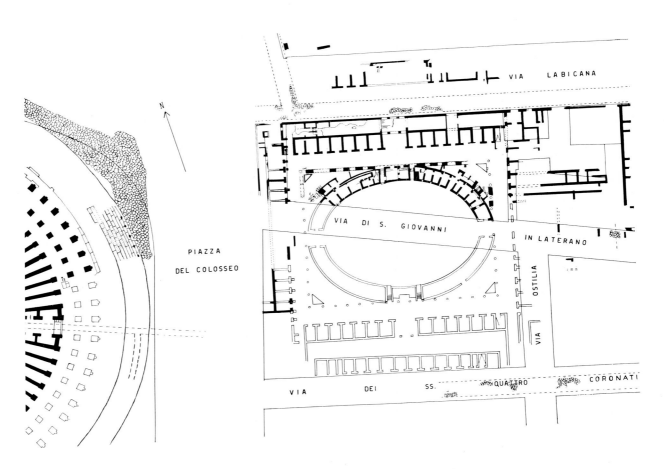

698 Site-plan of the Ludus Magnus, based on the 1960/61 excavations (Lucos Cozza).

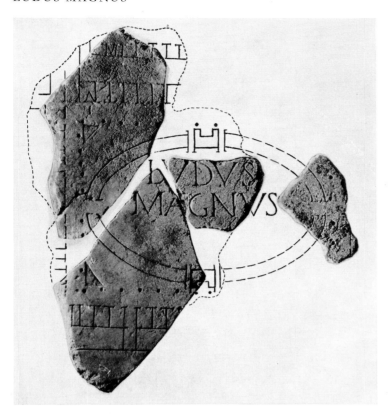

699 Fragment of the Severan marble plan with the inscription Ludus Magnus (CIL VI, 29844, No. 4). Detail of pl. XVII FUR.                    Fot 5929

700  Part of the Ludus Magnus excavated in 1937.                    Rip X  C/3667

701 Interior of the arena.   Fot 6385

702 The Ludus Magnus after further excavations and restoration in 1960/61.                    Fot 6390

MAGNA MATER, AEDES. A podium at the west corner of the Palatine has been attributed to the Temple of Magna Mater, which was built sometime after 204 B. C. to house the sacred black stone of the goddess, which had been brought to Rome from Pessinus. The temple was consecrated in 191 B. C. After a fire in 111 B. C., it was rebuilt by Q. Caecilius Metellus, who was consul in 109. It was restored again in 3 A. D., in the reign of Augustus, and a relief set into the garden façade of the Villa Medici shows the temple after this restoration. The ruins of the temple, which had been exposed since the beginning of the 19th century, were first identified as Magna Mater in 1873 by Visconti and Lanciani. During excavations in the cella in 1950, a great deposit of votive terracottas and numerous figurines of Attis were found; these, in conjunction with inscriptions, a statue of the goddess and marble fragments of a lion, which had already been discovered in the vicinity, confirm the identity of the temple as that of Magna Mater.

P. ROSA, Relazione, p. 77 f.; C. L. VISCONTI–R. LANCIANI, Guida del Palatino, 1873, p. 134 f.; O. RICHTER, Hermes XX, 1885, pp. 418–425; O. GILBERT, Philologus XLV, 1886, pp. 449–468; CH. HÜLSEN, RM X, 1895, pp. 3–28; R. LANCIANI, Ruins, pp. 132–135 (Bibl: p. 135); E. R. FIECHTER, RM XXI, 1906, p. 227; H. JORDAN, Top I, 3, pp. 51–54; K. ESDAILE, RM XXIII, 1908, pp. 368–374; H. GRAILLOT, Le culte de Cybèle, 1912, pp. 320–332; E. B. VAN DEMAN, AJA XVI, 1912, p. 393; Röm Gebälke I, p. 5 f.; T. FRANK, Buildings, pp. 96–98; P-A, p. 324 f.; L. FAGERLIND, ActaInstSueciae II, 1932, pp. 121 f., 130; H. KÄHLER, Die römischen Kapitelle des Rheingebiets, 1939, p. 8; G. LUGLI, Centro, pp. 431–434, 455 f. (Bibl: p. 434); id., Tecnica I, pp. 409, 456; II, Tav. XCVII, 2; M. E. BLAKE I, pp. 35, 178 f.; A. BARTOLI, MemPontAcc 3, VI, 1947, pp. 229–239; id., Rend PontAcc 3, XXIX, 1956/57, pp. 14–16; Fasti Archaeologici V, 1950, 4100; M. CAGIANO, AM, p. 40 No. 11; P. HOMMEL, Giebel, pp. 30–34; B. ANDREAE, AA, 1957, p. 182 f.; G. CARETTONI, JRS L, 1960, p. 200 f.

703 The Temple of Magna Mater on the Palatine.                                        Fot 382

704  The temple podium –
     east and north sides.
     Fot 380

705  The temple podium – west and north sides.                                Fot 6407

706 The statue of Magna Mater which was found in 1872 to the south of the temple, and fragments of a marble lion. Fot 5639

707 The front of the temple with the remains of an altar (on the left in the foreground).

Fot 378

708 The south end of a monumental stairway in front of the temple. The steps may have been used as seats for spectators
    of the ludi Megalenses.                                                                                  Fot 377

709 The Temple of Magna Mater on a Medici-Della Valle relief, set into the garden façade of the Villa Medici (s. a. Ara
Pietatis Augustae I, 77)                                                                                              Inst Neg 1838

MAGNA MATER IN CIRCO MAXIMO. A statue dedicated to the Magna Mater stood on the spina of the Circus Maximus, east of the central obelisk. In it, the Magna Mater is represented riding a lion. The Regionary Catalogue refers to it as "Aedes Matris Deum" (Notitia and Curiosum Regio XI). The statue of the Magna Mater on the lion in the Circus Maximus frequently appears on coins, reliefs, mosaics and terracotta lamps.

E. BRAUN, AnnInst, 1839, p. 247, Tav. N; E. HÜBNER, ib. 1863, p. 160 f.; K. ZANGEMEISTER, ib. 1870, p. 252 f.; O. KERN, RM V, 1890, p. 152 f.; W. H. ROSCHER II, p. 1667 f.; H. JORDAN, Top I, 3, pp. 138–141; H. GRAILLOT, Le culte de Cybèle, 1912, p. 335; DAREMBERG-SAGLIO, Dictionnaire (Circus) I, 2, figg. 1520, 1521, 1528, 1534; W. AMELUNG, VatCat III, pp. 128–130; P-A, p. 324; G. LUGLI, Centro, p. 604; G. V. GENTILI, BArte XLII, 1957, pp. 7–27.

710 Part of a fragment of a sarcophagus in the **Sala** Rotonda in the Vatican Museum. Magna Mater with the lion on the right of the obelisk.                                                                                    Inst Neg 3270

711 Detail of the Circus mosaic in the baths of the villa at Piazza Armerina. Magna Mater riding the lion, left of the obelisk. The carceres are at the right hand end of the mosaic.
Fot 5472

712 Sarcophagus relief in the Foligno Museum depicting the Circus Maximus. Magna Mater on the lion is to the right of the obelisk on the opposite side from the carceres.
Inst Neg 37.1338

MAGNA MATER, THOLUS. A round temple (tholus) of Magna Mater is thought to have stood near the Arch of Titus on the Sacra Via. Martial, in describing his route across the Forum to the Palatine, mentions a sanctuary of Bacchus, "tecta Lyaei", and a tholus of Cybele (Epigr. I, 70, 9 f.). It is possible that it is the sanctuary represented on a contorniate, which has the image of Diva Augusta Faustina on the observe side. The building on the Haterii relief, between the Colosseum and "Arcus in Sacra Via Summa", has been identified as the Tholus of Cybele, but, as the buildings on the relief are not in topographical order, it is impossible to determine their position. The triumphal arch surmounted by a quadriga, through which the statue of Magna Mater is seen, has not been identified. The statue of the goddess, standing at the top of a flight of thirteen steps leading up from an altar, seems to belong to a large temple, rather than to the small rotunda on the Sacra Via.

O. RICHTER, Hermes XX, 1885, pp. 418–425; CH. HÜLSEN, RM X, 1895, pp. 25–27; XVII, 1902, p. 96; W. H. ROSCHER II, p. 2917; G. SPANO, AttiAccNapoli XXIV, 1906, pp. 233 f., 250–253; H. JORDAN, Top I, 3, p. 103 f.; K. ESDAILE, RM XXIII, 1908, pp. 368–374; H. GRAILLOT, Le Culte de Cybèle, 1912, pp. 332–334; W. ALTMANN, Rundbauten, p. 71 f.; P-A, p. 325; L. DU JARDIN, Atti 3 CStR I, pp. 77–80; D. F. BROWN, AN, p. 171 f.; F. CASTAGNOLI, BCom LXIX, 1941, p. 66 f.; G. LUGLI, Centro, p. 219 f.; M. E. BLAKE II, p. 8.

713, 714 Contorniate of Diva Augusta Faustina, with a barrel-vaulted sanctuary of Cybele on the reverse face.
Fot 6410, 6411

715 The Haterii relief in the Museo Lateranense, showing a sanctuary of Magna Mater through a triumphal arch.
Inst Neg 39.565

MATIDIA, TEMPLUM. After the deification of Matidia, the mother of his wife Sabina, Hadrian erected a temple in her honour. It stood in the Campus Martius, east of the Pantheon. A coin, struck in 120 or 121 A.D., depicts the Temple of Matidia with the inscription "Divae Matidiae Socrui". The temple is shown between two aediculae, joined on either side to two-storeyed colonades. These evidently represent the BASILICA MARCIANAE and the BASILICA MATIDIAE, which are mentioned in the Regionary Catalogue (Reg. IX), as standing between the Pantheon and the Templum Antonini. A lead pipe, bearing the inscription "Templo Matidiae" (CIL XV, 7248) was found early in the 17th century; it branched north off the Aqua Virgo in Via del Seminario, and lay in the direction of the ruined columns and walls, between Piazza Capranica and Via dei Pastini, which presumably belonged to the Temple of Matidia. An engraving by Piranesi, entitled "Tempio di Giuturna", shows a row of five columns standing in an east-west direction, and two others in a different alignment (Antichità Romane I, Tav. XIV, fig. 1; Campus Martius, Tab. II, No. 26). All that remains visible to-day, is the stump of a cipollino marble column in the Vicolo della Spada d'Orlando. Two other columns to the west of it are said to be built into the house at No. 76 Piazza Capranica.

A. DONATUS, Roma vetus ac recens (2), 1648, pp. 292, 294; NARDINI-NIBBY III, p. 126; A. NIBBY, RomAnt II, p. 843 f.; PLATNER-BUNSEN, Beschreibung III, 3, pp. 145–147; F. CORSI, Delle pietre antiche, 1845, p. 98; F. REBER, Ruinen, p. 262; R. LANCIANI, BCom XI, 1883, pp. 5–16; id., Ruins, p. 502 f.; CH. HÜLSEN, RM XIV, 1899, pp. 141–153; H. DRESSEL, Coralla Numismatica in honour of B. V. Head, 1906, pp. 16–28; H. JORDAN, Top I, 3, pp. 575, XXIV; CH. HÜLSEN, ÖJh XV, 1912, pp. 132–142; R. PARIBENI, OP II, p. 57 f.; P-A, pp. 81, 331; G. LUGLI, Mon III, pp. 229–231; D. F. BROWN, AN, pp. 48–51; F. GNECCHI, Medaglioni Romani II, p. 5, No. 25.

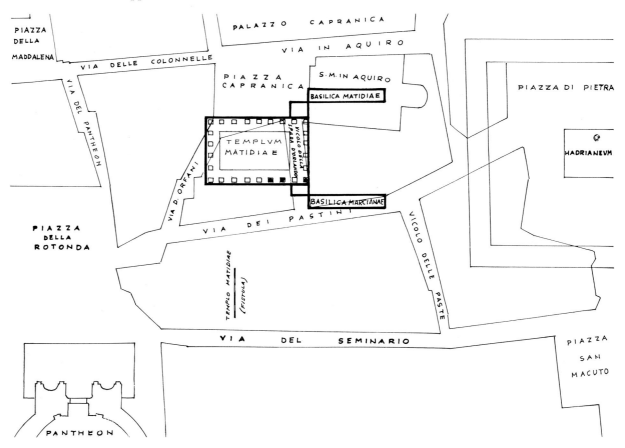

716 The presumed site of the Templum Matidiae, and the Basilicae Marcianae et Matidiae.

717 Coin of Hadrian, with the temple consecrated to
"Divae Matidiae Socrui".                    Fot 6409

718 Remains of walls and the stump of a column in Vicolo della Spada d'Orlando.                    Fot 6392

MAUSOLEUM AUGUSTI. In 28 B. C. Augustus built a monumental tomb for himself and his family, for which the word Mausoleum was used even in antiquity. The first to be buried there, in 23 B. C., was Marcellus, the son of Augustus' sister Octavia and the heir presumptive; then his grandsons Gaius and Lucius, and Augustus himself in 14 A. D. Nerva was the last Roman emperor to be buried there, in 98 A. D. In the middle ages, the tomb became a stronghold of the Colonna family; the fortress was destroyed in 1167. In the 15th and 16th centuries there was a garden in the ruins; and in the 18th century a wooden amphitheatre was built into it, and used for bull-fighting until the 19th century. Later, circus and theatrical performances took place there. In 1907, it was turned into a concert hall, with accomodation for 3500, and at the same time the first organized excavation was started, although small attempts had been made in 1519 and 1793. The excavations which started in 1907 were resumed in 1926, and by 1930 the crypt below the concert hall had been completely cleared. The final and definitive excavation of the monument began in 1934, during which houses surrounding the tomb were pulled down. After the last concert of the Orchestra of the Accademia di Santa Cecilia had taken place on the 13th May 1936, work started on the mausoleum itself. The excavation and restoration of the ancient structure were completed in October 1938.

A. BARTOLI, Disegni, Tav. CXI, fig. 197, CXII, figg. 199, 200, CXIV, fig. 204, CXV, fig. 205; A. NIBBY, Rom Ant II, pp. 520–532; F. REBER, Ruinen, pp. 287–292; R. LANCIANI, BCom X, 1882, pp. 152–155; id., Ruins, pp. 461–464; id., Storia II, pp. 13–19; O. HIRSCHFELD, Sitzungsberichte d. Berliner Akademie 1886, pp. 1149–1160; F. CERASOLI, BCom XXIII, 1895, p. 301 f.; H. JORDAN, Top I, 3, pp. 614–620; V. GARDTHAUSEN, RM XXXVI–XXXVII, 1921/22, pp. 111–144; A. M. COLINI-G.A. GIGLIOLI, BCom LIV, 1926, pp. 191–234; R. A. CORDINGLEY – I.A. RICHMOND, BSR X, 1927, pp. 23–35; P-A, pp. 332–335 (Bibl: p. 335); G. A. GIGLIOLI, Capitolium VI, 1930, pp. 532–567; G. GATTI, ib. X, 1934, pp. 457–464; A. MUÑOZ, ib. XIII, 1938, pp. 491–508; G. GATTI, BCom LXVI, 1938, pp. 273–275; id., L'Urbe III, 1938, 8, pp. 1–17; B. GOETZE, Ein röm. Rundgrab in Falerii, 1939, pp. 33–80; D. MUSTILLI, p. 21; G. LUGLI, Mon III, pp. 194–211; E. KORNEMANN, Klio XXXI, 1938, pp. 83–85; id., VI. Internat. Kongreß f. Archäologie, Berlin 1939, p. 471; A. M. COLINI, BCom LXVII, 1939, p. 206 f.; M. E. BLAKE I, pp. 171 f., 264 f., 345; C. PIETRANGELI, Scavi, p. 70 f.; G. LUGLI, Tecnica II, Tav. CXXXIV, 2; L. CREMA, ArchRom, p. 243 f.

719 The Mausoleum of Augustus. Air photograph.                                                          Fot 4371

720 The tombstone of Augustus' sister Octavia and her son Marcellus, found during the excavation of the crypt in 1927.
Rip X  C/504

721 The Tomb of Augustus after the excavations and restorations 1936–1938.                    Fot 1076

722 The base of the monument with the entrance.                                          Fot 1082

723 Perimeter wall and burial chamber (left).

Fot 1091

724 The concrete of the base with remains of opus quadratum during the excavations in 1937. Fot 1086

725 Tombstone of Agrippina the Elder (CIL VI, 886) who died in exile in 33 A. D., and was buried in the Mausoleum by her son Caligula after his accession in 37 A. D. (in the Museo Nuovo Capitolino).     Inst Neg 41.2310

MAUSOLEUM HADRIANI. The Mausoleum of Augustus was closed after the death of Nerva, and Trajan's ashes had been deposited in the base of the Columna Traiani. Hadrian, therefore, started to build a mausoleum for himself, his family and his successors, on the right bank of the Tiber in the GARDENS OF DOMITIA. The building was consecrated in 139 A. D. by his successor, and was dedicated to the deceased emperor and his already deified consort, "DIVA SABINA" (CIL VI, 984). Hadrian and Sabina, and L. Aelius Caesar, an adopted son, were buried in the mausoleum; also the Antonines, until Commodus (CIL VI, 984–995), for which reason it was also called the "Antoninorum Sepulcrum" (Hist. Aug., vita Severi 24). In later editions of the Regionary Catalogue (after 403 A. D.), the "Hadrianium" is described as a fortified bridgehead of the Pons Aelius. It was besieged by the Goths in 537, and in the battle, the defenders cast the marble statues which adorned it down on to their assailants. Originally, the mausoleum had a base 89 m. square, above which rose a marble-faced drum, 64 m. in diameter and 21 m. high, which enclosed the burial chamber. On the top was a mound of earth, planted with cypresses and crowned, either by a statue of Hadrian or by a quadriga.

A. NIBBY, Rom Ant II, pp. 488–518; H. JORDAN, Top II, pp. 166 f., 430–435, 580; R. LANCIANI, BCom XVI, 1888, pp. 129–131; TH. ASHBY, Top 1581, pp. 51–55; L. BORSARI, NSc, 1892, pp. 420–428; CH. HÜLSEN, RM VI, 1891, pp. 137–145; R. LANCIANI, Ruins, pp. 551–560; H. EGGER, Codex Escurialensis, 1906, p. 94; H. JORDAN, Top I, 3, pp. 663–667; E. RODOCANACHI, Le Château de St. Ange, 1909; M. BORGATTI, Annuario Accad. S. Luca I, 1909/11, pp. 121–125; CH. HÜLSEN, Boll. Assoc. Arch. Romana III, 1913, pp. 25–32; G. MCN. RUSHFORTH, JRS IX, 1919, p. 21; S. R. PIERCE, ib. XV, 1925, pp. 75–103; G. CULTRERA, MemLinc 5, XVII, 1923, p. 525 f.; P-A, pp. 336–338; M. BORGATTI, Castel Sant'Angelo in Roma, 1931; G. LUGLI, Mon III, pp. 693–708; id., Tecnica I, p. 605 f.; II, Tavv. CLXIX, 4, CCIV, 3; R. ARTOLI, Atti 4 CStR II, pp. 29–36; H. BLOCH, Bolli, pp. 253–256; D. E. STRONG, BSR XXI, 1953, pp. 129–147; L. CREMA, ArchRom, p. 484.

726 The Mausoleum of Hadrian.

727 The tomb chamber of the mausoleum.

Anderson 3085

728  The core of the drum which encloses the tomb chamber; originally it was faced with marble.                    Fot 1104

729  The tufa opus quadratum of the core of the drum.                          Fot 1103

730 Capital of a corner pilaster from the rectangular podium of the monument. Fot 1106

731 Frieze of bull's heads and garlands, found in 1891 in front of the entrance. Fot 1107

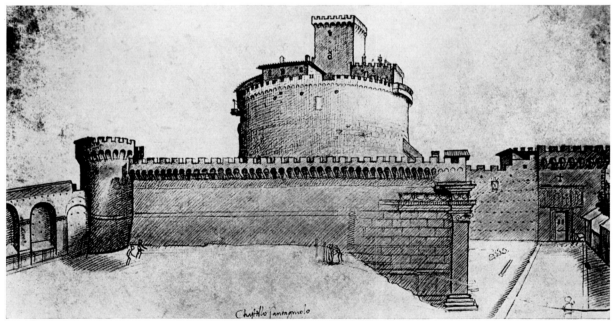

732 A view of the tomb in the last quarter of the 15th century (Codex Escurialensis fol. 30 v.). Inst Neg 2321

MERCATUS TRAIANI. The eastern exedra of Trajan's Forum is surrounded by a complex of buildings set against the slope of the Quirinal, and supporting the hill where it was hollowed out for the construction of the Forum. These buildings were erected in the first decade of the 2nd century A. D., before the Forum was built, and served as a market for general trading, and perhaps also for the public distribution of corn. There were 150 individual shops (tabernae), a great two-storeyed hall, and rooms with water tanks for the sale of fish and liquids; there were also offices for administration. Streets on three different levels provided access to the buildings; the street on the lowest level passed between the precinct wall of the Forum and the market, the middle one, with the mediaeval name of Via Biberatica (derived from Piperataria or Piperatica), led through the shops of the third storey. The upper street gave access to the shops facing the Quirinal. The buildings belonging to Trajan's Market were excavated in 1929/30.

A. NIBBY, RomAnt II, pp. 205–207; H. JORDAN, Top I, 2, p. 457 f.; G. BONI, NSc, 1907, pp. 414–427; C. RICCI, BArte V, 1911, pp. 445–455; id., Il mercato di Traiano, 1929; G. T. RIVOIRA, RomArch, p. 113; R. PARIBENI, OP II, pp. 80–82; P–A, p. 240 f.; G. GIOVANNONI, Architettura e Arti Decorative IX, 1929, pp. 281–287; G. LUGLI, Dedalo X, 1929/30, pp. 527–551; A. BOETHIUS, Roma IX, 1931, pp. 447–454, 501–508; R. M. RIEFSTAHL, Roma X, 1932, pp. 159–170; A. BOETHIUS–N. CARLGREN, ActaArch III, 1932, pp. 181–183; C. RICCI, VdI, pp. 115–120; A. M. COLINI, BCom LXI, 1933, pp. 253–257 (Bibl: pp. 254–256); R. PARIBENI, NSc, 1933, pp. 503–523; G. LUGLI, Historia VII, 1933, p. 22, fig. 6; A. VON GERKAN, RM LV, 1940, p. 16; A. PERNIER, Atti III StorArch, pp. 103–113; G. LUGLI, Centro, pp. 299–309 (Bibl: p. 309); id., Tecnica I, pp. 566 f., 602; II, Tavv. CLXVIII, 3, CCI, 1; H. BLOCH, Bolli, pp. 49–57; L. CREMA, ArchRom, p. 363 f.; G. INCISA DELLA ROCCHETTA, Miscellanea Bibliothecae Hertzianae, 1961, pp. 202–206.

733 The buildings of Trajan's Market, in the foreground is part of the perimeter wall of the Forum of Trajan.   Fot 484

734  Via Biberatica, seen from Via 4 Novembre.                                                                                          Fot 488

735  Via Biberatica, with the shops of the third storey.                              Fot 489

736  Via Biberatica above the hemicyclium of Trajan's Market.                                    Fot 490

737  The façade of the market building on Via Campo Carleo.                                       Fot 491

738 The façade of the hemicyclium. Fot 486

739  The great hall of Trajan's Market on Via 4 Novembre.                                    Rip X  C/2142

740  A court and the administration offices on the 3rd storey of the market.                    Rip X  C/440

741 Stairway with the great hall in the background, during excavations in 1929.                    Fot 3026

742 Street on the side of the market facing the Quirinal.

Fot 487

743  Shops on the Quirinal side in the Salita del Grillo; top right are remains of the republican city wall in opus quadratum.
Fot 3703

META ROMULI. Until the end of the 15th century, a pyramid tomb, known since the middle ages as the Meta Romuli, stood at the intersection of the ancient Via Cornelia and Via Triumphalis. In 1500, Pope Alexander VI wished to link St. Peter's with the Castel Sant'Angelo in preparation for the Holy Year, and the part of the pyramid which would have projected into the new Via Alexandrina (later Borgo Nuovo) was pulled down. The part of the pyramid, spared by the road, remained visible until the middle of the 16th century. It is mentioned in a document dated 5th February 1521, in connection with the transfer of property "in parte super area olim vulgariter nuncupata la meta": and it also appears on Bufalini's map of 1551, under the name of SEPULCRUM SCIPIONIS AFRICANI. The foundation of the pyramid was rediscovered in 1948 when the site at the north-east corner of Via della Conciliazione was being excavated for the foundation of the "Casa del Pellegrino".

NARDINI-NIBBY III, p. 367 f.; H. JORDAN, Top II, p. 405 f.; R. LANCIANI, MALinc I, 1889, pp. 525–527; id., Pagan and Christian Rome, 1893, p. 270 f.; id., Storia I, pp. 126, 161, 186–188; CH. HÜLSEN, Diss PontAcc 2, VIII, 1903, pp. 383–387; H. JORDAN, Top I, 3, p. 659 f.; H. EGGER, Codex Escurialensis, 1906, p. 63; G. TOMASSETTI, BCom XXXVI, 1908, pp. 26-30; M. MARCHETTI, ib. XLII, 1914, p. 395 f.; G. McN. RUSHFORTH, JRS IX, 1919, pp. 42, 56; CH. HÜLSEN, Chiese, p. 370 f.; P-A, p. 340; B. M. PEEBLES, RendPontAcc XII, 1936, pp. 21–63; G. LUGLI, Mon III, p. 678; G. GATTI, Fasti Archaelogici IV, 1949, 3771; id., BCom LXXIII, 1949, Appendice XVI, p. 107; Espl.Vat, p. 17.

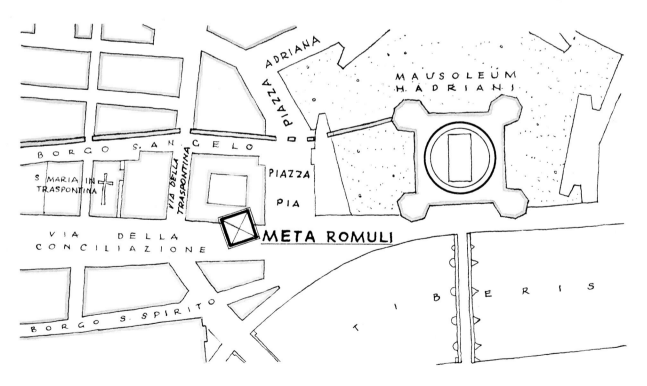

744 Site-plan of the Meta Romuli after the 1948/49 excavations (according to information by G. Gatti).

745  The Meta Romuli, between the Vatican Palace and the Castel Sant'Angelo, in a drawing in the Codex Escurialensis
     (fol. 7 v., 8).                                                                         Fot 6147

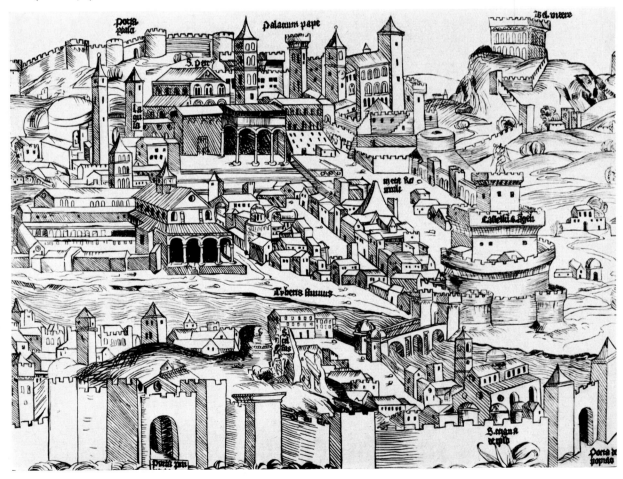

746  The pyramid entitled "Meta Romuli" in the Liber Chronicarum by Hartmann Schedel (Nuremberg 1493).  Fot 4268

META SUDANS. The ruins of a monumental fountain with the ancient name of Meta Sudans stood, until 1936, between the Arch of Constantine and the Colosseum. Although the fountain appears near the Colosseum on a coin of Titus, of 80 A.D., both ancient sources and recent research attribute its erection to Domitian, in whose reign the coin was presumably struck and put into circulation (A. v. Gerkan, RM XL, 1925, p. 28 f.). The ruins of the fountain were first excavated and examined in April 1743, and the half destroyed core of the cone was restored several times. The monument was completely excavated and studied, in 1933, before it was finally demolished. The place where it stood marked the meeting point of five regions of Augustan Rome: I Porta Capena, II Caelimontium, III Isis et Serapis, IV Templum Pacis, X Palatium.

s. a. Colossus Neronis I, 317.

F. DE FICORONI, Le Vestigia e Rarità di Roma, 1744, pp. 36–38; A. CASSIO, Corso delle Acque II, 1757, pp. 194–201; A. NIBBY, RomAnt I, pp. 370–372; PLATNER–BUNSEN, Beschreibung III, 1, p. 312 f.; R. LANCIANI, Ruins, p. 190 f. (Bibl: p. 191); H. JORDAN, Top I, 3, p. 24 f.; A. PASQUI, NSc, 1909, p. 428; E. B. VAN DEMAN, AJA XVI, 1912, p. 413; A. M. COLINI, RendPontAcc XIII, 1937, pp. 15–39; id., BCom LXVI, 1938, p. 247; G. LUGLI, Capitolium XVIII, 1943, p. 205; id., Centro, pp. 311–313; M. E. BLAKE II, p. 110 f.; L. CREMA, ArchRom, p. 578; M. BERNHART, Münzkunde, p. 137, Taf. 96, 1–3; BMC, Emp II, p. 262, pl. 50, 2; pl. 70, 1.

747  The Meta Sudans in front of the Colosseum.                    Brogi 3634

748 The excavation of the Meta Sudans in 1933; in the background is the base of the Colossus Neronis (s. a. I, 316,
    318) which, with the fountain, was removed in 1936.
                                                                            Rip X  C/2189

749 Coin of Titus of 80 A. D. with the Meta Sudans left
of the Colosseum.                        Fot 6414

750 The concrete core of the cone of the fountain. Most of the brick facing dates from a restoration early in the 19th
century.                                                                Alinari 17362

MILLIARIUM AUREUM. From the evidence of Roman writers the Milliarium Aureum, the Golden Milestone, erected by Augustus in 20 B. C., stood "in capite Fori Romani" (Plinius, Nat. Hist. III, 66), "sub aede Saturni" (Suetonius, Otho 6; Tacitus, Hist. I, 27). It was a marble column covered with gilt bronze which recorded the distances to the great cities of the empire. Part of the column was discovered and, in 1835, set up on the Umbilicus Romae (q. v. II, 1302), which, at that time, was wrongly identified as the Milliarium. To-day, this column drum lies below the Temple of Saturn, beside a circular marble plinth decorated with palmettes which was found in 1852, between the Rostra and the Basilica Iulia. During the excavation of Diocletian's monument to the Tetrarchs (s. Basis Decennalia I, 224), in October 1959, a concrete foundation was discovered south-east of the Hemicyclium of the Rostra; from its position and size, it may well be attributed to the Milliarium Aureum.

C. BUNSEN, BullInst, 1835, p. 78 f.; L. ROSSINI, Archi, p. 9, Tav. LII; E. BRAUN, BullInst, 1852, p. 81; G. MONTIROLI, Osservazioni sulla topografia della parte meridionale del Foro Romano, 1859, p. 13; H. JORDAN, Top I, 2, p. 244 f.; id., AnnInst, 1883, p. 56 f.; G. B. DE ROSSI, Piante iconografiche di Roma, 1879, p. 31 f.; O. RICHTER, Rekonstr. u. Geschichte der römischen Rednerbühne, 1884, pp. 35–39; id., Beiträge II, p. 12 f.; F. M. Nichols, Notizie dei Rostri, 1885, p. 5; R. LANCIANI, Ruins, p. 280; CH. HÜLSEN, FR, p. 75 f.; H. THÉDENAT, FR, pp. 133 f., 229–231; E. DE RUGGIERO, p. 374 f.; P-A, p. 342; G. LUGLI, Centro, p. 147; M. E. BLAKE I, p. 340.

751 Marble decoration of the base and the fragment of the shaft of the Milliarium Aureum.                    Fot 57

752 Concrete foundation of the Milliarium Aureum; in the background is the Umbilicus Romae and, on the right, the
    steps of the Hemicyclium.                                                      Fot 5788

MINERVA CHALCIDICA. The Temple of Minerva Chalcidica in the Campus Martius is attributed to Domitian, and is known from the Curiosum of the Constantinian Regionary Catalogue, where it is listed as standing between the Serapaeum and the Divorum. The Severan marble plan shows a circular building between the Porticus Divorum and the Temple of Isis and Serapis, of which the fragmentary inscription was first interpreted as "Lavacrum Agrippinae" (Bellori 1673), and later as "Lavacrum Agrippae" (Sjöqvist 1946). A recently discovered fragment of the marble plan, published in 1960, supplements the inscription, which now reads "Minerva" and makes it possible to identify the circular building as the Temple of Minerva Chalcidica. The schematic drawing of the marble plan shows a circular wall, surrounding a rectangular base, with a flight of steps on each side. This is supplemented by a drawing of Onofrio Panvinio (Cod. Vat. Lat. 3439 fol. 25 r.), based on the observations and measurements of Pirro Ligorio. The temple stood between the Piazza del Collegio Romano, Via della Gatta and Via di Santo Stefano del Cacco, below the modern building of the Questura, No. 3, Piazza del Collegio Romano (s. Arcus ad Isis I, 122).

G. P. BELLORI, Fragmenta vestigii veteris Romae, 1673, p. 23 f., Tab. V; R. LANCIANI. BCom XI, 1883, p. 42; id., Ruins, p. 461; CH. HÜLSEN, RM XVIII, 1903, pp. 39–46; E. PETERSEN, ib., p. 320; H. JORDAN, Top I, 3, pp. 570[30], 573; V. LUNDSTRÖM, Strena phil. Upsaliensis (Festskrift Persson), 1922, pp. 369–382; CH. HÜLSEN, Chiese, p. 346 f.; P-A, p. 344; G. LUGLI, Mon III, pp. 110–112; E. SJÖQVIST, ActaInstSuecia XII, 1946, pp. 99–105; F. CASTAGNOLI, L'Urbe XIII, 1950, 4, pp. 3–5; id., Palladio, N. S. II, 1952, p. 100 f.; E. NASH, RM LXVI, 1959, pp. 133–135; FUR, pp. 97, 99–101 (Bibl: p. 102), Tav. XXXI; F. CASTAGNOLI, AC XII, 1960, pp. 91–95.

753 Coin of Domitian with the round Temple of Minerva Chalcidica (BMC, Emp II, p. 241, pl. 67, 7).                    Fot 6437

754 Detail of pl. XXXI of the Severan marble plan.

Fot 4730

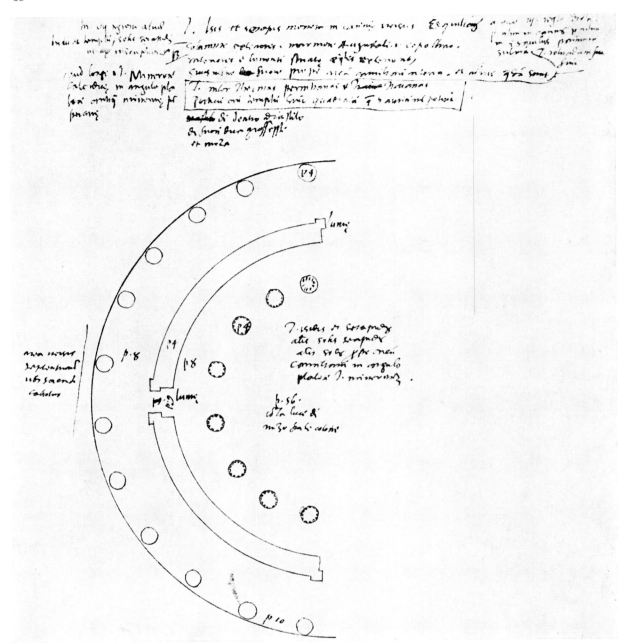

755  Drawing of the round temple by Onofrio Panvinio (Cod. Vat. Lat. 3439, fol. 25 r.).

MITHRAEUM PROPE CARCERES CIRCI MAXIMI. In 1931, when the Pantanella spaghetti factory, built 1878/79, was being converted into a scenery store for the Opera, the remains of an ancient building of the 2nd century B. C. were discovered; its purpose is not clear. It stands in the immediate vicinity of the Circus Maximus, less than 5 m. from the carceres, and only separated from them by the ancient street "AD DUODECIM PORTAS". The façade, with its broad stairway, is more likely to have belonged to a public building than to a private house, and it may have been connected with the circus games. In the second half of the 3rd century, a large part of the ground floor was converted into a Mithraeum. The floor and benches of this sanctuary were covered with marble, and the niches and consoles were probably adorned with statues and marble reliefs.

A. M. COLINI, BCom LIX, 1931, pp. 123–130; LXI, 1933, p. 279; A. W. VAN BUREN, Ancient Rome, 1936, p. 143 f.; C. PIETRANGELI, BCom LXVIII, 1940, pp. 143–173; G. LUGLI, Mon IV, 1, p. 157; id., Centro pp. 606–609; H. FUHRMANN, AA, 1941, pp. 517–521; M. J. VERMASEREN, De Mithrasdienst in Rome, 1951, pp. 45–51; id., Corpus I, pp. 181–187; Ni. 434–455; M. E. BLAKE II, p. 104 f.

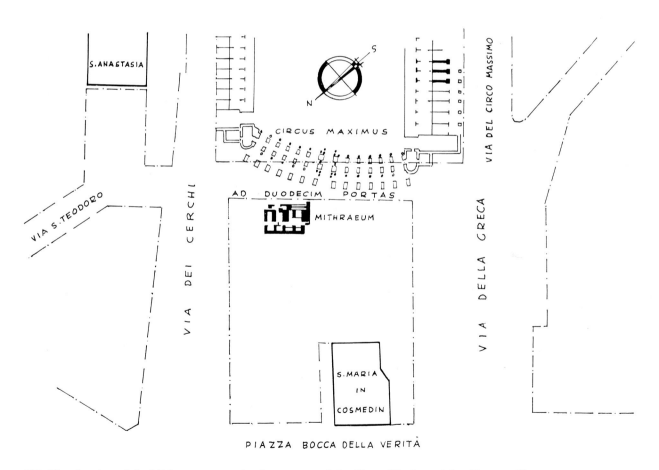

756 The site-plan of the Mithraeum opposite the carceres of the Circus Maximus (after Pietrangeli).

757 View towards the niche of the cult statue, from the entrance of the Mithraeum. Presumably statues of the torchbearers "Cautes" and "Cautopates" stood in the niches on either side in the foreground.                Rip X C/3849

758 The main hall of the Mithraeum, with the niche for the cult statue on the left. The circle on the floor is alabaster in a square of cipollino marble.                                    Rip X  C/3848

MITHRAEUM DOMUS BARBARINORUM. During building operations in the garden behind the Palazzo Barberini in 1936, some rooms of a Roman house of the 1st century A. D. were uncovered; the westernmost room had been converted into a Mithraeum at a later date. It is a rectangle of 11.85 m. × 6.25 m., and is roofed with a segmental barrel-vault. The cult image, on the south wall, is one of the few painted representations of Mithras; it shows the usual scene of the god killing the bull. The Mithraeum is situated between the garden façade of the Palazzo Barberini and the Salita S. Nicola da Tolentino.

G. Annibaldi, BCom LXVI, 1938, p. 251 f.; R. Horn, AA 1936, p. 475 f.; G. Lugli, Mon III, p. 320; id., Mon IV, 3, pp. 31–33; G. Gatti, BCom LXXI, 1943/45, pp. 97–100; G. Annibaldi, ib., pp. 101–108; M. J. Vermaseren, Corpus I, pp. 168–170; Ni. 389–395; M. E. Blake, II, p. 58.

759 The cult image of Mithras.                                          Fot 3589

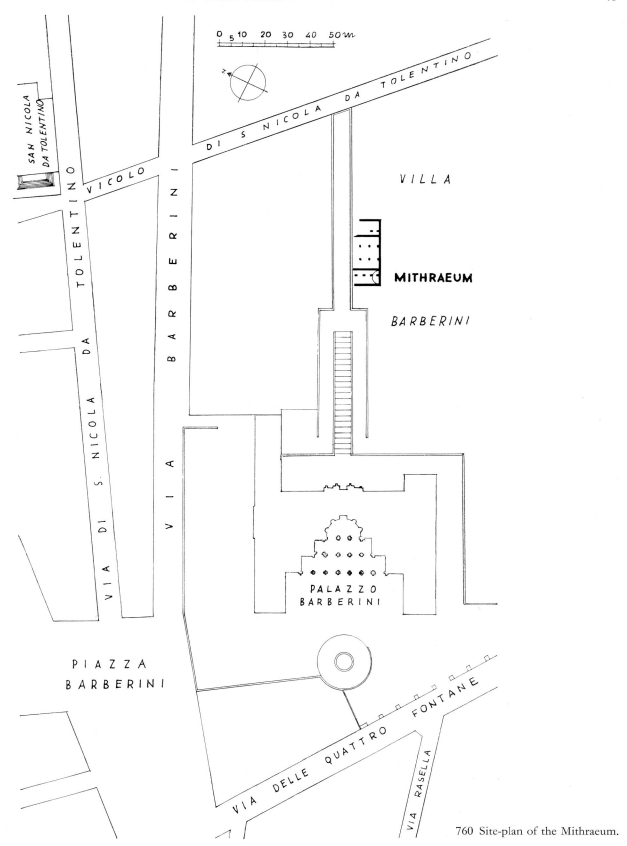

760 Site-plan of the Mithraeum.

761 Sacrificial area below the painted cult image.                          Fot 3587

MITHRAEUM DOMUS CLEMENTIS. Excavations under the church of S. Clemente, which were started by Father Joseph Mullooly in 1857, led to the discovery of a Mithraeum, in 1869. Early in the 3rd century, it had been built into a late 1st century private house (s. Domus Clementis I, 427). Later, when the cult of Mithras was suppressed, the interior decoration of the Mithraeum was destroyed, and it was filled up with earth. It was another thirty years before the Mithraeum and the adjacent rooms could be properly excavated, because water seeped in, and by 1885 the floor of the Mithraeum was flooded to a depth of 2.7 m. In 1912/14, a tunnel (Emissarium Clementinum) was built 14 m. below the street level; it was 700 m. long and diverted the water to a large sewer next to the Meta Sudans, beyond the Colosseum, thus making possible further archaeological exploration in the rooms of the ancient house.

G. B. DE ROSSI, BACrist 2, I, 1870, pp. 153–168; F. GORI, Il Buonarotti 2, V, 1870, pp. 289–299; TH. ROLLER, RA 2, XXIV, 1872, pp. 68–73; F. CUMONT, CRAI, 1915, pp. 203–211; L. NOLAN, The Basilica of S. Clemente (3), 1925, pp. 198–219; L. CANTARELLI, BCom XLIII, 1915, p. 69 f.; J. P. KIRSCH, Titelkirchen, pp. 38–40; P-A, p. 177; E. JUNYENT, RA Crist V, 1928, pp. 237–245; XV, 1938, pp. 150–152; id., Titolo, pp. 66–81 (Bibl: pp. 29, 31 f., 66 f.); C. CECCHELLI, S. Clemente, s. d. (1933), pp. 55–66 (Bibl: p. 74 f.); G. LUGLI, Mon III, pp. 542–547; M. J. VERMASEREN, Mededeelingen Rome 3, VI, 1950, pp. CIII–CXVIII; id., De Mithrasdienst in Rome, 1951, pp. 70–74; id., Corpus I, pp. 156–158, Ni. 338–348 (Bibl: p. 156); M. E. BLAKE II, p. 128.

762 The Mithraeum in the Roman house under S. Clemente. In front of the altar is an inscription "CAVTE SACR" (CIL VI, 748).

Anderson 22928

763  The altar of the Mithraeum in its present position in the centre aisle of the Mithraeum. Above the relief is the dedicatory inscription of CN ARRIUS CLAUDIANUS.                                                    Anderson 23657

764 The back of the altar with the representation of a snake. Anderson 25099

765  The left side of the altar, the torchbearer "Cautopates"
     with a lowered torch.                    Anderson 25098

766  The right side, the torchbearer "Cautes" with a raised
     torch.                                   Anderson 25097

MITHRAEUM DOMUS SANCTAE PRISCAE. In 1934, in the course of building operations, the Augustinian monks of S. Prisca discovered a Mithraeum under their church, and over a period of years they excavated it. The work was interrupted by the second World War, but was resumed in March 1953 by the Netherlands Historical Institute in Rome, and was completed in 1958. Behind and under the apse of the church, part of two Roman houses were identified, into which the Mithraeum had been built at the end of the 2nd century. The long walls are decorated with paintings, of which two layers are visible, the later is dated 220 A. D. The cult niche contains a large reclining figure of Oceanus-Saturnus, as well as the usual representation of Mithras killing the bull. On either side of the entrance to the Mithraeum are niches for the torchbearers, and the figure of "Cautes" survives.

A. FERRUA, La Civiltà Cattolica 17, II, 1940, pp. 298–309; id., BCom LXVIII, 1940, pp. 59–96; G. LUGLI, Mon IV, 3, pp. 56–59; H. FUHRMANN, AA, 1940, p. 478 f.; A. MERLIN, RA 6, XVII, 1941, pp. 40–45; F. CUMONT, CRAI, 1945, pp. 401–407; M. J. VERMASEREN, De Mithrasdienst in Rome, 1951, p. 55 f.; C. C. VAN ESSEN, Nederlands kunsthist. Jaarboek V, 1954, pp. 191–198; M. J. VERMASEREN – C. C. VAN ESSEN, The Aventine Mithraeum, Antiquity and Survival I, 1955, pp. 3–36; M. J. VERMASEREN, Corpus I, pp. 193–201, Ni. 476–500; II, p. 28 f.; C. C. VAN ESSEN, Palladio, N. S. IX, 1959, pp. 54–59.

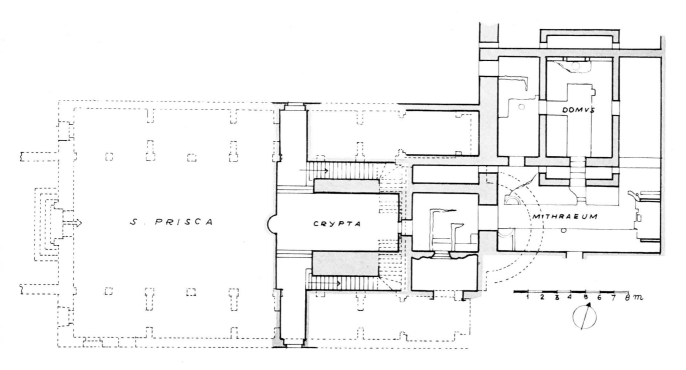

767 Site-plan of the Mithraeum under the church of S. Prisca.

768 Dedicatory inscription to the "Deus Sol Invictus Mithras".                    Fot 5291

769 View of the Mithraeum.                                                          Fot 5284

770  The cult-niche with Oceanus-Saturnus and Mithras.                    Fot 5285

771 Marble statue of "Cautes" in
the niche on the right of the
entrance.          Fot 1069

772 Wall painting on the west side of the right wall. Sacrificial procession with the "Suovetaurilia" (bull, ram, pig).
Fot 5265

773 Head of the servant who is leading the ram.                    Fot 5289

774 A side chapel to the north of the Mithraeum, showing side benches and centre niche set into the rear wall.  Fot 5915

MITHRAEUM THERMARUM ANTONINIARUM. When the Passeggiata Archeologica (now Via delle Terme di Caracalla) was being laid out, an undertaking sponsored by the Royal Commission of 1908, excavation of the service corridors beneath the Baths of Caracalla led, in 1912, to the discovery of a Mithraeum. It measures 23 × 9.70 m., and is the largest discovered in Rome. It is roofed with a cross vault resting on massive brick piers. The partly destroyed vault was restored in 1938, when the whole complex of subterranean service corridors was excavated.

E. GHISLANZONI. NSc, 1912, pp. 319–325; G. GATTI, BCom XL, 1912, pp. 155–147; La Zona Monumentale di Roma e l'opera della Commissione Reale, 1914, pp. 57–59; F. CUMONT – L. CANET, CRAI, 1919, pp. 313–328; A. D. NOCK, JHS XLV, 1925, p. 89; R. PARIBENI, MusNaz, p. 140, No. 288; P-A, p. 524; G. LUGLI, Mon I, pp. 428–432; id., Mon IV, 1, p. 160 f.; M. J. VERMASEREN, De Mithrasdienst in Rome, 1951, pp. 80–83; id., Corpus I, pp. 187–190, Ni. 457–463.

775 The Mithraeum in the Baths of Caracalla.

GFN C/6920

MURI AURELIANI. The city wall of imperial Rome was begun by Aurelian between 270 and 272 A. D., and was completed by Probus (276–282 A. D.). It is 18.837 km. long and has 381 towers, which project from the line of the wall every 100 Roman feet (29.60 m.), and give it additional strength. There are eighteen main gateways, and several smaller openings (posterulae). The original fortifications were from 7.50–8 m. in height and in certain places 10 m. The wall was twice reinforced and elevated. The first restoration is attributed to Maxentius, while its present form is mainly due to restorations by Honorius and Arcadius in 403 A. D. The wall continued to be the defence of Rome until the 20th September 1870, when the army of the Kingdom of Italy breached it with modern artillery, north-west of the Porta Pia, and entered the city. The greater part of the Aurelian fortifications are preserved; only on the right bank of the Tiber was the old wall replaced by a new line of defence under Urban VIII, in 1642/44.

s. a. Aqua Claudia I, 30; Circus Varianus I, 281; Horti Aciliorum I, 600, 601; Sepulcrum C. Sulpicii Platorini II, 1158.

W. GELL – A. NIBBY, Mura di Roma, 1821; C. CORVISIERI, ArchStorPat I, 1878, pp. 79–121, 137–171; H. JORDAN, Top I, 1, pp. 340–392; E. MÜNTZ, RA 3, VI, 1885, pp. 27–41; 3, VII, 1886, pp. 124–138, 224–242, 336–340; 3, VIII, 1886, pp. 33–39, 319–335; 3, IX, 1887, pp. 54–58; R. LANCIANI, BCom XX, 1892, 87–111; id., Ruins, pp. 66–73 (Bibl: p. 72); G. J. PFEIFFER, A. W. VAN BUREN, H. H. ARMSTRONG, Suppl. Papers Am. School of Class. Studies in Rome I, 1905, pp. 1–86; TH. ASHBY, Roma III, 1925, p. 317; I. A. RICHMOND, BCom LV, 1927, pp. 41–76; id., BSR X, 1927, pp. 12–22; id., The City Wall of Imperial Rome, 1930 (Bibl: p. 3 f.); P-A, pp. 348–350; G. LUGLI, Mon II, pp. 139–261; G. GATTI, BCom LXIV, 1936, pp. 67–70 (MS. Bruzza); A. M. COLINI, Celio, pp. 109–132, 330–333, 343; C. PIETRANGELI, Capitolium XX, 1945, pp. 1–8; id., BCom LXXII, 1946/48, pp. 221–223; H. BLOCH, Bolli, pp. 10 f., 313; F. P. JOHNSON, ClPhil XLIII, 1948, pp. 261–265; J. LE GALL, Tibre, pp. 287–294; G. CRESSEDI, NSc, 1956, pp. 42–45, 49 f.; G. LUGLI, Tecnica I, p. 616 f.; II, Tavv. CXXXIII, 4; CXXXIX, 3; CLXXVIII, 3; L. CREMA, ArchRom, p. 558.

776 The Aurelian Wall on the east side of the Pincio, below the Villa Medici.                    Fot 1236

777 The wall between Porta Pinciana and Porta Salaria, with the only tower which survives at its original height
(No. XXXIX at No. 10 Via Campania).                                                                    Fot 1235

778  The wall, immediately to the east of Porta Salaria; on the level of the rampart-walk is a latrine; in front of the wall
     is the Tomb of Q. Sulpicius Maximus (q. v.).                                                                Fot 1233

779 Posterula of the Via Nomentana, south of Porta Nomentana.                                        Fot 1301

90

780 Posterula of the Castra Praetoria, south of Via Montebello.

Fot 1302

781 The façade of an ancient house in Via di Porta Labicana, which was incorporated into the Aurelian Wall.   Fot 1231

782 The wall, south of Porta Tiburtina.                              Fot 5600

783 Posterula of the Horti Liciniani, on Via di Porta Labicana.                    Fot 1298

784 Covered rampart-walk in the upper part of a stretch of the wall, west of the Amphitheatrum Castrense.    Fot 5602

785 The arcades of two vaulted rampart-walks, lying one above the other, on Viale Castrense; the lower one dates
from the first and the upper from the second building period.                     Fot 5283

786 A posterula below the
Domus Lateranorum,
excavated by Parker in
1868.      Parker 1096

787 Part of the wall between Porta Asinaria and Porta Metrovia, directly west of the Posterula Lateranensis.   Parker 41

788 Towers east of Porta
Metrovia, which were
restored in the middle
of the 6th century by
Belisarius or Narses.
Fot 1230

789 The wall at Porta Latina.                                    Fot 1228

790 Covered rampart-walk inside the wall, between Porta Latina and Porta Appia.                Fot 6100

791 The interior of the wall, directly north of Porta Latina.                Fot 1229

792 The interior of the rampart-walk, between Porta Latina and Porta Appia.                    Fot 6097

793  The wall and towers
     near Porta Appia.
         Fot 1226

794  The wall between Porta Appia and Porta Ardeatina.                    Fot 1224

795  The posterula of Vigna Casali, with the street leading from it.                    Fot 1295

796 The Bastione di Sangallo, built by Antonio da Sangallo the younger, in 1534, under Paul III.          Fot 1221

797 Part of the Aurelian Wall which remains standing behind the Bastione di Sangallo, which took its place.   Fot 1223

798 The wall between Porta Ostiensis and the Tiber.                                    Fot 1219

799 Part of the wall which has been repaired, south of Monte Testaccio.              Fot 1217

800  The southern corner of the wall on the left bank of the Tiber, seen in an engraving by Giuseppe Vasi (Magnificenze
     V, 1754, Tav. 99).                                                                              Fot 3009

801  The part of the wall seen in Vasi's engraving outside the City Wall belonged to a river barrier. The corner of the
     Aurelian Wall, however, was destroyed in 1911, when the railway bridge was built.              Fot 1216

802 The remains of the wall on the left bank of the Tiber, in front of the slaughter-house (mattatoio). The modern tower is built on ancient foundations.          Fot 6093

803 Part of the Aurelian Wall below the Lungotevere Testaccio, between Ponte Aventino and Ponte Testaccio: travertine blocks from the Emporium (q. v. I, 464, 465) were used for its foundations.          Fot 1213

MURUS SERVII TULLII. According to tradition, the original city wall was built by Servius Tullius, the sixth King of Rome, who is thought to have reigned 578–534 B. C. However, the defences of Republican Rome, known as the "Servian Wall" – which is still visible in many places – date only from the period after the Gallic invasion of 386 B. C. The fortress walls of the Arx on the northern summit of the Capitol, and the remains of walls on the west slope of the Palatine, are earlier and may be attributed to the time of the Kings, in the 6th century B. C. The last thorough restoration and improvement of the wall took place in 87 B. C.

s. a. Auditorium Maecenatis I, 172, 175; Mercatus Traiani II, 743.

R. LANCIANI, AnnInst, 1871, pp. 40–85; H. JORDAN, Top I, 1, pp. 201–295; L. BRUZZA, AnnInst, 1876, pp. 72–105; J. H. PARKER, The primitive fortifications of Rome (2) 1878; R. LANCIANI, BCom IV, 1876, pp. 24–38, 121–134, 165–172, 210; L. BORSARI, BCom XVI, 1888, pp. 12–22; O. RICHTER, Über antike Steinmetzzeichen, 1885, pp. 7–13; G. PINZA, MALinc XV, 1905, pp. 746–753; id., BCom XL, 1912, pp. 67–81; D. VAGLIERI, NSc, 1907, pp. 504–511; F. BARNABEI, NSc, 1909, p. 221 f.; G. BONI, NSc, 1910, pp. 495–513; G. GATTI, BCom XXXVII, 1909, pp. 119–121; P. GRAFFUNDER, Klio XI, 1911, pp. 83–123; T. FRANK, AJA XXII, 1918, pp. 174–188; id., AJP XLV, 1924, p. 68 f.; id., Buildings, pp. 111–124; G. SÄFLUND, Gnomon III, 1927, p. 191 f.; P-A, pp. 350–355; A. MUÑOZ–A. M. COLINI, Campidoglio, 1930, pp. 34–38; G. SÄFLUND, Mura; A. VON GERKAN, Gnomon X, 1934, pp. 455–465; id., RM XLVI, 1931, pp. 153–158; LV, 1940, pp. 1–26; G. LUGLI, Historia VII, 1933, pp. 3–45; id., Mon II, pp. 99–138; P. DUCATI, Come nacque Roma, 1939, pp. 176–183; M. SANTANGELO, Quirinale, pp. 99–116; A. M. COLINI, Celio, pp. 31–35, 26 f.; H. LYNGBY, Eranos XLII, 1944, pp. 88–97; id., ForBoarium, pp. 63–106; M. P. QUONIAM, Mél LIX, 1947, pp. 41–64; M. E. BLAKE I, pp. 123–125 (Index p. 375); E. GJERSTAD–B. M. FELLETTI MAJ, NSc, 1948, pp. 321–325; A. VON GERKAN, Bonner Jahrbücher CXLIX, 1949, pp. 9–12; E. GJERSTAD, Studies pres. to D. M. ROBINSON I, 1951, pp. 412–422; id., ActaInstSueciae XVIII, 1954, pp. 50–65; XVII, 3, 1960, pp. 26–44; G. LUGLI, Tecnica I, pp. 258–266; II, Tavv. XL, XLI, XLII, XLVI, 1; L. CREMA, ArchRom, p. 26.

804 Part of the Servian Wall on the north-west slope of the Quirinal. It was discovered when the Largo di S. Susanna was being laid out in 1938.
Fot 1203

805 A cut through the wall in Via delle Finanze (now Via Antonio Salandra), for the construction of Via Giosuè Carducci.                                          Fot 1196

806 A cut through the wall on the north side of Via Carducci.                                          Fot 3688

807 The stretch of wall, 36 m. long, beside Via delle Finanze (now Via Antonio Salandra), during the excavation in 1909.
Fot 5204

808 Part of the retaining wall of the Agger Servianus, 24.85 m. in length, in the Piazza dei Cinquecento.          Fot 1178

809 Part of the outer line of the wall, 24.85 m. to the east of fig. 808.                                    Fot 1179

810 The wall in the Piazza dei Cinquecento, north-west of the Porta Viminalis (q. v.). Fot 1185

811 The wall in the Piazza dei Cinquecento with the railway station in the background. The Porta Viminalis is in the centre (right). Fot 1183

812 Outer side of the wall
    at the railway station,
    with later additions of
    brick.        Fot 1184

813 Inner side of the wall at the railway station.                          Fot 1182

814 Remains of the wall on the Esquiline – 45, Via Carlo Alberto – showing three courses of blocks.  Fot 1193

815 A stretch of the wall 23 m. long; in the centre a semicircular buttress faces inwards.          Fot 1187

816 Part of the wall incorporated in the south-east wall of the Auditorium Maecenatis, on the Esquiline.          Fot 774

817 The Servian Wall on the Aventine, in Via di S. Anselmo.                                   Fot 1199

818 Outer view of the wall on the Aventine, showing an arched opening for a catapult.                                   Fot 1198

819  The wall on the west slope of the Palatine.                                    Fot 1202

820  A corner of the wall on the west side of the Palatine, at the level of the Clivus Victoriae.                    Fot 5060

821  The wall at the foot of the Capitol, beside Via Teatro di Marcello.                                            Fot 1210

822 Fortress wall of the
    Arx, in the garden of
    S. Maria in Aracoeli;
    outer side.    Fot 1209

823 Section through the wall.                                                    Fot 1205

824  The eastern end of the
     fortress wall, opposite
     the north wall of the
     Tabularium.  Fot 1207

825  Juncture of two stretches of the wall at the foot of the Capitol, between the Museo del Risorgimento and the For-
     um Iulium.
                                                                         Fot 3306

826  Wall of a gate in the Servian Wall, in Piazza Magnanapoli.                    Fot 5663

827  Arched opening in the wall, for the installation of a catapult, in Palazzo Antonelli in Via Tre Canelle.

Anderson 40244

NAVALIA. The arsenal and shipyards of the Roman navy, the Navalia, lay on the left bank of the Tiber in the Campus Martius, opposite the "prata Quinctia in Vaticano" (Livy III, 26, 8; Pliny Nat. Hist. XVIII, 20). In 338 B. C., the ships captured at Antium were taken to the Navalia to be broken up, and their beaks, were used to decorate the orator's platform. When the Tiber embankment was being built in 1890/91, a tufa mole, some 50 m. long by 13.7 m. wide, was discovered; it was built out into the river, below the demolished Theatre of Apollo, some 160 m. upstream from the Pons Aelius. Judging by the technique of its construction and the building materials used, it may date from the 4th century B. C. and can be identified as the Navalia. With the building of the Pons Aelius (134 A. D.), the arsenal was apparently abandoned. The Navalia are not mentioned in literature after the 2nd century A. D. From a fragment of the Severan marble plan, bearing the word "NAVALEMFER", it has been inferred that a "Navale Inferius" existed, although neither the inscription nor the plan, nor anything in ancient literature allows us to accept the fact of a second marine arsenal.

A. DONATUS, Roma Vetus ac Recens (2), 1648, p. 252 f.; W. A. BECKER, Handbuch d. röm. Altertümer I, 1843, pp. 159–162; id., Zur römischen Topographie, 1845, p. 15 f.; L. PRELLER, Berichte d. Sächsischen Ges. d. Wiss. zu Leipzig I, 1849, p. 142 f.; H. JORDAN, Top I, 1, pp. 435–440 (Bibl: p. 435[49]); D. MARCHETTI, NSc, 1890, p. 153; 1892, p. 110 f.; id., BCom XIX, 1891, pp. 45–60; F. AZURRI, BCom XX, 1892, pp. 175–178; CH. HÜLSEN, DissPontAcc 2, VI, 1896, pp. 246–254; id., RM VII, 1892, pp. 322–326; R. LANCIANI, Ruins, pp. 525–527; L. BORSARI, Top, p. 58; E. PETERSEN, RM XV, 1900, pp. 352–354; A. MERLIN, L'Aventin dans l'antiquité, 1906, p. 122 f.; H. JORDAN, Top I, 3, pp. 143–145, 485 f., 600 f.; P-A, pp. 358–360; G. SÄFLUND, Eranos XXVIII, 1930, pp. 124–128; I. A. Richmond, Wall, p. 20; G. LUGLI, Mon II, pp. 295, 320–322; Mon III, p. 676; Centro, p. 576 f.; A. M. COLINI, BCom LXVI, 1938, p. 272 f.; M. E. BLAKE I, p. 51; J. LE GALL, Tibre, pp. 103–111, 191, 201 f.; G. CRESSEDI, RendPontAcc XXV–XXVI, 1949/51, pp. 55–65 (Bibl: p. 60); H. LYNGBY, For Boarium, pp. 97, 148; FUR, pp. 60 f., 228, Tav. XV, 2 (Bibl: p. 61).

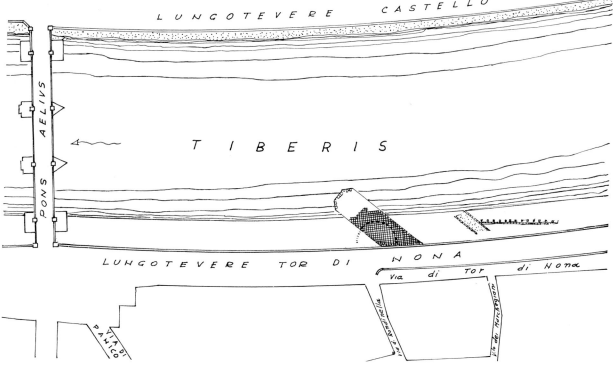

828 Site-plan of the wharf belonging to the Navalia, which was discovered under the destroyed Theatre of Apollo in 1890.

829  The remains of the mole projecting beyond the embankment, with the Pons Aelius and the Mausoleum Hadriani.
Fot 3664

830  The remains of the mole projecting into the Tiber, and the Pons Aelius.                    Fot 3665

NEPTUNUS, TEMPLUM. In 1837 the French architect V. Baltard found the remains of a temple in the southern part of the Campus Martius beneath some houses, Nos. 9 and 10, Via S. Salvatore in Campo. In 1872 Vespignani made a careful survey of it; and since 1876 it has been identified as the Temple of Neptune, which was either built or restored by Gn. Domitius Ahenobarbus. A coin of the gens Domitia of 42/41 B. C. shows the temple, although at that date it was apparently still unfinished, or even only vowed. The identification of the temple rests on the fact that, since the 17th century, a pair of matching reliefs, one of a lustratio and one of a marriage of Neptune, have been preserved in the neighbouring Palazzo Santacroce (Altar of Domitius Ahenobarbus), and it was supposed that they came from the temple under S. Salvatore in Campo. Both reliefs were acquired by Cardinal Fesch in 1811. The marriage of Neptune to Amphitrite was auctioned in Paris in 1816, and went to Munich, whereas the lustratio with the sacrifice of the Suovetaurilia has been in the Louvre since 1824.

L. CANINA, AnnInst, 1838, pp. 5–11; PLATNER–BUNSEN, Beschreibung III, 3, p. 30 f.; V. VESPIGNANI, BCom I, 1872/73, pp. 212–221; F. REBER, Ruinen, pp. 223–226; H. BRUNN, Sitzungsberichte d. Bayrischen Akademie 1876, pp. 342–354; A. FURTWÄNGLER, Intermezzi, 1896, pp. 35–48; H. JORDAN, Top I, 3, pp. 522–524; J. SIEVEKING, ÖJh XIII, 1910, pp. 95–101; E. MICHON, MonPiot XVII, 1910, pp. 147–157; R. BARTOCCINI, Atti e Memorie dell'Ist. Ital. di Numismatica III, 1, 1917, pp. 83–94; E. STRONG, SR I, pp. 10–14, II, p. 416; BMC, Rep II, p. 487 f., No. 93; P-A, pp. 329, 360 f.; F. W. GOETHERT, Zur Kunst d. röm. Republik, 1931, pp. 7–16 (Bibl: p. 63[1]); F. W. SHIPLEY, MAARome IX, 1931, p. 43 f.; G. LUGLI, Mon III, pp. 55–59; D. F. BROWN, Temples, p. 11; id., AN, pp. 191–193; O. VESSBERG, ActaInstSueciae VIII, 1941, p. 181 f.; F. CASTAGNOLI, CM, pp. 157–159; id., Arti Figurativi I, 1945, pp. 181–196 (Bibl: p. 192[1]); M. E. BLAKE I, p. 156; E. WELIN, Acta InstSueciae XVIII, 1954, pp. 178–180; F. PANVINI ROSATI, RINum LVII, 1955, pp. 76–78; I. SCOTT RYBERG, Rites, pp. 27–34; W. FUCHS, Die Vorbilder der neuattischen Reliefs, 1959, pp. 160–164; H. KÄHLER, Rom und seine Welt II, 1960, pp. 102–104.

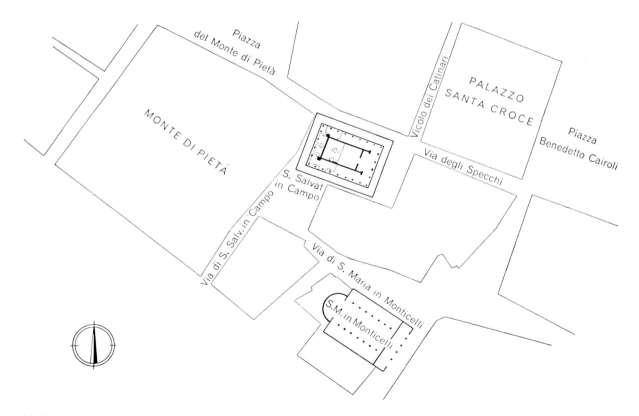

831 Site-plan of the temple between Via di S. Salvatore in Campo and Via degli Specchi, and of the Palazzo Santacroce.

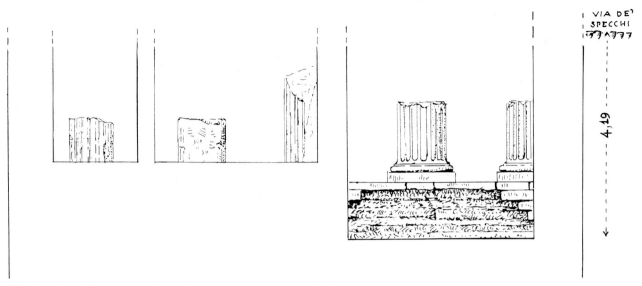

832 Remains of five columns from the front of the temple which lies beneath the houses Nos. 9 and 10, Via di S. Salvatore in Campo.

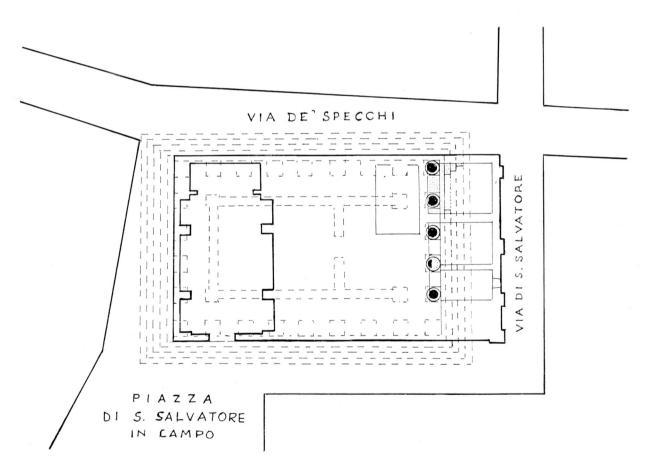

833 Presumed dimensions of the temple under S. Salvatore in Campo.

834 Coin of Gn. Domitius L. F. Ahenobarbus of 42/41 B. C. with the representation of the Temple of Neptune.

MCR B/253

835 The "Lustrum" relief, with a cast of the Neptune relief from the Antikensammlung in Munich, set together on a base in the Louvre.

Alinari 22555

NOVA VIA. The Nova Via, which skirted the northern edge of the Palatine was, with the exception of the Sacra Via, the only street in pre-imperial Rome to be called a "via". The others, if they had names, were called "vicus". The Nova Via branched off the Sacra Via near the Temple of Iuppiter Stator. The eastern stretch was called "Summa Nova Via", and at the north-west corner of the Palatine, above the Atrium Vestae, it was known as the "Infima Nova Via". Part of the street which led from the west slope of the Palatine to the Velabrum was later covered by Domitian's buildings. Since 1882, the Nova Via has been excavated to the level at which it lay in imperial times.

H. JORDAN, Top I, 1, p. 513 f.; R. LANCIANI, NSc, 1882, pp. 234–238, 413; 1884, p. 191; O. GILBERT, Rom II, pp. 114–117; III, p. 422 f.; O. RICHTER, Hermes XX, p. 428 f.; CH. HÜLSEN, RM XVII, 1902, p. 73 f.; id., FR, p. 195; TH. ASHBY, CR XIX, 1905, p. 76; H. THÉDENAT, FR, pp. 173 f., 356–358; E. DE RUGGIERO, p. 507 f.; E. B. VAN DEMAN, AJA XXVII, 1923, p. 392 f.; id., MAARome V, 1925, p. 121; P-A, p. 361 f.; I. A. POPESCU, Ephemeris Dacoromana IV, 1930, p. 3 f.; G. SÄFLUND, Mura, p. 195 f.; G. COZZO, Il luogo primitivo di Roma, 1935, p. 119 f.; G. LUGLI, Centro, p. 216 f.; M. E. BLAKE I, p. 255 f.; II, pp. 43 f., 117.

836 The Nova Via on the north slope of the Palatine. Left are the remains of a house (insula). In the background the street is seen bridged over by the substructures of the Domus Tiberiana.                                    Fot 128

837 The part of the street known as the "Summa Nova Via", on the north-east side of the Palatine.                    Fot 137

NYMPHAEUM AQUAE IULIAE. The branch of the Aqua Iulia which passes over Via Filippo Turati (s. I, 42), ended at a monumental fountain, the ruins of which stand to-day in the Piazza Vittorio Emanuele II. The brick façade of the nymphaeum, which dates from the time of Alexander Severus (222–235 A. D.), has a large central niche. From ancient times, marble trophies stood in arched openings on either side of it, until, in 1590, they were removed to the balustrade of the Piazza del Campidoglio. The trophies originally came from one of Domitian's victory monuments, and caused the nymphaeum to be called "C. Marii Trophaea" in the Renaissance. The mediaeval Mirabilia and Ordo Benedicti connected the monument with Marius and his victory over the Cimbri, calling it "Templum Marii, quod nunc vocatur Cimbrum" (CodTop III, pp. 28, 216). The Roman people, on the other hand, thought the trophies were armoured geese (oche armate, CodTop IV, p. 414, 5) and regarded the nymphaeum as a memorial to the geese which saved the Capitol during the Gallic invasion (CodTop IV, p. 365, 18–19; s. a. Iuno Moneta I, 635).

T. L. DONALDSON, Architectura Numismatica, 1859, pp. 270–282; H. JORDAN, Top II, pp. 517–520, 640, 665; id., Top I, 1, p. 478 f.; F. REBER, Ruinen, pp. 483–485; R. LANCIANI, Frontino, pp. 171–174 (393-395); E. MAASS, Die Tagesgötter in Rom u. den Provinzen, 1902, pp. 63–93; J. DURM, Baukunst der Römer (2), 1905, p. 475 f.; H. JORDAN, Top I, 3, pp. 348–350; W. HELBIG, Führer I, pp. 409–411 (Bibl: p. 410[1]); TH. ASHBY, Top 1581, pp. 115–117; K. LEHMANN-HARTLEBEN, RM XXXVIII–XXXIX, 1923/24, pp. 185–192; TH. ASHBY, The Years Work in Classical Studies XVII, 1923/24, p. 107; E. STRONG, SR I, p. 128 f.; P-A, p. 363 f.; E. B. VAN DEMAN, Aqueducts, p. 165 f.; G. LUGLI, Mon II, pp. 362–365; id., Tecnica I, p. 616; P. PECCHIAI, Il Campidoglio nel Cinquecento, 1950, p. 62; L. CREMA, ArchRom, p. 548.

838  The Nymphaeum of the Aqua Iulia in Piazza Vittorio Emanuele II.                    Fot 3079

839 The left hand trophy on the Capitol balustrade.
Inst Neg 59.130

840 The right hand trophy on the Capitol balustrade.
Fot 867

841 The nymphaeum with the trophies, before they were removed to the Capitol in 1590 (S. Du Pérac, I vestigi dell'antichità di Roma, 1575, fol. 27).
Fot 3047

NYMPHAEUM HORTORUM LICINIANORUM. The ten-sided, domed building in Via Giovanni Giolitti near the Stazione Termini was a pavilion in the Villa of the emperor P. Licinius Gallienus (253–268 A. D.), the HORTI LICINIANI. It is still known as the "Templum Minervae Medicae", a name which was erroneously conferred on it in the 17th century. The building dates from about the middle of the 3rd century A. D. The drum, penetrated by large windows, supports a dome, which is composed of a brick framework of ten radiating ribs, the intervening spaces being filled in with light-weight material. In 1828, part of the dome fell in, and in the following year the building was struck by lightening, and suffered further damage. The purpose of this richly-decorated building is not certain; it is more likely to have been a hall for ceremonial receptions or banquets, than a nymphaeum.

A. NIBBY. RomAnt II, pp. 331–339; G. B. DE ROSSI, Studi e Documenti di Storia e Diritto IV, 1883, p. 176 f. (note per la pianta del Nolli, No. 931); F. REBER, Ruinen, p. 485 f.; H. JORDAN, Top II, pp. 130–132; R. LANCIANI, Ruins, pp. 401–403; id., Storia III, pp. 158–161; G. GIOVANNONI, Annali d. Soc. degli Ingegneri e degli Architetti, 1904, pp. 165–201; J. DURM, Baukunst der Römer, (2), 1905, p. 283 f.; H. JORDAN, Top I, 3, pp. 359–361; W. ALTMANN, Rundbauten, pp. 81–84; G. T. Rivoira, RomArch, pp. 182–188; P-A, pp. 268, 364; P. GRIMAL, Mél LIII, 1936, pp. 282–285; G. LUGLI, Mon III, pp. 480–483; id., Studies pres. to D. M. Robinson II, 1953, p. 1212 f.; id., Tecnica I, pp. 670 f., 675; G. GIOVANNONI, La cupola del c. d. Tempio di Minerva Medica, 1943; G. CARAFFA, La cupola della sala decagona degli Horti Liciniani, 1944; G. DE ANGELIS D'OSSAT, Boll. del Centro Naz. di Studi di Storia dell'Arch. 1945, 4, pp. 3–6; L. CREMA, ArchRom, p. 634 f.

842 The Nymphaeum Hortorum Licinianorum in 1780. A drawing by Franz Innocenz Kobell (1749–1822); Munich, Graphische Sammlung.                                                                              GFN E/43725

843  Interior of the drum and springing of the dome.                                    Fot 887

844 Exterior view of the dome during restoration work in 1942.   Fot 3235

845 Exterior view of the ruin.                                                Inst Neg 42.274

OBELISCUS ANTINOI. The obelisk which stands to-day on the Pincio, in the middle of the Viale dell'Obelisco, belonged to the tomb or cenotaph of Antinous outside the Porta Maggiore on the ancient Via Labicana. At the beginning of the 16th century, it lay about 390 m. east of the Aurelian Wall, near the arches of the Aqua Claudia. An inscription of 1570, which was later fixed to one of the piers of the Acqua Felice (built in 1585), records the re-erection of the obelisk. In 1633, it was taken to the courtyard of the Palazzo Barberini. There it remained for more than 135 years, until Princess Cornelia Barberini presented it to Pope Clement XIV (1769–1777), and it was taken to the Giardino della Pigna in the Vatican Palace. Finally, Pius VII arranged for it to be set up on the Pincio, and in 1822 this work was executed by Valadier.

B. MARLIANO, Urbis Romae Topographia, ed. 1544, p. 117; M. MERCATI, Ob, p. 264; B. D'OVERBEKE II, p. 15, pl. b 11; G. ZOEGA, pp. 77–79, 189 f.; G. B. CIPRIANI, Su i 12 obelischi Egizj, 1823, p. 21 f.; R. LANCIANI, MALinc I, 1889, p. 491; id., Ruins, p. 396 f.; id., Storia III, p. 164 f.; O. MARUCCHI, BCom XIX, 1891, pp. 277–279; id., Ob, pp. 132–139; CH. HÜLSEN, RM XI, 1896, pp. 122–130; A. ERMAN, ib., pp. 113–121; id., Ob, pp. 10–17, 28–47; A. BARTOLI, Disegni III, Tav. CCLXXXII, fig. 467; p. 87; P. MARCONI, MALinc XXIX, 1923, p. 180; H. JORDAN, Top I, 3, p. 251; P-A, p. 366; A. LINDSSTRÖM, pp. 79–83; G. LUGLI, Mon III, p. 485 f.; A. M. COLINI, MemPont Acc 3, VIII, 1955, p. 168 f.; E. NASH, RM LXIV, 1957, pp. 250–254.

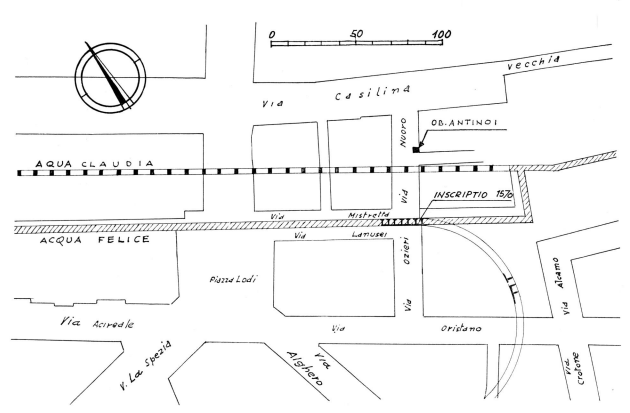

846  The original position of the Antinous Obelisk, between Via Labicana (now Via Casilina Vecchia) and the arches of the Aqua Claudia.

847  The re-erected obelisk in the Viale dell'Obelisco.                    Fot 909

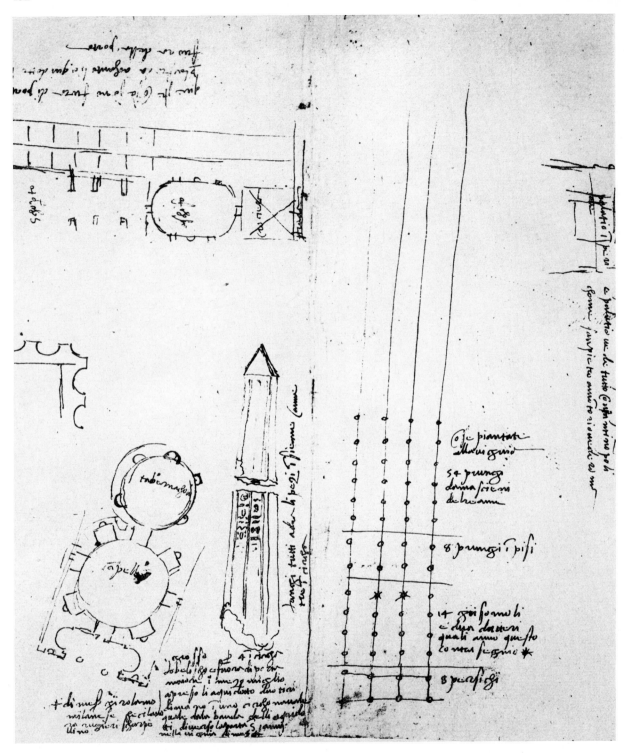

848 The earliest picture of the obelisk, a drawing by Antonio da Sangallo the Younger (about 1525) with a note: "fuora di porta maiore 1 mezo miglio apresso li aquidotto".    Fot 3053

849 An engraving by Bonaventura van Overbeek at the end of the 17th century. It shows the obelisk, broken into three pieces, in the courtyard of the Palazzo Barberini.                                                Fot 3063

850 The inscription of 1570, which records the re-erection of the obelisk. It is attached to a pier of the Acqua Felice (built in 1585) between Via Oziero and Via Nuoro.                                                Fot 700

OBELISCUS AUGUSTI IN CAMPO MARTIO. In 10 B. C. Augustus erected an obelisk, which he had brought from Heliopolis, in the Campus Martius. It stood about 89 m. west of the Ara Pacis, and served as a gnomon for a marble sundial, inlaid with bronze lines, which extended to the north of it. According to the Itinerary of the Anonymous Einsidlensis (2.5, 4.3), it was still standing in the 8th century. Parts of the dial were discovered in 1463, when a chapel (later the Sacristy) was built at S. Lorenzo in Lucina; and in 1502 the base of the obelisk and its inscription were found. The obelisk was excavated in 1748, as is recorded in an inscription on a house at No. 3, Piazza del Parlamento. Forty years later, preparations for its re-erection were started, and between 1788 and 1792 the base, and the four broken pieces of the shaft, were taken to Piazza di Montecitorio, where the obelisk was repaired with fragments from the column of Antoninus Pius (s. Columna Antonini Pii I, p. 270). It was re-erected on the 14th July 1792.

A. M. BANDINI, De Obelisco Caesaris Augusti e Campi Martii ruderibus nuper eruto, 1750; G. ZOEGA, pp. 72–74; F. CANCELLIERI, Mercato, pp. 170–172; G. B. CIPRIANI, Su i 12 obelischi Egizj, 1823, p. 20 f.; A. NIBBY, RomAnt II, pp. 265–270; G. B. DE ROSSI, Studi e Documenti di Storia e Diritto III, 1882, pp. 55–57, 59 f.; CIL VI, 702; O. MARUCCHI, Ob, pp. 104–114; R. LANCIANI, Ruins, pp. 464–466 (Bibl: p. 466); id., Storia I, pp. 83, 136, 169; IV, p. 151; id.,

BCom XLV, 1917, p. 23; TH. ASHBY, BSR II, 1904, p. 3, pl. 69 d; H. JORDAN, Top I, 3, pp. 610–612; M. L. W. LAISTNER, JRS XI, 1921, p. 265 f.; C. MOHLBERG, RendPontAcc 3, IV, 1926, pp. 263–265; P-A, p. 366 f., A. LINDSSTRÖM, pp. 42–51; G. LUGLI, Mon III, pp. 191–194; G. MARCHETTI-LONGHI, Atti 5 CStR II, pp. 531–544; G. GATTI, BCom LXVIII, 1940, pp. 266–268; E. NASH, RM LXIV, 1957, p. 237.

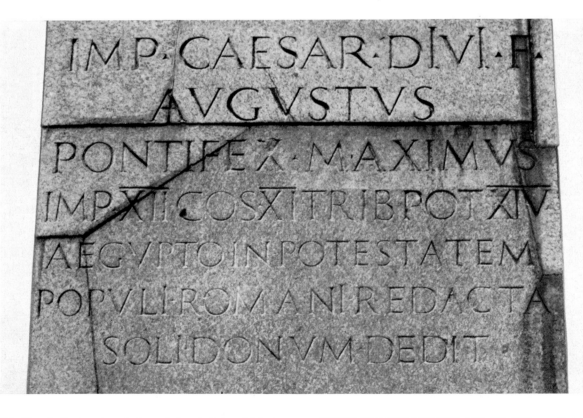

851 The dedicatory inscription of the obelisk, which Augustus "SOLI DONUM DEDIT" (CIL VI, 702).        Fot 5648

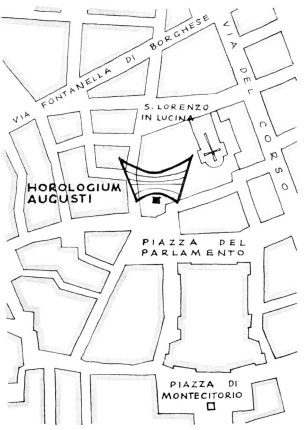

852 The original position of the obelisk, near S. Lorenzo in Lucina, and its present position in the Piazza di Montecitorio (from Lugli-Gismondi, Forma Urbis Romae, 1949).

853 The excavation of the obelisk in 1748 (Giuseppe Vasi, Le magnificenze di Roma, Bd. II, XI).           Fot 3052

854  The Obelisk of Augustus in the Piazza di Montecitorio, its position since 1792.                    Fot 4369

OBELISCUS AUGUSTI IN CIRCO MAXIMO. Of two obelisks brought to Rome by Augustus in 10 B. C., one was erected in the Campus Martius, and the other on the spina of the Circus Maximus. It was removed later to the east side of the spina, to make room in the centre for a second obelisk, which Constantine intended to bring to Rome. In 357 A. D., Constantius brought this larger obelisk from Alexandria, and set it up in the centre of the spina (s. Obeliscus Constantii). In the meantime, the obelisk of Augustus had stood alone on the east side, and in this position it is shown on a mosaic in the villa at Piazza Armerina, thus dating the mosaic between 326 A. D., the date of Constantine's last residence in Rome, and 357 A. D. (s. Magna Mater II, 711). In 1587, the obelisk was unearthed from the east side of the circus; the base with its inscription (CIL VI, 701) had already been discovered under Gregory XIII (1572–1585). Sixtus V intended to erect it in front of S. Croce in Gerusalemme (Marliani, ed. 1588; engraving by Bordino in 1588), but eventually decided on the Piazza del Popolo where, in March 1589, it was re-erected under the direction of Domenico Fontana.

I. F. BORDINUS, De rebus praeclare gestis a Sixto V. Pon. Max., 1588; B. MARLIANI, Urbis Romae Topographia, 1588, p. 67 f. (adnotatio); M. MERCATI, Ob, pp. 282, 387–390; G. Zoega, p. 72; A. Nibby, Rom Ant II, pp. 276–280; PLATNER-BUNSEN, Beschreibung III, 3, pp. 207–210; E. STEVENSON, BCom XIV, 1888, p. 277 f.; O. MARUCCHI, Ob, pp. 48, 51–90; R. LANCIANI, Storia IV, pp. 148–150; id., BCom XLV, 1917, p. 23 f.; H. JORDAN, Top I, 3, p. 124; M. MARCHETTI, BCom XLII, 1914, p. 114 f.; M. L. W. LAISTNER, JRS XI, 1921, p. 265 f.; TH. ASHBY, Roma I, 1923, p. 345 f.; P-A, p. 367; A. LINDSSTRÖM, pp. 30–41; G. LUGLI, Centro, p. 600; L. GIGLI, Studi Romani III, 1955, pp. 580–584; E. NASH, RM LXIV, p. 235 f.; G. V. GENTILI, BArte XLII, 1957, pp. 9, 22 f.; M. CAGIANO DE AZEVEDO, Scritti in onore di M. Salmi, 1961, p. 26.

855 The Obelisk of Augustus, excavated in the eastern half of the Circus Maximus, wood-cut by Girolamo Franzini of 1588 in Pompilio Totti, Ritratto di Roma Antica, 1627.                                            Fot 3056

856  The Obelisk of Augustus from the Circus Maximus in the Piazza del Popolo, where it has stood since 1589.

Fot 5269

OBELISCUS CAPITOLINUS. This obelisk stood near S. Maria in Aracoeli on the Capitol until 1542; its provenance
is unknown. It occupied a position at the foot of the steps, which a that time led from the Piazza del Campidoglio
to the church and monastery of S. Maria in Aracoeli, as is shown in seven drawings by Marten van Heemskerck,
and other views of the 16th century. Against the theory that it stood there in antiquity may be argued, not only
that according to the drawings its base stood far above the ancient level, but also that it consists of two pieces,
a small original Egyptian pointed fragment, 2.68 m. long, with hieroglyphs and a plain granite shaft about
5 m. long. When Pope Paul III was altering the Piazza del Campidoglio, he started to build a new access to
the monastery of S. Maria in Aracoeli, and the obelisk was taken down in 1542, and stored above the little
cemetery of the church. When a plan to re-erect it in the Piazza was not carried out, the Conservatori decided
on the 11th September 1582 to present it to Ciriaco Mattei, who set it up in his Villa Caelimontana. The villa
fell into disrepair with the decline of the Mattei family at the end of the 18th century. In 1813, a new owner,
Don Manuel Godoy, Principe de la Paz, found the obelisk thrown down; after putting the gardens in order he
had it re-erected in its present position, on the south side of the villa, in May 1817.

G. ZOEGA, p. 80 f.; G. B. CIPRIANO, Su i 12 obelischi Egizj, 1823, p. 23; A. NIBBY, RomAnt II, p. 289 f.; C. Re, BCom X, 1882, p. 112; A. MICHAELIS, RM VI, 1891, p. 31; O. MARUCCHI, Ob, pp. 101–103; E. RODOCANACHI, Le Capitole Romain (3), 1912, p. 143 f.; HEEMSKERCK I, p. 7 f., fol. 6, 11, 61; II, fol. 12, 16, 72, 92; P-A, p. 367; A. LINDSSTRÖM, pp. 63-66; P. PECCHIAI, Il Campidoglio nel Cinquecento, 1950, p. 64; H. SIEBENHÜNER, Das Kapitol in Rom, 1954, pp. 30, 67, 132[18]; E. NASH, RM LXIV, 1957, pp. 235, 254[80]; J.–J. GLOTON, Mél LXXIII, 1961, p. 455 f.

857  The Obeliscus Capitolinus on the right of S. Maria in Aracoeli (Heemskerck II, fol. 16 r.).                    Fot 4761

858  The Obeliscus Capitolinus seen from the Forum (Heemskerck I, fol. 6 r.).                    Fot 3530

859  The obelisk with a view over the Forum to the Colosseum (Heemskerck I, fol. 11).           Fot 4762

860  The Obeliscus Capitolinus in the Villa Caelimontana.                          Fot 912

OBELISCUS CONSTANTII. In addition to the two obelisks which he brought to Rome, Augustus also planned to bring one of the obelisks from the Temple of Ammon at Thebes, which had been erected by Totmoses III in the 15th century B. C. Constantine carried out this intention to the extent that the obelisk, destined for the spina of the Circus Maximus, was transported down the Nile to Alexandria; but when Constantine died in 337 A. D., it remained there. Twenty years later, his son Constantius brought it to Rome. In the meantime the Obelisk of Augustus (q. v. II, p. 137) had been moved to the east side of the Circus Maximus, and the new obelisk was set up in the centre of the spina. On the four sides of its base, an inscription in 24 hexameters (CIL VI, 1163) records the transportation of the obelisk, and its re-erection in Rome, following the triumph with which Constantius celebrated his victory over Magnentius, in 357 A. D. In February 1587, the obelisk was found at a depth of 7 m., broken in 3 pieces. The inscription was still legible, but it was destroyed and the fragments were used to repair the obelisk when, in 1588, it was re-erected in front of S. Giovanni in Laterano by Domenico Fontana.

M. MERCATI, Ob, pp. 277–290, 377–387; G. ZOEGA, pp. 67–69; F. CANCELLIERI, Mercato, p. 176 f.; A. Nibby, RomAnt II, pp. 257–261; S. BIRCH, Records of the past IV, 1875, pp. 9–16; O. MARUCCHI, BCom XIX, 1891, pp. 256–266; id., Ob, pp. 8–50; L. BORSARI, BCom XXVI, 1898, p. 25; H. JORDAN, Top I, 3, p. 132; R. LANCIANI, Storia I, p. 45; IV, pp. 148–151; id., BCom XLV, 1917, p. 24; TH. ASHBY, Top 1581, p. 107; P-A, p. 367 f.; A. LINDSSTRÖM, pp. 90–101; G. LUGLI, Centro, p. 602; G. LEFEBVRE, Mélanges Picard II, 1949, pp. 586–593; E. NASH, RM LXIV, 1957, p. 237.

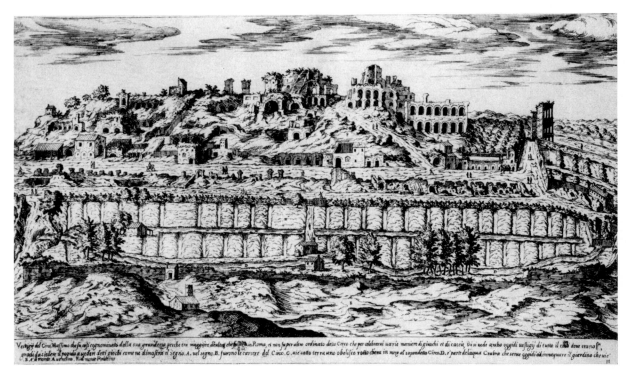

861 A picture of the Circus Maximus in 1575, with a note of the place where the obelisk lay buried "C, uie' sotto terra uno obelisco rotto ch'era in mezo al sopradetto Circo" (S. Du Pérac, I vestigi dell'antichità di Roma, 1575, fol. 11).
Fot 3058

862  The Obelisk of Constantius in the Piazza di S. Giovanni in Laterano, where it has stood since 1588.    Alinari 47306

OBELISCUS HORTORUM SALLUSTIANORUM. The obelisk of the Gardens of Sallust is a copy of Augustus' Obelisk in the Circus Maximus, which was made in the imperial period. It stood on the Collis Hortorum (Pincio), between the Porta Salaria and Porta Pinciana. It is mentioned in the 8th century Einsiedeln Itinerary, where it is called a "piramis". The overturned obelisk is shown in almost all the pictorial maps of the 16th century (Bufalini 1551, Pinardo 1555, Paciotto 1557, Cartario 1576, Du Pérac-Lafréry 1577). Its foundation was discovered when the Lutheran Church was built, in 1912, in the street block bounded by Via Sicilia, Via Toscana, Via Sardegna, and Via Abruzzi. Pope Clement XII had the obelisk taken to the Lateran in 1734, and it was intended that it should be set up in front of the new façade by Alessandro Galilei. This plan was never carried out and the obelisk lay near the Scala Santa until, in 1789, Pius VI had it re-erected in front of SS. Trinità dei Monti. The ancient base, which had been visible until the end of the 17th century, became buried and lost, and was rediscovered in 1843, in the Villa Ludovisi. In 1890 the City of Rome, to whom it had been presented, transferred this block of granite to a storehouse near the reservoir of the Aqua Marcia in Via Gaeta. In 1926, it was taken from there to the Capitol, and became a memorial to the fallen Fascists. Since 1954, the base has stood in the garden south-east of S. Maria in Aracoeli, opposite the Republican Wall.

M. MERCATI, Ob, pp. 255–259; B. D'Overbeke II, p. 17, pl. b. 12; G. ZOEGA, pp. 76 f., 616 f.; F. CANCELLIERI, Mercato, p. 164 f.; G. B. CIPRIANI, Su i 12 obelischi Egizj, 1823, p. 19 f.; A. NIBBY, RomAnt II, pp. 281–283; H. JORDAN, Top II, p. 344; TH. SCHREIBER, Die antiken Bildwerke der Villa Ludovisi, 1880, p. 144, No. 127; E. SARTI, ArchStorPat IX, 1886, p. 436; R. LANCIANI, MALinc I, 1889, p. 460 f.; id., Ruins, p. 415; O. MARUCCHI, Ob, pp. 140–147; H. JORDAN, Top I, 3, p. 434 f.; CH. HÜLSEN, Diss PontAcc 2, IX, 1907, p. 395 f.; E. KATTERFELD, RM XXVIII, 1913, pp. 95 f., 106–109; M. MARCHETTI, BCom XLII, 1914, p. 373 f.; R. BONFIGLIETTI, Capitolium IV, 1928, pp. 416–418; P-A, p. 368; A. LINDSSTRÖM, p. 84–88; C. RICCI, VdI, p. 35; G. LUGLI, Mon III, p. 332 f.; M. SANTANGELO, Quirinale, p. 180 f.; P. PECCHIAI, La scalinata di Piazza di Spagna, 1941, pp. 95–105; G. FELICI, Villa Ludovisi, 1952, p. 242 f.; E. NASH, RM LXIV, 1957, pp. 239–245, 250; J.-J. GLOTON, Mél LXXIII, 1961, pp. 457, 465–467.

863 The Obeliscus Hortorum Sallustianorum with its base in the Villa Ludovisi, in about 1680 (Bonaventura d'Overbeke II, pl. b, 12).
                                                                                                      Fot 3065

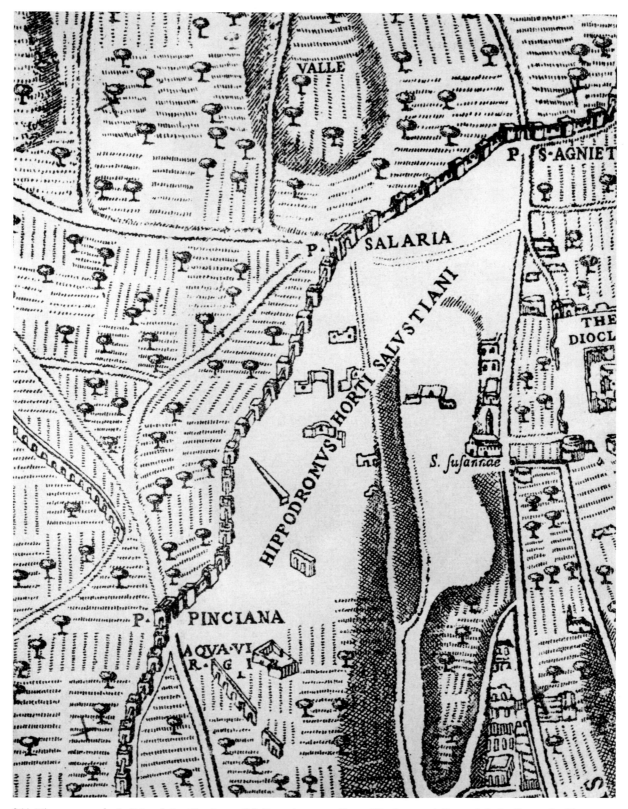

864 The upturned obelisk of the Gardens of Sallust, between Porta Pinciana and Porta Salaria (from the Francesco Paciotto plan of 1557).                    Fot 3060

865  Sketch of the excavation of 1912 between Via Toscana
     and Via Sicilia, with the foundation of the Obelisk of
     the Gardens of Sallust (after RM XXVIII, 1913, p. 94).

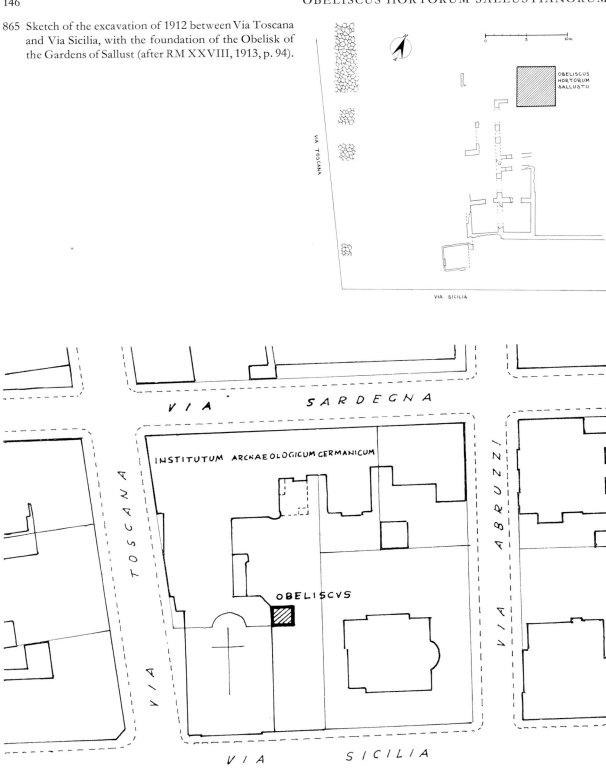

866  The ancient position of the obelisk in the street block enclosed by Via Sicilia, Via Toscana, Via Sardegna, and Via
     Abruzzi.

867 The base of the obelisk in the garden south-east of S. Maria in Aracoeli.          Fot 898

868 The Obelisk of the Gardens of Sallust in front of SS. Trinità dei Monti, where it has stood since 1789.     Fot 896

OBELISCUS ISEI CAMPENSIS – DI DOGALI. Several of the Roman obelisks came from the Iseum and Serapaeum (the Temple of Isis) in the Campus Martius; they were found near S. Maria sopra Minerva and the neighbouring Dominican convent. The last one was excavated in 1883, in Via Beato Angelico, between the apse of the church and the Biblioteca Casanatense. From its size, and the dedication to Ramses II, it must be the counterpart of the obelisk which now stands in front of the Pantheon. In June 1887, the newly-discovered obelisk was set up in front of the old railway station – the Stazione Termini – as a memorial to the 500 Italian soldiers who fell in the Battle of Dogali in Abyssinia, on the 25th January 1887. Because it obstructed the traffic, it was removed, 37 years later, to its present position in the public gardens between Viale delle Terme and Via delle Terme di Diocleziano. The removal, transportation and re-erection of the obelisk were carried out between the end of July 1924 and the 31st May 1925.

R. LANCIANI, NSc, 1883, p. 244; id., BCom XI, 1883, pp. 34, 60; E. SCHIAPARELLI, ib., pp. 72–103; O. MARUCCHI, Ob, pp. 96–100; H. JORDAN, Top I, 3, p. 570 f.; U. CONTE, Capitolium I, 1925/26, p. 152 f.; P-A, p. 369; A. LINDSSTRÖM, pp. 63, 65, 67; G. LUGLI, Mon III, p. 110; P. ROMANO, Roma nelle sue strade e nelle sua piazze, s. d. (1947), p. 142 f.; E. NASH, RM LXIV, 1957, p. 238.

869  The obelisk from the Iseum in the Campus Martius set up in front of the Rome railway station as a memorial to the soldiers killed at the Battle of Dogali.

GFN D/2186

870 The Obelisk of Dogali in the gardens in Viale delle Terme, its position since 1925.                    Fot 899

OBELISCUS ISEI CAMPENSIS – DI S. MACUTO. The obelisk which now stands in front of the Pantheon was probably discovered when the apse of S. Maria sopra Minerva was rebuilt in 1374. For a long time it lay neglected, against a wall of the church of S. Macuto; but in the middle of the 15th century it was set up in the Piazza di S. Macuto (s. Poggii Bracciolini descriptio Urbis ad Nicolaum V [1447–1455] ap. Urlichs, Cod. Topographicus, p. 241). Early in the 18th century, there was a scheme to erect it in front of the Palazzo Quirinale, between the two horse-tamers; however, nothing came of this project, for which even the model had been prepared, and later one of the obelisks from the Mausoleum of Augustus occupied the position (s. II, 877). In 1711, Pope Clement XI had the obelisk of the Piazza di S. Macuto (popularly known as the "Guglia di S. Mautte") erected on top of the fountain in the Piazza della Rotonda, in front of the Pantheon.

A. FULVIO, Delle antichità della città di Roma, 1543, p. 166; L. MAURO, Antichità di Roma, 1558, p. 100; M. MERCATI, Ob, p. 264 f.; A. DONATUS, Roma vetus ac recens (2), 1648, p. 403; A. CASSIO, Corso dell'acque I, 1756, pp. 301–303; G. ZOEGA, p. 79; G. P. CHATTARD, Nuova descrizione del Vaticano III, 1767, p. 132; F. CANCELLIERI, Mercato, p. 177 f.; G. B. CIPRIANI, Su i 12 obelischi Egizj, 1823, p. 18; A. NIBBY, RomAnt II, pp. 272–274; C. L. URLICHS, Codex Urbis Romae Topographicus, 1871, p. 241; P. ADINOLFI II, p. 371; O. MARUCCHI, Ob, pp. 91–95; P-A, p. 369; A. LINDSSTRÖM, pp. 63, 65; G. LUGLI, Mon III, p. 109; M. ARMELLINI, Chiese di Roma (3) I, 1942, p. 383 f.; C. PIETRANGELI, BCom LXXII, 1946/48, p. 204; E. NASH, RM LXIV, 1957, p. 239.

871 The obelisk from the Iseum in the Piazza di S. Macuto, with the Church of S. Ignazio (engraving by G. B. Falda about 1665).                                                                                                  Fot 3062

872 The obelisk in the Piazza della Rotonda, its position since 1711.                    Fot 900

OBELISCUS ISEI CAMPENSIS – PIAZZA DELLA MINERVA. This, the smallest of the Roman obelisks, was found in 1665 in the garden of the Dominican monastery adjoining S. Maria sopra Minerva. Pope Alexander VII (Chigi) commissioned Gian Lorenzo Bernini to erect it in the Piazza della Minerva. From Bernini's drawings, the sculptor Ercole Ferrata created the base, with the elephant supporting the obelisk, which stands in front of S. Maria sopra Minerva. The obelisk was placed in position on the 3rd February 1667, and the monument was unveiled on the 11th June of the same year.

A. KIRCHER, Obelisci Aegyptiaci nuper inter Isaei Romani rudera efossi interpretatio hieroglyphica, 1666; G. ZOEGA, p. 79 f.; G. B. CIPRIANI, Su i 12 obelischi Egizj, 1823, p. 17 f.; F. CANCELLIERI, Mercato, p. 177.; A. NIBBY, RomAnt II, pp. 263–265; R. LANCIANI, BCom XI, 1883, p. 45 f.; O. MARUCCHI, Ob, pp. 115–119; I. I. BERTHIER, L'église de la Minerve à Rome, 1910, pp. 21 f., 443; P-A, p. 369; E. ROSSI, Roma VII, 1929, p. 372; A. LINDSSTRÖM, pp. 67–69; W. S. HECKSCHER, Art Bulletin XXIX, 1947, pp. 155–182; E. NASH, RM LXIV, 1957, p. 239; J.–J. GLOTON, Mél LXXIII, 1961, pp. 458–460.

873 Obelisk from the Temple of Isis in the Piazza della Minerva, found in 1665 in the nearby Dominican monastery.     Fot 906

OBELISCUS ISEI CAMPENSIS – URBINO. The obelisk made up from several fragments, which now stands between the Palazzo Ducale and the Church of S. Domenico in Urbino, originally came from the Iseum in the Campus Martius. The fragments were probably found with the Obelisk of S. Macuto (q. v. II, p. 150) in about 1374. At the time of Paul IV (1555–1559), two of them were built into the wall of a house near the Church of S. Macuto, which from 1539–1725 had the title of S. Bartolomeo ed Alessandro dei Bergamaschi. These fragments, and another, which was in the Collegio Romano, were presented by the Jesuits to Cardinal Alessandro Albani on 16th August 1729*. In 1739, the cardinal presented the assembled obelisk, surmounted by a cross over the Albani coat-of-arms, to his native city of Urbino. One of the fragments of the obelisk was drawn in Rome by Marten van Heemskerck between 1532 and 1535, and the same fragment is illustrated in Athanasius Kircher's book (p. 134, IV).

A. KIRCHER, Obelisci Aegyptiaci nuper inter Isaei Romani rudera effossi interpretatio hieroglyphica, 1666, p. 134 f.; F. CANCELLIERI, Mercato, p. 164[5]; A. NIBBY, RomAnt II, p. 290; A. M. UNGARELLI, Interpretatio obeliscorum Urbis Romae, 1842, p. 133 f.; R. LANCIANI, BCom XI, 1883, pp. 41–44; HEEMSKERCK I, p. 34, fol. 63; B. POCQUET DU HAUT JUSSÉ, Mél XXXVI, 1916/17, pp. 96–101; P-A, p. 396 f.; E. CALZINI, Urbino e i suoi monumenti, 1897, p. 94; L. SERRA, Urbino, catalogo delle cose d'arte e di antichità, 1932, p. 81 f.; A. LINDSSTRÖM, pp. 61–64, 68 f.

* The presentation is recorded in the Diario of Francesco Valesio. A misprint in Cancellieri (Mercato, p. 164) who copied Valesio's text, gave the date as 1792 instead of 1729. Nibby (RomAnt II, p. 290) gives Valesio's note according to Cancellieri and alters the date to 1702 – at which time Alessandro Albani was only nine years old. This was copied by Lanciani (BCom XI, 1883, p. 41), and repeated by Platner-Ashby p. 369.

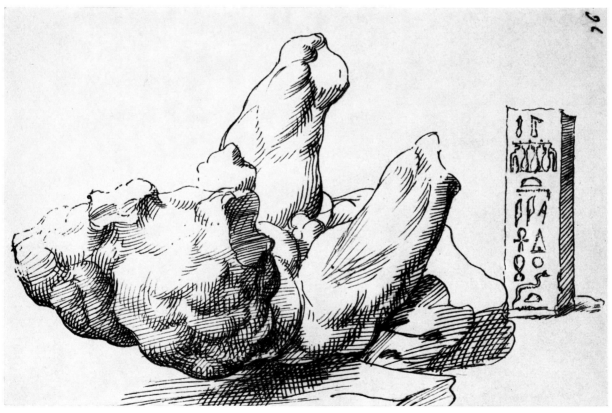

874 A drawing by Marten van Heemskerck of about 1534. A fragment of the Obelisk of Urbino is shown near the Torso Belvedere (Skizzenbücher I, fol. 63).

Fot 5293

875 The obelisk beside the Palazzo Ducale; the fragment which was drawn by van Heemskerck is visible above the
granite plinth.                                                                                            Fot 5279

OBELISCI MAUSOLEI AUGUSTI. The two obelisks which stood in front of the Mausoleum of Augustus were probably placed there by Domitian. They were discovered, shortly before 1527, near the church of S. Rocco (s. Fulvius, ed. 1527, fol. 71). In 1586 the obelisk, which had been lying in front of the church, in what is now Via di Ripetta, was taken to the Piazza dell'Esquilino, where it was re-erected under the direction of Domenico Fontana. The second obelisk, which had been lying behind the church, became buried under earth and rubble. In 1781 it was rediscovered when a drain was being laid, and in 1782 it was excavated and taken to the Piazza del Quirinale to be erected between the horse-tamers. The work began in 1783 and was completed in October 1786.

A. FULVIUS, Antiquitates Urbis, 1527, fol. 71 v; L. MAURO, Le Antichità di Roma, 1558, p. 94; U. ALDO-VRANDI, ib., p. 314; M. MERCATI, Ob, pp. 247–255, 372–377; G. ZOEGA, pp. 75 f., 616, 632–634, 644; F. CANCELLIERI, Mercato, pp. 164, 167–169; A. NIBBY, RomAnt II, pp. 261 f., 280 f.; PLATNER-BUNSEN, Beschreibung III, 2, pp. 294–296; R. LANCIANI, BCom X, 1882, pp. 152, 154 f.; id., Storia II, p. 15; IV, p. 152; O. MARUCCHI, Ob, pp. 147–149; H. JORDAN, Top I, 3, p. 620; M. MARCHETTI, BCom XLII, 1914, p. 382; TH. ASHBY, JRS IX, 1919, p. 188 (fol. 75 v); A. BARTOLI, Disegni II, Tavv. CXIII, CXXXII, fig. 241; CLXXXIV, fig. 319; P-A, p. 370; A. LINDS-STRÖM, pp. 72–78; G. A. GIGLIOLI, Capitolium VI, 1930, p. 562; G. LUGLI, Mon III, p. 199 f.; C. PIE-TRANGELI, Roma XX, 1942, pp. 441–452; E. NASH, RM LXIV, 1957, p. 237 f.

876 The obelisk from the Mausoleum of Augustus, re-erected in front of the apse of S. Maria Maggiore in 1587.                                              Fot 894

877 Obelisk from the Mausoleum of Augustus, re-erected in the Piazza del Quirinale 1783–1786.                    Fot 895

OBELISCUS MEDICEUS. The obelisk which Cardinal Ferdinando de' Medici erected in the villa he had acquired on the Pincio in 1576, was found on the site of the Temple of Isis, behind S. Maria sopra Minerva. The obelisk of Dogali and that of S. Macuto, both of a similar size, were also found there (q. v.). Aldovrandi (Memorie 37) reported in 1556, that the obelisk had been discovered a few years earlier, near the church door, where it was also seen by Pirro Ligorio (Codex Bodleianus fol. 75 v. ap. Lanciani, BCom XI, 1883, p. 42) and Lucio Mauro (Antichità p. 98) who wrote that it was "dietro a questa chiesa sulla porta picciola, ch'è presso l'altar maggiore".* It stood in the Villa Medici, in front of the garden façade of the palace, until 1788. Then, it was taken to Florence and in 1790 re-erected in the Boboli Gardens, on the garden side of the Pitti Palace.

L. MAURO, Le antichità di Roma, 1558, p. 98; U. ALDOVRANDI, ib., p. 314; id., Memorie, 1556, No. 37 (C. Fea, Misc. filologica critica e antiquaria I, 1790, p. 221); M. MERCATI, Ob, p. 246; NARDINI–NIBBY III, p. 128; B. D'OVERBEKE II, p. 19, pl. b 13; R. LANCIANI, BCom XI, 1883, pp. 41–44; id., Storia III, pp. 114, 121; A. PELLEGRINI, Bessarione, rivista di studi orientali, anno V, 1901, vol IX, nn. 59–60, pp. 5–14; P-A, p. 369; A. LINDSSTRÖM, pp. 63–66; E. NASH, RM LXIV, 1957, p. 239; J.–J. GLOTON, Mél LXXIII, 1961, p. 456 f.

* Contemporary reports agree that the obelisk was discovered in one piece "steso in terra", in the middle of the 16th century. Therefore, it cannot have anything to do with the Urbino Obelisk, as Lanciani asserts (BCom XI, 1883, p. 41), as that obelisk was composed of pieces of different obelisks, one of which was drawn by Marten van Heemskerck about 1534 (s. Obeliscus Isei Campensis – Urbino II, 874).

878 The Medici Obelisk from the Iseum in the Campus Martius in front of the garden façade of the Villa Medici in Rome (painting by an unknown 18th century artist – Maraini Collection, Rome).                    GFN E/43693

879  The Medici Obelisk in the Boboli Gardens in Florence, in front of the garden façade of the Pitti Palace.    Fot 915

OBELISCUS PAMPHILIUS. The obelisk which stands on Bernini's fountain in the Piazza Navona was found in the Circus of Maxentius on the Via Appia, lying in the centre of the spina, broken in five pieces. When Champollion first deciphered its inscription in 1822, he established that it was definitely not Egyptian, but Roman work. It gives the names of Domitian, Divus Vespasianus and Divus Titus. Since it was Domitian who rebuilt the Iseum after the fire of 80 A. D., and as the inscription refers to the "restoration of that which was destroyed", it can be assumed that the obelisk was originally set up in the Isis Temple. Maxentius must have removed it to his circus on the Via Appia, early in the 4th century. In April 1647, Pope Innocent X (Pamphili) saw the obelisk lying near the Via Appia, and had it taken to the Piazza Navona, to be erected over Bernini's central fountain. The fragments arrived at their destination in August 1648, and a year later, on the 14th August 1649, the re-erection of the obelisk was completed.*

A. KIRCHER, Obeliscus Pamphilius, 1650; M. MERCATI, Ob, p. 263 f.; G. ZOEGA, pp. 74 f., 83, 587, 646; G. B. CIPRIANI, Su i 12 obelischi Egizj, 1823, p. 17; F. CANCELLIERI, Mercato, p. 35 f.; A. NIBBY, Rom Ant II, pp. 270–272; I. ROSELLINI, I monumenti del l'Egitto e della Nubia, parte I, tomo II, 1833, p. 442 f.; O. MARUCCHI, Ob, pp. 125–131; id., BCom XLV, 1917, pp. 103–124; id., RendPontAcc 3, II, 1923/24, p. 113 f.; G. FARINA, BCom XXXVI, 1908, pp. 254–274; A. ERMAN, Ob, pp. 4–10, 18–28; TH. ASHBY, JRS IX, 1919, p. 188; P-A, p. 369; A. LINDSSTRÖM, pp. 69–71; G. LUGLI, Mon III, p. 222 f.; P. ROMANO–P. PARTINI, Piazza Navona, s. d. (1953), pp. 120 f., 132–136; E. NASH, RM LXIV, 1957, p. 238; J.–J. GLOTON, Mél LXXIII, 1961, pp. 460–462.

* The almost unanimously accepted date of the transporting and re-erection of the obelisk – 1651 – is wrong. The obelisk, surmounted by a dove (the Pamphili arms), was erected in 1649, but the fountain was not actually dedicated until the 16th June 1651.

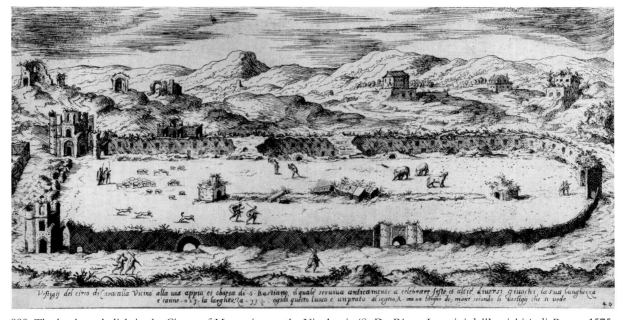

880 The broken obelisk in the Circus of Maxentius on the Via Appia (S. Du Pérac, I vestigi dell'antichità di Roma, 1575, fol. 40).

Fot 3057

881  The Obeliscus Pamphilius above Bernini's Fountain of the Four Rivers in Piazza Navona.                    Fot 913

OBELISCUS VATICANUS. The obelisk which stands in the centre of the Piazza San Pietro was brought from Heliopolis at the time of Caligula, and set up in the Circus Gai et Neronis (q. v. I, 270). It was transferred to its present position in 1586; before that, it stood south of St. Peter's, in front of the round church of S. Andrea. Excavations in 1957–1959 established that this was its original position. When it was re-erected in the Piazza San Pietro, under the direction of Domenico Fontana, the ball, which had previously surmounted it, was replaced by a cross. In 1587 the ball was presented to the City of Rome, and was used to adorn the Marforio fountain on the Piazza del Campidoglio. In 1692 it was placed at the north end of the balustrade, on a column drum; in 1848 this was replaced by the seventh milestone from the Via Appia, and the ball was taken to the Palazzo dei Conservatori, where it is exhibited in the Sala dei Bronzi.

M. MERCATI, Ob, pp. 239–244, 365–371; D. FONTANA, Del metodo tenuto nel trasportare l'obelisco Vaticano, 1590, fol. 3 r.–36 v.; G. ZOEGA, pp. 69–71; G. B. CIPRIANI, Su i 12 obelischi Egizj, 1823, pp. 12–15; A. NIBBY, RomAnt II, pp. 283–289; PLATNER-BUNSEN, Beschreibung II, 1, pp. 156–165; H. JORDAN, Top II, pp. 429, 625; CIL VI, 882; R. LANCIANI, Ruins, p. 549 f. (Bibl: p. 551); id., Storia IV, pp. 144–147; O. MARUCCHI, Ob. pp. 149–151; H. JORDAN, Top I, 3, p. 657; G. McN. RUSHFORTH, JRS IX, 1919, pp. 43, 56 f.; A. GRAF, Roma nella memoria e nelle imaginazioni del Medio Evo, 1923, pp. 226–234; CH. HÜLSEN, Roma I, 1923, pp. 412–418; H. ST. Jones, Cons, p. 171; P–A, p. 370 f.; A. LINDSSTRÖM, pp. 52–58; G. ZUCCHETTI, Ecclesia IX, 1950, pp. 523–526; G. CECCHELLI, Capitolium XXV, 1950, pp. 53–71; SCHÜLLER-PIROLI, 2000 Jahre Sankt Peter, 1950, p. 192 f.; P. PECCHIAI, Il Campidoglio nel cinquecento, 1950, pp. 64 f., 73; J. M. C. TOYNBEE–J. WARD PERKINS, The shrine of St. Peter, 1956, pp. 9–12, 20–22; E. NASH, RM LXIV, 1957, p. 234 f.; C. PIETRANGELI, Capitolium XXXII, 1957, 2, p. 10; M. GUARDUCCI, La tomba di S. Pietro, 1959, pp. 34–37; F. CASTAGNOLI, RendPontAcc 3, XXXII, 1959/60, pp. 97–121; J.–J. GLOTON, Mél LXXIII, 1961, pp. 440, 448–451.

882 The Obeliscus Vaticanus in its former position, south of St. Peter's (Heemskerck II, fol. 7 r.).　　　Fot 4763

883  The obelisk in the Piazza S. Pietro, its position since 1586.                    Fot 903

PALATINUS MONS. According to tradition, the first Roman settlement was on the Palatine, and it was there that Romulus founded the city in the middle of the 8th century B. C. Remains of hut settlements have been found on both summits of the hill; on the GERMALUS to the west, and on the PALATIUM to the east. The foundations of three huts were excavated in 1948, between the Temple of Magna Mater and the Scalae Caci, where, according to literary tradition, the "casa Romuli" stood, an antiquity which was preserved until the 4th century A. D. (CodTop I, p. 128). In 1912/1914, a hutted settlement was discovered under the Domus Flavia on the Palatium. The steep slopes of the hill were partly supported by buttresses, and partly covered by buildings. During a vain search for the Lupercal in 1938/40, buildings of the imperial epoch were uncovered on the south-west corner of the hill. In the same way, the remains of an imperial building were found when Vignola's gateway of the Farnese Gardens was re-erected in 1958, at the east side of the hill.

C. L. VISCONTI – R. LANCIANI, Guida del Palatino, 1873; E. HAUGWITZ, Der Palatin, seine Geschichte und seine Ruinen, 1901; H. JORDAN, Top I, 1, pp. 162–178; V. REINA–U. BARBIERI, NSc, 1904, pp. 43–46; S. B. PLATNER, ClPhil I, 1906, pp. 69–80; D. VAGLIERI, NSc, 1907, pp. 185–205; id., RendLinc 5, XVII, 1908, pp. 201–210; L. PIGORINI, RendLinc 5, XVI, 1907, pp. 669–680; XVIII, 1909, pp. 249–262; J. B. CARTER, AJA XII, 1908, pp. 172–183; P. GRAFFUNDER, RE, Rom, 1914, pp. 1011–1016; T. FRANK, Buildings, pp. 91–109; E. TÄUBLER, RM XLI, 1926, pp. 212–226; CH. HÜLSEN, Forum und Palatin, 1926, pp. 68–75; P-A, pp. 101 f., 374–380 (Bibl: pp. 377, 380); I. A. POPESCU, Ephem. Dacoromana IV, 1930, pp. 3–5; A. M. COLINI, BCom LXIV, 1938, p. 282; V. BASANOFF, MemLinc 6, IX, 1939, pp. 5–109; A. M. COLINI, BCom LXVII, 1939, p. 208 f.; G. Bovini, ib., p. 209; G. DE ANGELIS d'Ossat, BCom LXII, 1934, pp. 75–87; P. BAROCELLI, BCom LXX, 1942, p.131 f.; G. LUGLI, Capitolium XVIII, 1943, pp. 203–210; id., Eranos XLI, 1943, pp. 11–13; id., Centro, pp. 242, 389–427, 447–455 (Bibl: pp. 389–393, 427); M. MARELLA VIANELLO, Antichità I, 1947, pt. 3, pp. 3–34; K. ZIEGLER, RE, Palatium, 1949, pp. 5–81; F. CASTAGNOLI, Studies pres. to D. M. Robinson I, 1951, pp. 389–399 (Bibl: p. 389 f.); S. M. PUGLISI, MALinc XLI, 1951, pp. 3–98; P. ROMANELLI, ib., pp. 101–124; A. DAVICO, ib., pp. 125–134; P. ROMANELLI, Bull. Paletnologia Ital. N. S. 9, LXIV, 1954/'55, pp. 257–260; G. CARETTONI, ib., pp. 261–276; B. ANDREAE, AA 1957, pp. 141–146; M. E. BLAKE II, p. 124; R. BLOCH, The origins of Rome, 1960, pp. 66–75; G. CARETTONI, JRS L, 1960, pp. 197–203; E. GJERSTAD, ActaInstSueciae XVII, 3, 1960, pp. 45–131.

884 Air photograph of the Palatine                                    Fot 4797

885 Reconstruction of the wooden frame of an
    8th century hut on the Germalus (Architect
    A. Davico).                    GFN E/33227

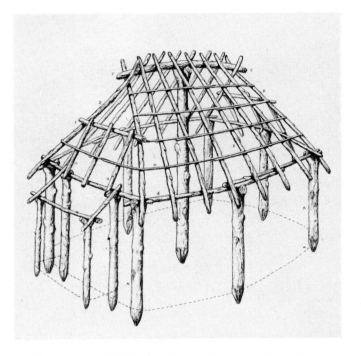

886 Foundations of a hut with post holes.                                    GFN E/27102

887 A reconstruction of a hut belonging to the archaic settlement on the Germalus.   Fot 6402

888 The remains of three huts on the Germalus.

GFN E/27100

889  An archaic cistern on the Germalus, west of the Domus Augusti.                    Arch Vat IX–20–7

890 Remains of an imperial building on the east side of the Palatine, discovered in 1958.                    Fot 5118

891  Two storeys of barrel-vaulted rooms of a building on the east side of the Palatine, discovered during the re-erection
of Vignola's gateway in 1958.                                                                        Fot 5117

892  Remains of buildings of the imperial era on the south-west corner of the Palatine, excavated in 1938/40.    Fot 421

893 North-east corner of the Palatine with the buttresses of the precinct of the Temple of Iuppiter Ultor (q. v.).  Fot 423

894 Buttress walls on the north-east side of the Palatine, above the remains of an "insula".

Fot 228

PANTHEON. The temple in the Campus Martius which was built by Agrippa, either during or after his third consulate in 27 B. C., faced south. After the fire in 80 A. D., it was restored by Domitian. In 110 A. D., after being struck by lightning it was again burnt down, and was rebuilt by Hadrian with its front to the north, so that the front row of the columns of the pronaos now stands on the foundations of the rear wall of Agrippa's temple. The domed building, which is almost entirely preserved, was started in 118/119 A. D. and presumably was consecrated between 125 and 128 A. D., during Hadrian's sojourn in Rome. A restoration by Septimius Severus and Caracalla is recorded in an inscription on the architrave (CIL VI, 896). In 608 A. D., the East Roman emperor Phocas presented the Pantheon to Pope Boniface IV, who consecrated it as the Church of S. Maria ad Martyres. For a thousand years it was a source of valuable building material. The emperor Constantius II helped himself to the bronze roof tiles in 663 A. D., and Pope Urban VIII removed the bronze beams from the pronaos. They were melted down to make 80 cannons for the Castel Sant' Angelo, and the bronze columns of the baldacchino in St. Peter's.

F. GORI, ArchStor II, 1877, pp. 244–256, 273–288; R. LANCIANI, NSc, 1881, pp. 255–269 (Bibl: p. 256 f.); 1882, pp. 340–345 (Bibl: p. 340); G. CHEDANNE, CRAI, 1892, pp. 122–125, 171, 401, 408 f.; CH. HÜLSEN, RM VIII, 1893, pp. 305–318; L. BELTRAMI, NSc, 1892, pp. 88–90; id., Il Pantheon, 1898; R. LANCIANI, BCom XX, 1892, pp. 150–159; id., Ruins, pp. 473–486; F. G. MOORE, AJA III, 1899, pp. 40–43;

J. DURM, Baukunst d. Römer (2), 1905, pp. 550–572; R. LANCIANI, Storia II, pp. 236–240; H. JORDAN, Top I, 3, pp. 581–589; F. CERASOLI, BCom XXXVII, 1909, pp. 280–289; TH. ASHBY, Top 1581, pp. 128–132; G. CASCIOLI, DissPontAcc 2, XV, 1921, p. 373 f.; G. T. RIVOIRA, RomArch, pp. 122–131; A. M. COLINI – I. GISMONDI, BCom LIV, 1926, pp. 67–92; G. BELTRAMI, Roma V, 1927, p. 471; id., Il Pantheon

895 The Pantheon.                                                                              Fot 931

rivendicato ad Adriano, 1929; G. Cozzo, Ingegneria Romana, 1927, pp. 257–297; A. von Gerkan, Gnomon V, 1929, pp. 273–277; P. Gentizon, RA 5, XXX, 1929, pp. 121–123; P-A, pp. 382–386 (Bibl: p. 385 f).; C. Montani, Capitolium VIII, 1932, pp. 417–426; F. W. Shipley, Agrippa, pp. 55–65; J. Guey, Mél LIII, 1936, pp. 198–249; G. Lugli, Mon III, pp. 123–150 (Bibl: p. 124 f.); B. Goetze, Ein röm. Rundgrab in Falerii, 1939, pp. 47–49; K. Lehmann, Art Bulletin XXVII, 1945, p. 22 f.; H. Bloch, Bolli, pp. 14–19, 102–117; M. E. Blake I, p. 161; K. Ziegler, RE, Pantheon, 1949, pp. 729–741; C. H. O. Scaife, JRS XLIII, 1953, p. 37; F. Sanguinetti, Palladio N. S. VI, 1956, p. 78 f.; P. Mingazzini, AC IX, 1957, p. 108 f.; G. Lugli, Tecnica I, p. 666 f.; A. von Gerkan, Göttinger gel. Anzeigen CCXII, 1958, p. 197; R. Vighi, Il Pantheon, 1959; L. Crema, ArchRom, pp. 375–381; V. Bartoccetti, S. Maria ad Martyres, s. d. (1960), pp. 7–25.

896 The rotunda and dome of the Pantheon, seen from the south-east.                                     Fot 933

897 View into the interior with the leaves of the ancient door in the foreground.

Sopr Lazio 4357

898 The interior of the Pantheon.

899 The coffering of the dome, and the relieving arches of the drum.
Sopr Lazio 9804

900 The Pantheon in 1534, with a bell tower which was built in 1270. The collapsed left side of the pronaos was restored between 1662 and 1666 (Heemskerck I, fol. 10). Fot 4766

901  The Pantheon with Bernini's bell towers, erected at the time of Urban VIII, and removed in 1883.        Fot 6401

PLUTEI TRAIANI. The pair of marble reliefs dating from the reign of Hadrian, which came to light in the Roman Forum, in 1872, between the Comitium and the Column of Phocas, are known as the "Plutei" or "Anaglypha Traiani". One of the panels shows the burning of the records on the occasion of a remission of taxes, which took place in 118 A. D. (CIL VI, 967). The left hand relief depicts an emperor standing on a Rostra, and a statue of Trajan receiving the thanks of a mother for the "institutio alimentaria" (CIL IX, 1455; XI, 1147). In the background of each panel, we see the buildings which surrounded the Forum on its west, south and east sides, systematically displayed – from the Rostra which was at the west end of the Forum, at the right, to the Rostra Aedis Divi Iuli, at the left. The right hand end of the right hand panel lacks a block of marble, 1.30 m. wide, on which presumably the Temple of Concord was shown. After this we see the Temple of Vespasian, an arch without decoration, the Ionic Temple of Saturn, and the Vicus Iugarius, followed by the arcades of the Basilica Iulia. The panel terminates with the statue of Marsyas with the fig tree which is repeated on the other panel, after which come more arches of the Basilica Iulia. An interval at the side of the Basilica Iulia indicates the Vicus Tuscus, after which comes the Temple of Castor. The emperor stands on the Rostra of the Temple of Julius Caesar; his attendants ascend the ramp of the Rostra, passing through an archway. This must be the central opening of the Arch of Augustus. For better protection, the reliefs were removed in 1949 from the place where they were discovered, and set up inside the Curia.

G. HENZEN, BullInst, 1872, pp. 274–281; E. BRIZIO, AnnInst, 1872, pp. 309–330; C. L. VISCONTI, Deux actes de Domitien en qualité de censeur représentés dans les bas-reliefs du double pluteus, 1873; F. M. NICHOLS, The Roman Forum, 1877, pp. 60–76; H. JORDAN, Top I, 2, pp. 219–226, 246–250; L. CANTARELLI, BCom XVII, 1889, pp. 99–115; XXVIII, 1900, p. 145 f.; XLVIII, 1920, p. 169 f.; CH. HÜLSEN, RM IV, 1889, p. 239 f.; E. PETERSON, RM XIV, 1899, pp. 222–229; J. H. MIDDLETON I, pp. 345–348; A. S. JENKINS, AJA V, 1901, pp. 58–82; CH. HÜLSEN, RM XVIII, 1903, p. 20 f.; id., FR, p. 91–96; TH. ASHBY, CR XX, 1906, p. 132 f.; O. RICHTER, Beiträge II, pp. 25–30; J. B. CARTER, AJA XIV, 1910, pp. 310–317; E. DE RUGGIERO, pp. 366–369; H. THÉDENAT, FR, pp. 129 f., 260–262; J. SIEVEKING, Festschrift P. Arndt, 1925, p. 28 f.; W. SCHEEL, RM XLIII, 1928, pp. 234–238; E. STRONG, SR I, pp. 138–142; W. SESTON, Mél XLIV, 1927, pp. 154–183; P-A, pp. 453–455; S. PANTZERHIELM THOMAS, Symbolae Osloenses X, 1932, pp. 122–145; E. SVENBERG, Eranos XXXI, 1933, pp. 121–140; O. MARUCCHI, Le Forum Romain et le Palatin (3), 1933, pp. 138–148 (Bibl: p. 139); J. M. C. TOYNBEE, The Hadrianic School, 1934, p. 244; W. H. GROSS, Bildnisse Traians, 1940, p. 53; G. LUGLI, Centro, pp. 160–164, 167; id., MonMin, p. 107 f.; M. HAMMOND, MAARome XXI, 1953, pp. 127–183; E. WELIN, SFR, pp. 89–93; S. STUCCHI, Mon, pp. 82–88; B. ANDREAE, AA 1957, p. 162 f.; H. KÄHLER, Rom und seine Welt II, 1960, pp. 262–265.

902 The left marble panel with the monument to Trajan for the "institutio alimentaria".                    Fot 6458

903 The Suovetaurilia of the completely preserved left panel.  Fot 6639

904 The Suovetaurilia of the right panel.  Fot 6640

905 The right panel, with the burning of the records on the occasion of a remission of taxes in 118 A. D.  Fot 6457

PONS AELIUS. In connection with the building of his mausoleum on the right bank, Hadrian built a bridge across the Tiber which was completed in 134 A. D. (CIL VI, 973). In antiquity, the bridge was called the Pons Aelius or Pons Hadriani; and in the middle ages it was known as the "Pons Sancti Petri", or "Pons Sancti Angeli". It kept its original form until the end of the last century. When the course of the Tiber was being altered, and new embankments were built, the bridge was drastically altered in 1892–1894. During this work, the ancient ramps were uncovered, the one on the left bank was about 33 m. long, and the one on the right bank 22 m. These were destroyed, and two smaller arches of the ancient bridge were replaced by two larger ones on each side of the three ancient central arches. Nicholas V furnished the bridge with a new balustrade, after the old one had been broken in the Holy Year of 1450, causing the death of 172 pilgrims. In place of the ancient statues, which are shown on a medallion of Hadrian (F. Gnecchi, Medaglioni Rom. II, Tav. 42, 4), the modern Ponte S. Angelo was decorated with angels of the School of Bernini, in 1667–1669. In 1527, Clement VII placed the statues of St. Peter and St. Paul at the east end of the bridge.

s. a. Navalia II, 829, 830.

A. NIBBY, RomAnt I, pp. 159–166; H. JORDAN, Top I, 1, p. 416; R. LANCIANI, BCom XVI, 1888, p. 129 f.; L. BORSARI, NSc, 1892, pp. 231–233, 412–428; C. L. VISCONTI, BCom XX, 1892, pp. 263–266; CH. HÜLSEN, RM VIII, 1893, pp. 321–323; R. LANCIANI, BCom XXI, 1893, pp. 14–26; id., Ruins, pp. 22–24; S. R. PIERCE, JRS XV, 1925, pp. 95–98; P–A, p. 396 f.; M. BORGATTI, Castel Sant'Angelo in Roma, 1931, pp. 61–67; G. LUGLI, Mon II, pp. 310–315; J. LE GALL, Tibre, pp. 211–215.

906 Pons Aelius.                                                                        Fot 589

907 The ancient central arches of the Pons Aelius.                    Fot 3667

908 The Pons Aelius before the embankment was built in 1892.          Fot 4321

909 Ancient ramp on the left bank of the Tiber, discovered in 1892 and then destroyed.                    Fot 2966

910 The ramp on the left bank of the Tiber seen from the north. Fot 3202

911 The ramp on the left bank of the Tiber seen from the south. Fot 3201

PONS AEMILIUS. The arch, known as the Ponte Rotto, which stands below the island, belonged to the Pons Aemilius, the first stone bridge over the Tiber. The piers were built in 179 B. C. by the censors M. Fulvius Nobilior and M. Aemilius Lepidus, and were not connected by stone arches until 142 B. C. In the middle ages, the bridge was called Pons Senatorum (Mirabilia 9, CodTop III, 26), or Pons S. Mariae, after a picture of the Madonna in a small chapel which stood on the bridge. Since the 13th century, numerous repairs to the bridge are recorded. During a flood in 1557 two of the arches fell; they were rebuilt by Gregory XIII for the Holy Year of 1575. However, after the flood of 14th December 1598 had carried away its eastern half, the bridge was not repaired again. In 1853, the three arches which were still connected to the right bank of the Tiber were joined by an iron suspension bridge to the left bank; but in 1885 this was removed, also two of the ancient arches on the right bank, so that to-day all that remains of the Pons Aemilius is a single arch in the middle of the river.

A. NIBBY, RomAnt I, pp. 193–199; P. ADINOLFI I, pp. 24–28; H. JORDAN, Top I, 1, pp. 409–414, 420 f.; O. RICHTER, Befestigung des Janiculums, 1882, pp. 18–20; R. LANCIANI, NSc, 1885, p. 157 f.; id., Ruins, p. 20 (Bibl: p. 21); O. GILBERT, Rom III, pp. 257–260; CH. HÜLSEN, RM VI, 1891, p. 147; M. BESNIER, L'Ile Tibérine, 1902, pp. 128–130; R. LANCIANI, Storia II, pp. 22–28; IV, pp. 49, 84; TH. ASHBY, Mél XXVI, 1906, pp. 180 f., 189–193; id., Top 1581, p. 58; R. DELBRÜCK, HB I, pp. 12–22; II, Taf. 2; M. MARCHETTI, BCom XLII, 1914, p. 390; T. FRANK, Buildings, pp. 139–141; P-A, p. 397 f.; G. LUGLI, Mon II, pp. 298–303; G. GATTI, BCom LXVIII, 1940, p. 136 f.; M. E. BLAKE I, pp. 178, 198; J. LE GALL, Tibre, pp. 75–80, 106; id., RA 6, XLVII, 1956, pp. 34–39; L. CREMA, ArchRom, p. 12; H. COHEN, Monnaies Imp. II, 1882, p. 27, Antoninus Pius, 17, 18; D. O. ARRIVABENE, Capitolinum XXXVII, 1962, p. 135.

912 The Ponte Rotto, the remains of the Pons Aemilius.                                                    Fot 585

913 The arch of the Pons Aemilius
seen from the island.    Fot 5594

914 The west side of the Pons Aemilius connected with the left bank of the river by a suspension bridge, before the
destruction of the arches on the right bank in 1885.                                      Fot 6434

PONS AGRIPPAE. In 1887, an inscribed cippus (CIL VI, 31545) was found on the Tiber bank, about 660 m. upstream from the Ponte Sisto. It had been set up by the "curatores riparum", between 41 and 44 A. D., and testified to the existence of a Pons Agrippae, which until then had been unknown. In the same year the foundations of a bridge were discovered, both in the river-bed and on the banks. This bridge crossed the Tiber 160 m. north-west of the Ponte Sisto, from what is now the Lungotevere Tebaldi, in the direction of the tomb of C. Sulpicius Platorinus and the Transtiberine section of the Aurelian Wall. These remains are identified as the Pons Agrippae. According to a fragment of the Fasti Ostienses (NSc, 1939, p. 361), the bridge was restored by Antoninus Pius in 147 A. D.

L. BORSARI, NSc, 1887, pp. 322–327; G. GATTI, BCom XV, 1887, pp. 306–313; L. BORSARI, BCom XVI, 1888, pp. 92–98; CH. HÜLSEN, RM IV, 1889, p. 285 f.; id., RM VI, 1891, p. 135 f; R. LANCIANI, Ruins, p. 21 f.; P-A, p. 398; F. W. SHIPLEY, Agrippa, p. 66 f.; G. LUGLI, Mon II, p. 308 f.; G. CALZA, NSc, 1939, pp. 361, 364; M. E. BLAKE I, pp. 45, 161; H. RIEMANN, RE, Pons Agrippae, 1952, pp. 2455–2461; J. LE GALL, Tibre, pp. 157, 210 f.

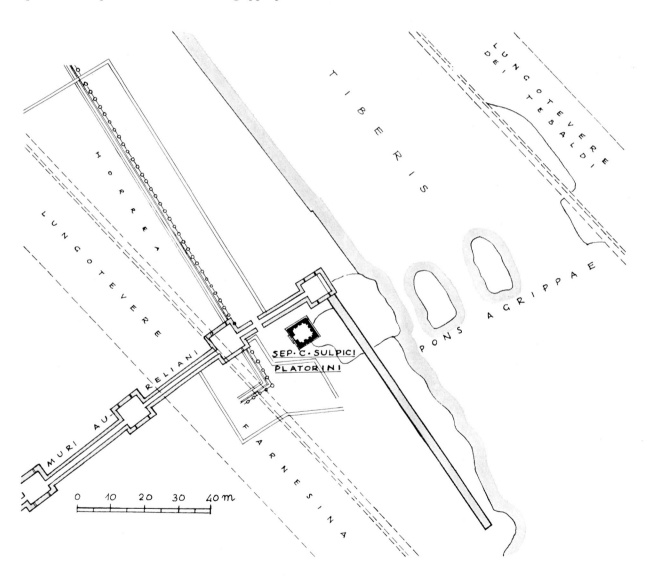

915 Site-plan of the remains of the Pons Agrippae discovered in 1887.

PONS AURELIUS. Sixtus IV built the Ponte Sisto on the foundations of the ancient Pons Aurelius in 1473/75, the name of which is handed down in the Regionary Catalogue (Reg. XIV). In later literary sources it is also called Pons Antoninus, Ianicularis, Tremulus, Valentinianus and, after its destruction, Ruptus and Fractus (CodTop III, p. 26; IV, p. 128). Its founder was probably Marcus Aurelius Antoninus Caracalla. The bridge and a triumphal arch standing at the entrance to the Campus Martius were restored in 366–67 A. D. by the emperors Valens and Valentinianus (CIL VI, 31402–31412). Remains of the arch, and its marble and bronze decoration, were found in the bed of the Tiber in 1878, when the left side of the river was drained. The foundations of the piers of the ancient bridge were also visible.

A. NIBBY, RomAnt I, pp. 178–183; H. JORDAN, Top I, 1, p. 417 f.; II, pp. 192–195; P. ADINOLFI I, pp. 18–22; R. LANCIANI, NSc, 1878, p. 343 f.; id., BCom VI, 1878, pp. 241–248; IX, 1881, p. 11; id., Ruins, pp. 24–26; A. MAYERHÖFER, Die Brücken im Alten Rom (2), 1884, pp. 87–116; L. BORSARI, NSc, 1887, p. 325 f.; G. GATTI, NSc, 1892, p. 50; F. BARNABEI, ib., p. 234 f.; CH. HÜLSEN, RM VII, 1892, p. 329; D. MARCHETTI, BCom XX, 1892, pp. 139–145; G. DEHN, RM XXVI, 1911, pp. 238–259; R. PARIBENI, RM XXVIII, 1913, pp. 113–121; TH. ASHBY, Top 1581, p. 58; P-A, p. 398 f.; R. PARIBENI, MusNaz, p. 206, No. 550; p. 307, No. 1073; G. LUGLI, Mon II, pp. 315–318; J. LE GALL, Tibre, pp. 295–301; F. CASTAGNOLI, BCom LXXIV, 1951/52, p. 52; F. GNECCHI, Medaglioni Romani II, Tav. 61, 1; H. RIEMANN, RE, Pons Valentiniani, 1952, pp. 2469–2482; R. A. STACCIOLI, Capitolium XXXIII, 1958, 2, pp. 3–5.

916 The arch of the Ponte Sisto on the right bank of the Tiber with remains of the foundations of the Pons Aurelius.

Fot 596

917  The Ponte Sisto built on the remains of the Pons Aurelius in 1473/75.                    Fot 594

918  The pier of the Ponte Sisto on the right bank; it is built on the foundations of the Pons Aurelius and indicates
     the greater width of the ancient bridge.                                                  Fot 595

PONS CESTIUS. The bridge, which connects the right bank of the Tiber with the island, was called the Pons
Cestius in the 4th century Regionary Catalogue. Its builder was presumably a certain Cestius, who was curator
viarum between 62 and 27 B. C. In 370 A. D., a hastily erected new bridge was dedicated, as the Pons Gratiani
(CIL VI, 1175, 1176); among other ancient building material used in its construction was travertine from the
nearby Theatre of Marcellus. In 1885/1889, when the channel to the west of the island was widened from 48 to
76 m., the bridge was taken down. In 1892 a new bridge was completed, the centre arch of which was rebuilt
to its original design and measurements, 347 of the 563 ancient travertine blocks being used again. In place of
the small side arches of the Pons Gratiani, with openings of 5.80 m., the new side arches were built to the
same width as the centre arch, increasing the total length of the bridge from 48 m. to 80.40 m.

FLAVIO BIONDO-LUCIO FAUNO, Roma Ristaurata,1543, II, 79–81; A. NIBBY, RomAnt I, pp. 167–174; F. RE-BER, Ruinen, pp. 319–321; H. JORDAN, Top I, 1, pp. 418–420; P. ADINOLFI I, pp. 22–24; R. LANCIANI, NSc, 1885, p. 188; 1886, p. 159; L.Borsari, BCom XVII, 1889, pp. 165–172; Ch. HÜLSEN, RM IV, 1889, pp. 282–285; P. BONATO, Annali della Soc. degli ingegneri e degli architetti italiani IV, 1889, parte II, pp. 139–151; R. LANCIANI, Ruins, p. 18 f.; M. BES-NIER, L'Ile Tibérine, 1902, pp. 106–119; P-A, p. 399 f.; G. LUGLI, Mon II, pp. 306–308; id., Tecnica I, pp. 239, 325, fig. 61; M. E. BLAKE I, p. 146 f.; J. LE GALL, Tibre, pp. 208 f., 301–305.

919 Ponte Cestio, seen from the south.                                                    Fot 582

920  Ponte Cestio, seen from the north.                                         Fot 5597

921  The Pons Gratiani, built on the remains of the Pons Cestius before it was destroyed in 1885. Under the parapet is
the dedicatory inscription to Gratianus (CIL VI, 1176).                         Fot 2964

PONS FABRICIUS. The bridge which connected the left bank of the Tiber to the island was built in 62 B. C. by the curator viarum L. Fabricius. Inscriptions over the arches of the bridge (CIL VI, 1305, 31594) record the date and the name of the builder. The left arch of the bridge also bears an inscription of the consuls in 21 B. C., M. Lollius and Q. Lepidus, referring either to a restoration of the left side of the bridge, or to the final approval of the structure by the authorities ("COS. EX. S. C. PROBAVERUNT"), 41 years after the building started. In the middle ages, the bridge was also known as the Pons Iudaeorum (CodTop I, p. 26) "ubi Iudaei habitare videntur" (letter of Benedict VIII of 1018). The later name of Ponte dei Quattro Capi, which is given in Albertini's Opusculum de mirabilibus Urbis Romae of 1510 (CodTop IV, p. 466), derives from the four-headed herms which served as the piers of the bronze balustrade on the ancient bridge. They were incorporated into the new parapet, which was built by Innocent XI in 1679.

A. NIBBY, RomAnt I, pp. 174–178; H. JORDAN, Top I, 1, p. 418 f.; C. L. URLICHS, Cod. Urb. Romae Topographicus, 1871, p. 204; P. ADINOLFI I, p. 21 f.; CH. HÜLSEN, RM VI, 1891, p. 135[1] f.; J. H. MIDDLETON II, p. 367 f.; R. LANCIANI, Ruins, p. 17 f.; M. BESNIER, L'Ile Tibérine, 1902, pp. 93–105; T. FRANK, Buildings, p. 142 f.; TH. ASHBY, Practical engineering in ancient Rome (Brit. Assoc., section H, Anthropology, 1925) p. 6; P-A, p. 400; G. LUGLI, Mon II, pp. 303–305; M. E. BLAKE I, pp. 146, 172; J. LE GALL, Tibre, pp. 205–208; L. A. HOLLAND, Janus and the bridge, 1961, pp. 212–218.

922 Pons Fabricius, seen downstream.

923  Pons Fabricius, seen upstream.                                                          Fot 579

924  The arch adjoining the left bank of the Tiber with the inscriptions of Fabricius, and of the consuls Lollius and
     Lepidus.                                                                                Fot 5650

PONS MULVIUS. The Via Flaminia, which was built in 220 B. C., crossed the Tiber by the Pons Mulvius* which, at the latest, must date from the building of the road. In literature, the bridge is first mentioned in connection with an historical event in 207 B. C. (Livy XXVII, 51, 2). The stone bridge, the remains of which are preserved in the modern structure, was built in 109 B. C. by the censor M. Aemilius Scaurus. For more than 2000 years it has served as the principal entrance to the city of Rome, and in its long history it has been damaged many times by wars and floods. After the 14th century, the broken end arches of the bridge were replaced by wooden gangways; these were burnt several times in subsequent battles, but remained unchanged, even after extensive restorations had been effected by Nicholas V and Calixtus III, in 1451–1458. Finally, the bridge was completely restored, in 1805, by Giuseppe Valadier. During the defence of Rome by Garibaldi in 1849, the arch at the north end of the bridge was blown up, and the roadway rendered unusable. The damage was repaired in the same year.

G. A. GUATTANI, Memorie enciclopediche romane I, 1806, pp. 5–8; A. NIBBY, RomAnt I, pp. 183–193; id., Analisi della carta de'dintorni di Roma (2) II, 1848, pp. 580–588; H. JORDAN, Top I, 1, p. 415; G. TOMASSETTI, ArchStorPat VI, 1883, pp. 207–221; id., La Campagna Romana III, 1913, pp. 232–236; R. DEL-BRÜCK, HB I, pp. 3–11; TH. ASHBY, JRS XI, 1921, p. 137; T. FRANK, Buildings, p. 141 f.; E. MARTINORI, Via Flaminia, 1929, pp. 36–48; E. AMADEI, Capitolium IX, 1933, pp. 548–558; M. E. BLAKE I, p. 134; H. H. BALLANCE, BSR XIX, 1951, pp. 79–84; J. LE GALL, Tibre, pp. 86–91; id., RA 6, XLVII, 1956, p. 38 f.

* The Pons Mulvius is the only Roman bridge which has not altered its name, although the name itself has changed its form in the course of time. Milvius, Molbius (CodTop I, passim) in antiquity and, since the 14th century, Pons Mollis, Ponte Mole and Ponte Molle.

925 Pons Mulvius, west side.                                                                 Fot 602

926  The ancient arches of the Pons Mulvius, east side.                                      Fot 605

PONS NERONIANUS. The remains of the bridge, which was called Pons Neronianus in the Mirabilia (CodTop III, p. 26)*, can be seen at low water immediately below the Ponte Vittorio Emanuele. It crossed the river in line with the Via Recta, whose course from Via Flaminia (Via del Corso) to the bridge through Vicolo del Curato, Via dei Coronari, Via di S. Agostino, and Via delle Coppelle, is still recognizable in the modern street plan. From the fact that it is not mentioned in the 4th century Regionary Catalogue, it may be assumed that the bridge was destroyed before the time of Constantine. The erection of an "ARCUS ARCADII, HONORII ET THEODOSII" near the west end of the bridge, after Stilicho's victory over the Goths at Pollentia in 405 A. D. (CIL VI, 1196), does not mean that the bridge was still in existence in the 5th century; the Aurelian Wall had stood between its remains and the triumphal arch, since the end of the 3rd century. With the building of the City Wall along the left bank of the Tiber, the bridge could no longer have served the traffic which passed from the Via Flaminia, across the Campus Martius, to the Gardens of Agrippina on the right bank; even if it had been accessible from the POSTERULA DE EPISCOPO. However, the position of this gate is not positively stated in mediaeval sources.

FLAVIO BIONDO–LUCIO FAUNO, Roma Ristaurata, 1543, I, 41; A. NIBBY, RomAnt I, pp. 205–207; H. JORDAN, Top I, 1, p. 416 f.; C. CORVISIERI, ArchStor Pat I, 1878, pp. 144–156; P. ADINOLFI I, p. 76 f.; R. LANCIANI, BCom XXI, 1893, p.20³; id., Ruins, p. 24; O. RICHTER, Topographie der Stadt Rom (2), 1901, p. 68; H. JORDAN, Top I, 3, p. 503 f.; A. PASQUI, NSc, 1909, pp. 11–14; G. GATTI, BCom XXXVII, 1909, p. 124 f.; P-A, pp. 401, 33 f.; I. A. RICHMOND, Wall, pp. 25, 238; G. LUGLI, Mon II, p. 309 f.; J. LE GALL, Tibre, pp. 211, 311; M. E. BLAKE II, p. 36.

* Other names: Pons Triumphalis, Pons ruptus ad S. Spiritum in Sassia, Pons Vaticanus, Ponte d'Orazio (Mem. Flaminio Vacca 93).

927 The remains of the Pons Neronianus in the year 1754, when the centre pier was still preserved to a height of 4.56 m. (G. Vasi, Magnificenze di Roma V, Tav. 87).

Fot 2967

928 Two piers of the Pons Neronianus showing the direction of the ancient bridge; to the left Ponte Vittorio Emanuele.                                                                                           Fot 597

929  A pier of the Pons Neronianus on the left bank of the Tiber.                          Fot 3695

PONS THEODOSII. Until 1877, the remains of an ancient bridge stood in the Tiber below the Aventine. It crossed the river in the direction of S. Sabina and, in the absence of other evidence, was identified as the PONS PROBI of the Constantinian Regionary Catalogue. Q. Aurelius Symmachus, Praefectus Urbi from 384–385 A. D., reported in two official memoranda and wrote in letters to the Praefectus Praetorio Eusignius and to Licinius (Epist. IV, 70; V, 76) about the rebuilding of the bridge, which was begun in 381, but was still not completed in 387. The bridge is called the "Pons Marmoreus Theodosii" (CodTop III, p. 26) in the Mirabilia; and in the Graphia Aureae Urbis it is called "Pons Theodosii in Riparmea" – Riparmea = Ripa Romaea = Ripa Grande (CodTop III, p. 84). It was already destroyed at the beginning of the 11th century, and in letters of Benedict VIII of 1018 and Leo IX of 1049, it is referred to as the "Pons Fractus iuxta Marmoratam". In 1484, Sixtus IV had the bridge pulled down to its foundations, and 400 large cannon balls were made out of the travertine facing of its arches and piers.

A. NIBBY, RomAnt I, pp. 199–205; C. L. URLICHS, Cod. Urbis Romae Topographicus, 1871, p. 203 f.; H. JORDAN, Top I, 1, p. 421 f.; II, p. 195; R. LANCIANI, BCom V, 1877, p. 167; O. GILBERT, Rom III, p. 262; C. L. VISCONTI, BCom XX, 1892, p. 261 f.; R. LANCIANI, Ruins, p. 16 f.; TH. ASHBY, Top 1581, p. 86; P-A, p. 401; G. LUGLI. Mon II, pp. 296–298, 318; M. E. HIRST, BSR XIV, 1938, p. 147 f.; J. LE GALL, Tibre, pp. 305–311.

930 The remains of the piers of the Pons Theodosii before their destruction in 1877.                                    Alinari 6762

931 The piers of the Pons Theodosii with the right bank of the Tiber. Fot 4719

PORTA APPIA. The original gateway in the Aurelian Wall, through which the Via Appia left the city, had two arches; the remains of the western arch are still visible on the inner side of the gate. The Porta Appia took its name, as did most of the other gateways, from the road which passed through it. In the middle ages it was known as Porta d'Accia, Datia or Dazza, but never quite lost its original name (CodTop IV, p. 112). The modern name of Porta S. Sebastiano comes from the church of S. Sebastiano fuori le Mura, and appears for the first time as "Porta San Bastiano" on the occasion of Charles V's entrance into Rome in 1536. The present gateway is a restoration by Honorius and Arcadius (401/402 A. D.). Later, incorporating the so-called Arco di Druso (q. v.), a vantage-court was built; but apparently it was never used for defence, since there are no traces of hinges, doors or any other means of shutting the rear gate of the court.

A. NIBBY, RomAnt I, p. 149 f.; H. JORDAN, Top I, 1, p. 366; F. REBER, Ruinen, p. 538; R. LANCIANI, Storia II, p. 59; R. SCHULTZE, Bonner Jahrbücher CXVIII, 1909, p. 343; G. TOMASSETTI, La Campagna Romana II, 1910, pp. 32–36; I. A. RICHMOND, BCom LV, 1927, pp. 59–63; P-A, p. 402 f.; G. B. GIOVE-NALE, BCom LVII, 1929, pp. 183–214; LIX, 1931, pp. 106–115; I. A. RICHMOND, Wall, pp. 121–142; G. LUGLI, Mon II, pp. 223–235; id., Tecnica II, Tav. LIII, 2; G. C. GUIDI, Roma XXI, 1943, pp. 14–17.

932 Porta Appia, outer side.                                                                               Fot 5839

933 View of the inner side of the Porta Appia with the vantage-court closed by the "Arco di Druso" (L. Rossini, Le porte antiche e moderne del recinto di Roma, 1829). Fot 6171

934 Inner side of the Porta Appia, shortly after the vantage-court was opened in 1870. Fot 5972

PORTA ARDEATINA. When the Bastione di Sangallo was built between 1537 and 1542, the gateway was destroyed which lay between the Porta Appia and Porta Ostiensis, and between the 20th and 21st towers west of Porta Appia.* The gate, which was not flanked by towers, stood at an angle in the wall, and thus allowed the Via Ardeatina, proceeding from the north-west, to leave the city without changing direction. From a measured drawing by Sangallo (Uffizi, Disegni di architettura No. 1517), it appears that the opening of the gateway was 13.60 m. distant from the nearest tower to the east, and 15.85 m. from the nearest tower to the west.

s. a. Muri Aureliani II, 796, 797.

A. NIBBY, RomAnt I, p. 151; H. JORDAN, Top I, 1, p. 367 f.; CH. HÜLSEN, RM IX, 1894, pp. 320–327; R. LANCIANI, FUR, fol. 45, 46; E. ROCCHI, Le piante iconografiche e prospettiche di Roma del secolo XVI, 1902, pp. 183 f., 239; Tav. XXXII; G. TOMASSETTI, La Campagna Romana II, 1910, p. 410 f.; P-A, p. 403; G. B. GIOVENALE, BCom LIX, 1931, p. 62 f.; I. A. RICHMOND, Wall, pp. 217–219; CodTop II, p. 149[3]; IV, p. 244; C. PIETRANGELI, Capitolium XX, 1945, pp. 1–8; C. C. VAN ESSEN, Mededeelingen Rome 3, IX, 1957, pp. 142, 147.

* Richmond's erroneous assertion that the gateway lay "between the twelfth and thirteenth towers west of Porta Appia" (Wall, p. 217) is repeated in CodTop II, p. 149. It originates with Hülsen, RM IX, 1894, p. 326 – he, however, counted the towers west of Porta Ardeatina. From Richmond's own reckoning of the towers of Sector L, west of Porta Appia (Wall, p. 270), the site of the gateway must have been between the 20th and 21st towers (s. a. Lanciani, FUR, fol. 45,46).

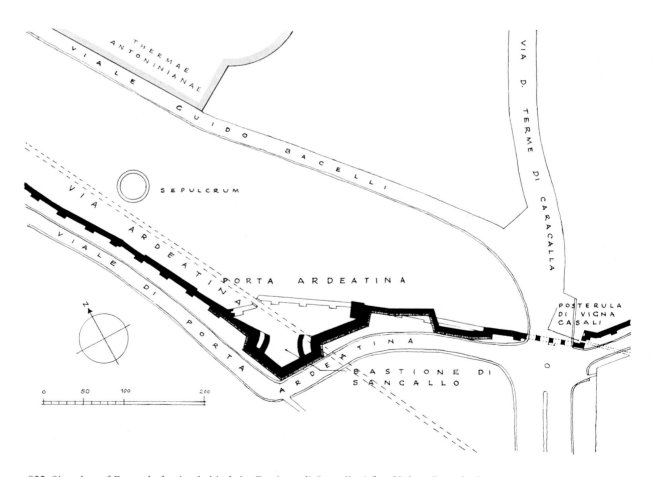

935 Site-plan of Porta Ardeatina behind the Bastione di Sangallo (after Hülsen-Rauscher).

936 Remains of the Aurelian Wall behind the eastern end of the Bastione di Sangallo. Fot 1223

937 Remains of a tower at the western end of the Bastione di Sangallo. Fot 1281

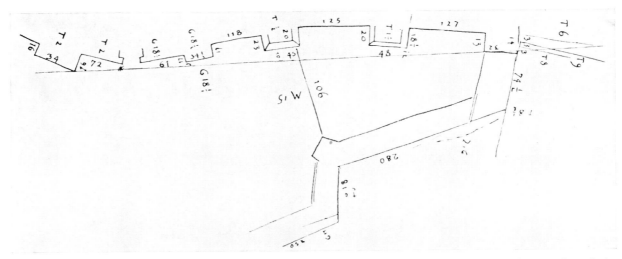

938 Drawing by Sangallo, with the measurements of the towers and the intervening curtains of the wall, and the
opening for the Porta Ardeatina.                                                                    Fot 3015

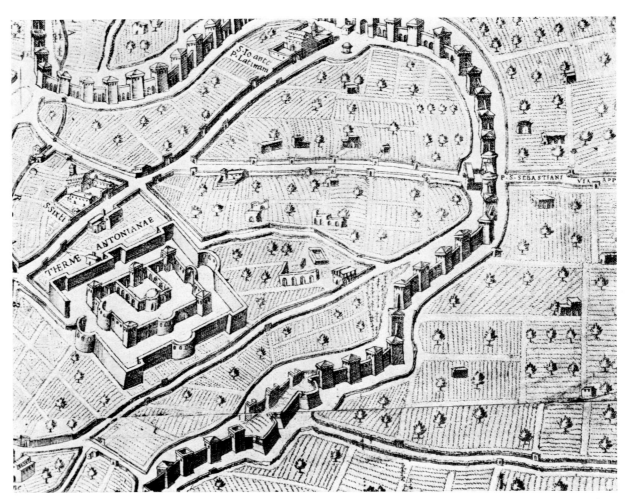

939 A detail from the map of Mario Cartario of 1576, with three towers of the Aurelian Wall still preserved behind the
Bastione di Sangallo. The Porta Ardeatina was between the last tower of the preserved part of the wall and the
first tower below the Bastione di Sangallo.                                                          Fot 3014

940 Stefano du Pérac's "Urbis Romae Sciografia" of 1574, showing Porta Ardeatina in an angle of the wall. At that time,
the ruined gateway could still be seen.                                                                        Fot 3016

PORTA ASINARIA. The Porta Asinaria, like Porta Ardeatina, was originally a modest opening in the Aurelian Wall, without its own towers. Later, in the time of Honorius, the gateway was enlarged and provided with semicircular towers, in which system of fortification two rectangular wall towers were incorporated. The Porta Asinaria was walled up for the first time by King Ladislaus of Naples, after the conquest of Rome in 1408, but it was reopened only a few weeks later. It was again walled up under Pius IV in 1564/65, and in 1574 it was replaced by the Porta S. Giovanni. During the restoration and reopening of the gateway in 1951/1954, the vantage-court and its gate were excavated.

A. NIBBY, RomAnt I, pp. 146–148; F. REBER, Ruinen, p. 535 f.; H. JORDAN, Top I, 1, p. 363; TH. ASHBY, BSR IV, 1907, p. 42 f.; L. MARIANI, BCom XLV, 1917, p. 194; G. e F. TOMASSETTI, La Campagna Romana IV, 1926, pp. 20–26; I. A. RICHMOND, BCom LV, 1927, p. 64 f.; P-A, p. 404; G. B. GIOVENALE, BCom LIX, 1931, pp. 65–68; I. A. RICHMOND, Wall, pp. 144–159; G. LUGLI, Mon II, pp. 210–214; A. M. COLINI, Celio, pp. 122–124; P. SCARPA, Capitolium XXVIII, 1953, pp. 87–92; G. GATTI, ib. XXIX, 1954, pp. 97–104; A. M. COLINI, Studi Romani II, 1954, p. 314 f.

941  Porta Asinaria after it was reopened in 1954.                                        Fot 3698

942 The rectangular wall tower on the west of the Porta Asinaria incorporated into the circular tower of the gateway.　Fot 1265

943 Porta Asinaria, inner side with the vantage-court and rear gate.　Fot 1267

Porta Aurelia. Until 1642, the Porta Aurelia stood in the Aurelian Wall, on the site of the modern Porta San Pancrazio. It was flanked by two rectangular towers, and had a vantage-court with an inner gate. Between 1642 and 1644, Urban VIII replaced the Aurelian Wall on the Janiculum, which had fallen into disrepair, with a new wall. He had a new gateway built by Marco Antonio de Rossi, in which the vantage-court and inner gate, which had been restored a century earlier by Paul III (1534–1549), were evidently preserved. In June 1849, the new gateway was severely damaged by the assault of the French against Garibaldi's army which was defending the Roman Republic. In 1854, Pius IX replaced it with a new gateway designed by Virginio Vespignani.

A. Nibby, RomAnt I, p. 153 f.; H. Jordan, Top I, 1, pp. 375–380; G. Tomassetti, La Campagna Romana II, 1910, pp. 465–467; P-A, p. 404; I. A. Richmond, Wall, pp. 221–223; G. B. Giovenale, BCom LIX, 1931, pp. 74–76; G. Lugli, Mon II, p. 254 f.; G. Matthiae, Capitolium XXII, 1947, p. 71.

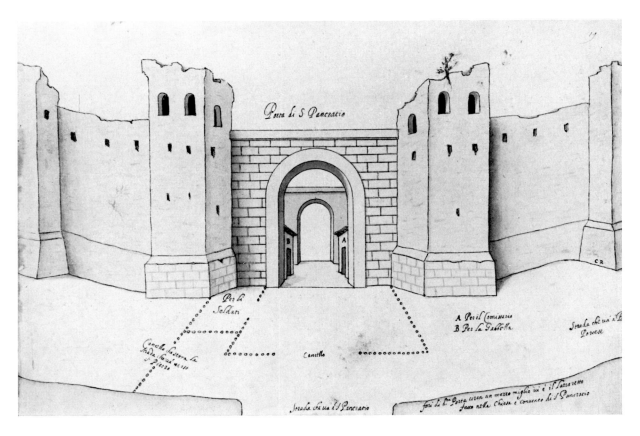

944 The Porta Aurelia, a drawing by Carlo Rainaldi of 1633 (Cod. Vat. Barb. Lat. 4411, fol. 19).                    Fot 3005

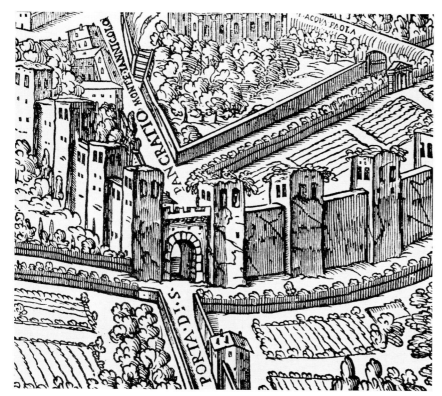

945 The Porta Aurelia before it was pulled down by Urban VIII. Maggi's Plan of the City 1625.                    Fot 3010

946 The Porta San Pancrazio which was built 1642/44 in place of Porta Aurelia (L. Rossini, Le porte antiche e moderne del recinto di Roma, 1829).                                                                    Fot 6405

PORTA CHIUSA. The name of this gateway, beside the south wall of the Castra Praetoria, is modern; its ancient name is unknown. In the 15th and 16th centuries it was known as the "Porta Interaggeres" (CodTop IV, pp. 431, 489). It stands across the line of the road which led to Tivoli from the Porta Viminalis in the Servian Wall, and appears to date from the reconstruction of the gateways at the time of Honorius. The well-preserved outer side is visible behind modern buildings, Nos. 4–6, Via Monzambano; but the inner side, which lies in the area of No. 25 A, Viale di Castro Pretorio, is built over by modern houses. Excavations in 1868 did not go down to the ancient level, but confirmed that, like the Porta Metrovia (q. v.), the gateway had been in the form of a tower. In 1585/86 under Sixtus V, a branch of the Acqua Felice was carried through it.

s. a. Castra Praetoria I, 255.

W. GELL–A. NIBBY, Le Mura di Roma, 1820, p. 339; J. H. PARKER, Archaeologia XLII, 1869, p. 17 f., plate II; H. JORDAN, Top I, 1, p. 355; TH. ASHBY, BSR III, 1906, pp. 86, 199 f.; P-A, p. 406; G. B. GIOVENALE, BCom LIX, 1931, pp. 63–65; I. A. RICH-MOND, Wall, pp. 181–184; G. LUGLI, Mon II, pp. 188–191; G. ZANGHIERI, Boll. dell'Ist. Storico e di Cultura dell'Arma del Genio, fasc. 27, giugno 1948, p. 69 f.; CodTop II, p. 205[3].

947 Inner side of the Porta Chiusa during the 1868 excavation (drawing by Ciconetti from Archaeologia XLII, 1869).
Fot 3012

948 Outer side of the Porta Chiusa.                                    Rip X D/194

PORTA FLAMINIA. The Via Flaminia, which was built in 220 B. C., left the city through this gateway. Originally it was flanked by two semicircular towers, the remains of which were discovered when the rectangular bastions on the north side were pulled down in 1877. These bastions were a later reinforcement of the gateway, but had ancient foundations, and were faced with marble; in the time of Sixtus IV (1471–1484), they were either strengthened or restored. Pius IV had the Porta Flaminia, which since the end of the 14th century had been called the Porta del Popolo after the adjacent church, rebuilt by Nanni di Baccio Bigio in 1561/63.* The inner side of the gateway was designed by Bernini for the entrance of Queen Christina of Sweden, in 1655.

W. GELL–A. NIBBY, Le Mura di Roma, 1820, pp. 301–308; A. NIBBY, RomAnt I, pp. 138–141; R. LANCIANI, NSc, 1877, p. 269 f.; 1878, pp. 34 f., 138; 1880, p. 468; C. L. VISCONTI–V. VESPIGNANI, BCom V, 1877, pp. 184–252; VIII, 1880, pp. 169–182; IX, 1881, pp. 174–188; H. JORDAN, Top I, 1, p. 353; I, 3, p. 463; R. LANCIANI, Storia I, p. 80; III, p. 234 f.; TH. ASHBY–S. R. PIERCE, Town Planning Review XI, 1924, pp. 76–79; G. TOMASSETTI, La Campagna Romana III, 1913, pp. 201–208; P-A, p. 407 f.; G. B. GIOVENALE, BCom LIX, 1931, pp. 79–83; I. A. RICHMOND, Wall, pp. 191–200; G. LUGLI, Mon II, p. 165 f.

* Even to-day the north side of the Porta del Popolo is almost universally attributed to Vignola; but from the building accounts it appears that it was built to the design of Nanni di Baccio Bigio, and under his direction (H. Willich, G. Barozzi da Vignola, 1906, p. 90 f.; R. Lanciani, Storia III, p. 234; E. B. Mac Dougall, Journ. Society of Architectural Historians XIX, 1960, p. 106[32]).

949 The inner side of the Porta Flaminia with Bernini's central arch (1655). The side arches were added in 1878. Fot 1241

950 The inner side of the gateway after restoration by Pius IV. An engraving by Israel Sylvestre  (about 1640–1644).
Fot 3520

951 The ancient arch of the Porta Flaminia. A drawing by Marten van Heemskerck (about 1537).        Fot 3532

952  The outer side of the Porta Flaminia before the towers were pulled down in 1877.                    Parker 1353

Porta Latina. The plan of this gateway, with its two semicircular towers, belongs to the first period of Aurelian's Wall, but the arch with its row of windows above the gateway, dates from the time of Honorius. The gateway had a vantage-court with an inner gate, which can be seen on pictorial plans of the 16th and 17th century, and in pictures up to the 18th century (s. H. Egger, Römische Veduten I, Taf. 82). In the course of its history, the gateway was walled up several times; in May 1408 it was closed by King Ladislaus of Naples (s. a. Porta Asinaria II, p. 204), but it was opened again in September 1409. From 1656 to 1669 it was closed to prevent the plague from spreading. At the beginning of the 19th century, owing to the abandonment of the Via Latina, the gateway became superfluous, and in 1808 it was again walled up. It has remained closed, except for a short period in 1827, until 1911, when it was finally reopened.

s. a. Muri Aureliani II, 789.

A. Nibby, RomAnt I, p. 148 f.; H. Jordan, Top I, 1, p. 366; Th. Ashby, BSR IV, 1907, p. 13; H. Grisar, Roma alla fine del mondo antico, 1908, p. 544 f.; G. e F. Tomassetti, La Campagna Romana IV, 1926, pp. 6–9; I. A. Richmond, BCom LV, 1927, p. 57; id., Wall, pp. 100–109; P-A, p. 408 f.; G. B. Giovenale, BCom LIX, 1931, pp. 91–96; G. Lugli, Mon II, pp. 220–222; id., Tecnica II, Tav. LXXIV, 4.

953 Porta Latina, outer side.                                                    Fot 1276

PORTA METROVIA. The ancient name of the gateway, which is situated between Porta Asinaria and Porta Latina, is unknown. It is often mentioned in mediaeval literature under a variety of names. The earliest literary evidence is in the description of the Wall in the 8th century Einsiedeln manuscript, where it is referred to as the Porta Metrovia (CodTop II, p. 206). The original gate was a modest opening, between two towers in the Aurelian Wall, which gave access to the city from the PALUDES DECENNIAE. The road which led to the Porta Metrovia continued inside the Wall, in the direction of Porta Querquetulana, in the Servian Wall (s. Arcus Dolabellae et Silani I, p. 113). Later, perhaps in the time of Maxentius, the gateway was strengthened by building a tower behind it. In 1122 Pope Callixtus II diverted the Marrana through the gateway, thus bringing water to the fields and gardens within the Wall as well as draining the PALUDES DECENNIAE. It is not known when the gateway was walled up.

W. GELL–A. NIBBY, Le Mura di Roma, 1820, p. 364 f.; A. NIBBY, RomAnt I, p. 148; H. JORDAN, Top I, 1, p. 364; CH. HÜLSEN, BCom XIX, 1891, p. 355 f.; CIL VI, 31893 b; TH. ASHBY, BSR IV, 1907, pp. 40–42; M. MARCHETTI, BCom XLII, 1914, p. 82, No. 14; F. LAIS, Il Rivo dell'Acqua Mariana (2), 1920, p. 27; G. e F. TOMASSETTI, La Campagna Romana IV, 1926, pp. 13–19, 157–159; I. A. RICHMOND, BCom LV, 1927, p. 63 f.; id., Wall, pp. 142–144; P-A, p. 409; G. B. GIOVENALE, BCom LIX, 1931, p. 68 f.; G. LUGLI, Mon II, p. 218 f.; CodTop II, p. 147; A. M. COLINI, Celio, pp. 129–132, 440 f.

954 The inner side of the Porta Metrovia in the Aurelian Wall (L. Rossini, Le porte antiche e moderne del recinto di Roma, 1829).
Fot 6404

955 Porta Metrovia, the gateway tower with an inscription recording the restoration of the gateway in 1157 (left) and
1579 (right). Fot 1272

956  The walled up gateway in the Aurelian Wall, outer side.                                Fot 1271

PORTA NOMENTANA. The gate in the Aurelian Wall through which the Via Nomentana left the city, lay about 75 m. south-east of the Porta Pia. It was flanked by two semicircular towers, and was the only Roman gateway to retain its original Aurelian type of fortification. The north tower has been preserved, but the south tower was pulled down in 1826*, when the tomb of Q. Haterius was discovered beneath it. The Porta Nomentana was walled up under Pius IV in 1564, and was replaced by the Porta Pia, built from Michelangelo's design.

s. a. Sepulcrum Q. Haterii II, 1111.

W. GELL–A. NIBBY, Le Mura di Roma, 1820, p. 324 f.; A. NIBBY, Memorie Romane d'antichità e di belle arti III, 1826, pp. 456–458; H. JORDAN, Top I, 1, pp. 344[10] f., 355; G. TOMASSETTI, ArchStorPat XI, 1888, p. 156; I. A. RICHMOND, BCom LV, 1927, p. 55 f.; id., Wall, pp. 93–100; P-A, p. 410; G. B. GIOVENALE, BCom LIX, 1931, pp. 72–74; E. MARTINORI, Via Nomentana, 1932, p. 12 f.; G. LUGLI, Mon II, pp. 175–178.

* It is generally thought that 1827 was the date of its demolition, and that Cardinali was the author of the excavation report (CIL VI, 1426). In fact, the report was written by Nibby, who states, in Memorie Romane of 1826, that the excavation took place at the beginning of that year; later, in RomAnt II, 1839, p. 519, he himself gives the erroneous date of 1827.

957 Porta Nomentana, the gateway has been walled up since 1564.                                        Fot 1244

PORTA OSTIENSIS. This gateway is first mentioned by Ammianus Marcellinus (XVII, 4, 14), describing the journey of the Obeliscus Constantii (q. v.) "per Ostiensem portam" to the Circus Maximus, in 357 A. D. The original gateway in the Aurelian Wall was flanked by two semicircular towers, as in the later reconstruction, and during the first building period it had two arches, corresponding with the still extant rear gates of the vantage-court. In spite of its massive walls, this vantage-court was not used for defence (s. Porta Appia II, p. 198); the entrances to its perimeter walls, and to the gateway towers, lay outside the vantage-court on the city side, and therefore could not be guarded from it. The modern name of Porta San Paolo, which derives from the Basilica of S. Paolo fuori le Mura, is mentioned as early as the 6th century A. D., in the writings of Procopius (Bellum Gothicum II, 4, 3; III, 36). Procopius came to Rome with Belisarius, in 536 A. D.

W. GELL–A. NIBBY, Le Mura di Roma, 1820, pp. 377–380; A. NIBBY, RomAnt I, p. 151 f.; H. JORDAN, Top I, 1, p. 368 f.; R. LANCIANI, MALinc I, 1889, pp. 511–513; id., The destruction of Ancient Rome, 1899, p. 54; G. TOMASSETTI, ArchStorPat XVII, 1894, pp. 75–81; R. SCHULTZE, Bonner Jahrbücher CXVIII, 1909, p. 342 f.; I. A. RICHMOND, BCom LV, 1927, pp. 57–59; id., Wall, pp. 109–121; P-A, p. 410 f.; G. B. GIOVENALE, BCom LIX, 1931, pp. 96–106; G. LUGLI, Mon II, pp. 241–247; C. PIETRANGELI, BCom LXXII, 1946/48, p. 214 f.

958 Porta Ostiensis, the city side with the gates of the vantage-court.                                        Fot 1286

959 Porta Ostiensis, outer side. Fot 1283

960 Porta Ostiensis, with the vantage-court and double gate behind. Fot 1287

PORTA PINCIANA. An ancient road (Via Salaria Vetus ?), which corresponded to the modern Via di Porta Pinciana, left the city by the gateway which to-day stands at the end of Via Vittorio Veneto. It was originally a postern beside one of the towers, and was turned into a main gateway at the time of Honorius or Maxentius, by the addition of a second round tower. Its original name is not known; the hill on which it stood was still called Collis Hortorum at the time of Aurelian. In the course of the 4th century, a large part of the hill was acquired by the gens Pincia, and the names Mons Pincius and Porta Pinciana may have come into use at that time. The gateway had a vantage-court, the walls of which stood until the 19th century. It was walled up in 1808, and when a new quarter of the city was laid out in the grounds of the former Villa Ludovisi, it was re-opened in 1887/88.

W. GELL–A. NIBBY, Le Mura di Roma, 1820, pp. 317–319; A. NIBBY, RomAnt I, p. 141 f.; H. JORDAN, Top I, 1, p. 354; C. L. VISCONTI, BCom XVI, 1888, p. 41; G. TOMASSETTI, ArchStorPat XI, 1888, pp. 153–156, 159–161; CH. HÜLSEN, RM IV, 1889, p. 269 f.; R. LANCIANI, BCom XX, 1892, p. 102; L. MARIANI, BCom XLV, 1917, pp. 214–216; P-A, p. 412; I. A. RICHMOND, Wall, pp. 159–169; G. B. GIOVENALE, BCom LIX, 1931, pp. 84–91; G. LUGLI, Mon II, pp. 170–172; CodTop II, p. 143.

961 The Porta Pinciana, outer side.                                                          Fot 1242

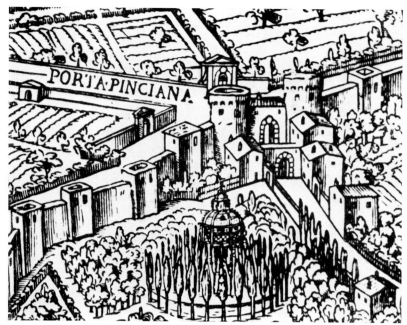

962 The Porta Pinciana with its vantage-court and the inner gate, from the map of Maggi-Maupin-Losi of 1625.          Fot 6126

963 The Porta Pinciana, inner side.                    Fot 1243

Porta Portuensis. This gateway, which was built during the reign of Aurelian as the entrance for Via Portuensis, retained its original double arch until its demolition in 1643. In 403 A. D., it was restored by Honorius, as
was reported in an inscription over the arches (CIL VI, 1188). The gateway was about 100 m. distant from the
Tiber, and 453 m. from the new Porta Portese. Pictures of it, before it was pulled down under Urban VIII,
show a vantage-court with an inner gate, and the eastern arch walled up.*

F. Nardini, Roma Antica, 1666, p. 36; Nardini–
Nibby I, p. 68; A. Nibby, RomAnt I, p. 153; H. Jor-
dan, Top I, 1, p. 371 f.; R. Lanciani, BCom XX,
1892, p. 286 f.; id., FUR, 34,39; G. Tomassetti,
ArchStorPat XXII, 1899, pp. 451–455; Th. Ashby,
Roma III, 1925, p. 317; P-A, p. 412; I. A. Richmond,
Wall, pp. 200–205; G. B. Giovenale, BCom LIX,
1931, pp. 56–58; G. Lugli, Mon II, pp. 250–252;
G. Matthiae, Arti Figurative II, 1946, pp. 49, 57[2];
id., Capitolium XXII, 1947, pp. 68–72.

* Richmond's assertion (Wall, p. 202) that the western arch was walled up, cannot be accepted in face of the evidence of the drawings by Rainaldi
in 1633 (fig. 965), and Nardini (ed. 1666, p. 36).

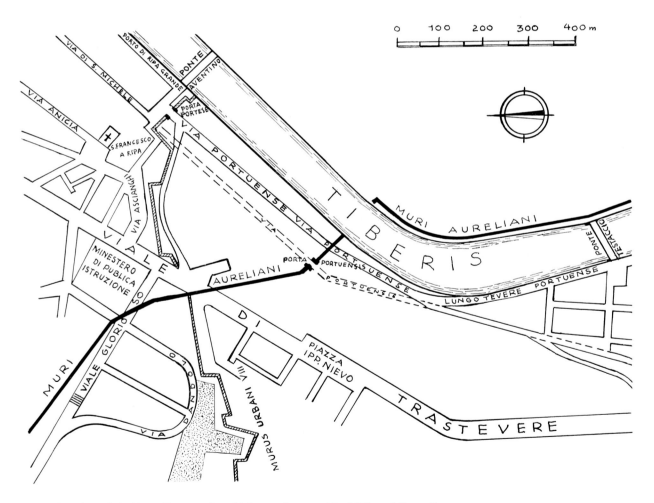

964 Site-plan of the Porta Portuensis, which was destroyed in 1643, and Porta Portese.

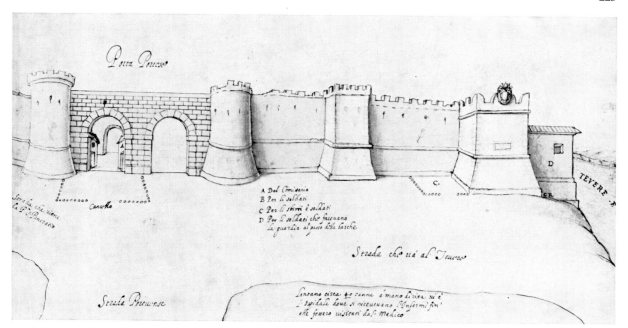

965 Porta Portuensis, a drawing by Carlo Rainaldi in 1633 (Cod. Vat. Barb. Lat. 4411, fol. 18).          Fot 3006

966 Porta Portuensis on the Maggi-Maupin-Losi pictorial plan of 1625.          Fot 3011

967  Porta Portese, which was begun by Urban VIII and completed by Innocent X. It stood 453 m. north of the demolished
     Porta Portuensis, which it replaced.                                                                    Fot 1289

PORTA PRAENESTINA. Aurelian incorporated the two monumental arches that carried the Aqua Claudia and the Anio Novus over the Via Praenestina and the Via Labicana (s. I, 32) into his city wall, making them into a fortified double-gateway. At the time of Honorius, the gateway received its final form, with two rectangular towers in front of the aqueduct arches, and a round tower between the two openings. A still preserved inscription, recording the restoration of the gateway by Honorius in 403 A. D. (CIL VI, 1189), was on the upper curtain of the Porta Labicana, which possibly had been closed since the 6th century. Since the 10th century the gateway has also been known as the PORTA MAGGIORE. It was pulled down in 1834/1838, after which the arches of the Aqua Claudia continued to be used as the gateway, until 1915, when the hinges of the gates were removed. The last excavation, in 1955/57, revealed the foundations of the vantage-court and the ancient roads.

W. GELL–A. NIBBY, Le Mura di Roma, 1820, pp. 348–350; A. NIBBY, RomAnt I, pp. 117, 145 f.; L. CANINA, AnnInst, 1838, pp. 213–219; H. JORDAN, Top I, 1, p. 357; F. REBER, Ruinen, pp. 528–532; TH. ASHBY, BSR I, 1902, p. 150; id., Top 1581, p. 92 f.; G. TOMASSETTI, La Campagna Romana III, 1913, pp. 380–384; L. MARIANI, BCom XLV, 1917, pp. 195–207; P-A, p. 412 f.; G. B. GIOVENALE, BCom LIX, 1931, pp. 48–56; I. A. RICHMOND, Wall, pp. 205–217; G. LUGLI, Mon II, pp. 199–206; A. PETRIGNANI, Porta Maggiore, il suo ripristino e la sistemazione delle adiacenze, 1938; CodTop II, p. 146; A. M. COLINI, Celio, p. 113; id., Capitolium XXXII, 1957, 11, pp. 3–9; G. MARCHETTI-LONGHI, Capitolium XXX, 1955, pp. 318–325; L. CREMA, ArchRom, p. 224; M. E. BLAKE II, p. 27 f.

968 Porta Praenestina and Porta Labicana (L. Rossini, Le porte antiche e moderne del recinto di Roma, 1829).  Fot 6406

969 Window gallery and the inscription
of Honorius, all that remains of the
Porta Labicana.              Fot 1262

970 Porta Maggiore (Praenestina) after the 1955/57 excavations.                    Fot 5671

971 North side of the vantage-court.
Fot 5652

972 Foundations of the vantage-court with Via Labicana (right) and Via Praenestina on a higher level (left).
Rip X B/4459

973 Via Labicana and the inner side of the arches of
the Aqua Claudia.
Fot 3699

974 Inner side of the Porta Praenestina with the vantage-court and its gate (G. Cassini, Nuova raccolta delle migliore
vedute di Roma, 1775, fol. 54).                                                                    Fot 4775

PORTA SALARIA. The Via Salaria proceeded from the Porta Collina in the Servian Wall, and left the city by a gateway between the Porta Pinciana and the Porta Nomentana. Until its destruction in 1871, the gateway retained its original form of the time of Aurelian, flanked by two semicircular towers. On the 20th September 1870, the Porta Salaria was severely damaged by artillery fire; it was removed by Virginio Vespignani and replaced by a new gateway in 1873. When the towers were demolished, the tomb of Q. Sulpicius Maximus (q. v.) was discovered under the east tower, and that of Cornelia (q. v.), daughter of L. Scipio, under the west tower. The modern gate was removed in 1921 to relieve traffic congestion.

W. GELL–A. NIBBY, Le Mura di Roma, 1820, p. 321; A. NIBBY, RomAnt I, p. 142 f.; C. L. VISCONTI, Il sepolcro del fanciullo Q. Sulpicio Massimo, 1871, p. 3 f., Tav. I, 1; H. JORDAN, Top I, 1, p. 354; G. TOMASSETTI, ArchStorPat XI, 1888, p. 158; R. LAN-CIANI, MALinc I, 1889, p. 461; N. PERSICHETTI, RM XXIII, 1908, pp. 286–288; G. McN. RUSHFORTH, JRS IX, 1919, pp. 19, 46; P-A, p. 416; G. B. GIOVENALE, BCom LIX, 1931, pp. 70–72; I. A. RICHMOND, Wall, pp. 185–190; G. LUGLI, Mon II, p. 173 f.

975 The Porta Salaria before 1870.

Parker 7

976  The new Porta Salaria erected in 1873. On the site of the ancient towers are: left the tomb of Q. Sulpicius Maximus,
     and right, that of Cornelia.                                                                    GFN  C/9008

977  The ancient Porta Salaria during its destruction in 1871, with the tomb of Sulpicius Maximus on the left.  Parker 2069

PORTA SEPTIMIANA. The gateway nearest to the Tiber in the northern sector of the Transtiberine wall, stood above an ancient street which corresponded to the modern Via della Lungara, and connected that part of the city within the wall, with the Via Cornelia. In mediaeval and Renaissance literature, the name of the gateway is the subject of much imaginary speculation (CodTop III, pp. 18, 80; IV, pp. 39 f., 100, 113 f., 168, 455, 465). It may well be ancient and date back to Septimius Severus; a "porta nominis sui" which lay near his "balneae in Transtiberina regione" is mentioned in the Historia Augusta (Severus 19). After being included in the Aurelian Wall, the Porta Septimiana is not officially mentioned again until 1123. The ruined gateway was completely rebuilt in 1498 by Alexander VI. Its present state is the result of a restoration under Pius VI in 1798.

ANDREAS FULVIUS, Antiquitates Urbis, 1527, fol. XI v.; L. MAURO, Le antichità della città di Roma, 1558, p. 105 f.; F. CANCELLIERI, Mercato, p. 241; A. NIBBY, RomAnt I, p. 154; H. JORDAN, Top I, 1, p. 373; II, p. 378; R. LANCIANI, Storia I, p. 161; G. TOMASSETTI, La Campagna Romana II, 1910, p. 476 f.; M. MAR-CHETTI, BCom XLII, 1914, p. 83; A. v. DOMASZEWSKI, Sitzungsber. der Heidelberger Akademie d. Wissenschaften 1916, 7. Abh., p. 5 f.; Ch. HÜLSEN, Chiese, p. 468 f., No. 61; P-A, p. 416 f.; I. A. RICHMOND, Wall, pp. 223–227; G. B. GIOVENALE, BCom LIX, 1931, p. 76; G. LUGLI, Mon II, pp. 256–258.

978 The Porta Septimiana, rear view.

PORTA TIBURTINA. The conduits of the Aquae Marcia, Tepula and Iulia crossed the road to Tivoli by means of a monumental arch (s. Aqua Marcia I, 44, 45), which was built by Augustus in 5 B. C., and which was incorporated in the Aurelian Wall as a gateway. Honorius added a second outer arch, and massive rectangular towers. The restoration of the gateway, which included building a vantage-court with a rear gate, is recorded in an inscription on the outer side (CIL VI, 1190). In the middle ages, the Porta Tiburtina was also called Porta Taurina, from the bull's head decoration on the arch of the aqueduct, and Porta Sancti Laurentii, after the church of S. Lorenzo fuori le Mura (CodTop III, pp. 135, 181). The vantage–court, with the great rear gate, was pulled down under Pius IX in 1869.

W. GELL–A. NIBBY, Le mura di Roma, 1820, p. 341 f.; A. NIBBY, RomAnt I, p. 144 f.; H. JORDAN, Top I, 1, p. 356; II, p. 166; R. LANCIANI, BCom XX, 1892, p. 111; id., Ruins, p. 75; id., The destruction of Ancient Rome, 1899, p. 189 f.; TH. ASHBY, BSR III, 1906, p. 87 f.; G. TOMASSETTI, ArchStorPat XXX, 1907, pp. 337–342; L. MARIANI, BCom XLV, 1917, pp. 207–215, Tavv. XVIII, XIX; P-A, p. 417; G. B. GIOVENALE, BCom LIX, 1931, pp. 58–62, Tav. II; I. A. RICHMOND, Wall, pp. 170–181; E. MARTINORI, Via Tiburtina, 1932, pp. 76–79; TH. ASHBY, Aqueducts, p. 145 f.; G. LUGLI, Mon II, pp. 192–195; L. CREMA, ArchRom, p. 209.

979 Porta Tiburtina, outer side.

980 Porta Tiburtina, inner side.

Fot 1251

PORTA VIMINALIS. Since the recent enlargement of Piazza dei Cinquecento, in 1939/50, the remains of this gate in the Servian Wall stand isolated, between two long stretches of the wall in front of the Stazione Termini. This part of the wall first came to light in 1876, when the so-called Monte della Giustizia, the highest point of the former Villa Montalto-Negroni, was removed to make way for the new Railway Station.

H. JORDAN, Top I, 1, pp. 214, 222 f.; R. LANCIANI, BCom IV, 1876, pp. 168 f., 172, 210, Tav. XVIII; id., Frontino, p. 93; id., FUR, 17; J. H. MIDDLETON I, p. 133; TH. ASHBY, BSR III, 1906, p. 85 f.; M. MAR- CHETTI, BCom XLII, 1914, p. 80 f.; T. FRANK, Build- ings, pp. 122–124; P–A, p. 419; G. SÄFLUND, Mura, pp. 63–66, 155 f., 205, 225 f.; G. LUGLI, Mon II, p. 130; M. E. BLAKE I, p. 38 f.

981 Remains of the Porta Viminalis in the Piazza dei Cinquecento.                                    Fot 1186

PORTICUS ABSIDATA. The Porticus Absidata, which is listed in Regio IV in the Constantinian Regionary Catalogue, can be identified on a fragment of the Severan marble plan as the semicircular building behind the temple in the Forum of Nerva (FUR, Tav. XX, 16a). Excavations in 1940 revealed the curved foundation wall of the porticus, which adjoins the perimeter wall of the Forum Augustum to the west, and the Forum Pacis to the east.

H. JORDAN, Top II, pp. 99 f., 319; R. LANCIANI, MemLinc XI, 1883, p. 24, Tav. III, 1; id., MALinc I, 1889, pp. 528–530; L. DUCHESNE, Mél IX, 1889, pp. 350–352; id., RM XXII, 1907, p. 429 f.; H. JORDAN, Top I, 3, p. 328 f.; A. BARTOLI, Disegni III, Tav. 278, fig. 463; P-A, p. 419 f.; A. M. COLINI, BCom LXV, 1937, p. 31; LXVIII, 1940, p. 226 f., Tav. Agg. A; P. H. VON BLANCKENHAGEN, FlArch, pp. 43–45; G. MARCHETTI-LONGHI, Rend PontAcc XXV–XXVI, 1949/51, pp. 194–221; G. LUGLI, Centro, p. 271; M. E. BLAKE II, p. 106; L. CREMA, ArchRom, p. 277; FUR, p. 73, Tav XX.

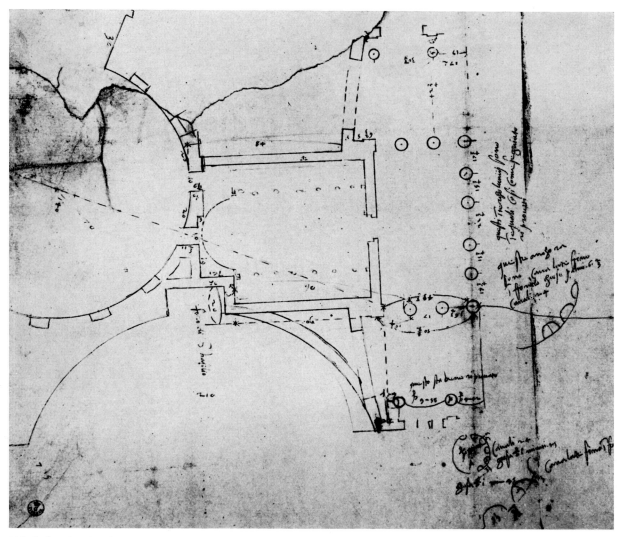

982 A drawing by Antonio da Sangallo the younger, with the Porticus Absidata (left), the Temple of Minerva (centre) and the eastern exedra of the Forum of Augustus (below). Fot 2982

983 Porticus Absidata and the perimeter wall of the Forum of Augustus (left).                    Fot 505

984 The curved foundation wall of the Porticus Absidata with the perimeter wall of the Forum Pacis on the right.
Rip X  C/3906

PORTICUS AEMILIA. In 193 B. C., the aediles, L. Aemilius Lepidus and L. Aemilius Paulus, built a large market-hall, known as the Porticus Aemilia. It was 487 m. long and 60 m. wide and stood to the south-west of the Aventine, outside the Servian Wall; it was intended for receiving and distributing goods and foodstuffs which were brought up the Tiber. It lay parallel to the river, about 90 m. distant from it. It was rebuilt in 174 B. C., and the remains of walls of opus incertum belonging to this new building may be seen in the Via Rubattino and Via B. Franklin, and parallel to Via G. Branca between Via Rubattino and Via Florio. The remains of numerous walls belonging to the market-hall, and extending as far as Via della Marmorata were discovered, and removed, when the Testaccio quarter of the city was being built in 1885/1925. The Porticus Aemilia, together with the Horrea Galbae (q. v. I, 589, 590), is shown on a fragment of the Severan marble plan (FUR, Tav. XXIV).

NARDINI–NIBBY III, p. 314 f.; A. PASQUI, NSc, 1911, p. 205 f.; G. MANCINI, ib., p. 318; G. GATTI, BCom XXXIX, 1911, p. 89 f.; F. FORNARI, NSc, 1915, p. 166 f.; R. LANCIANI, Ruins, p. 40, fig. 199 (p. 508); id., FUR, 40; H. JORDAN, Top I, 3, p. 173; P-A, p. 420; G. GATTI, BCom LXII, 1934, pp. 123–149; id., L'Urbe II, 1937, 9, p. 12 f.; A. BOETHIUS, Dragma M. P. Nilsson dedicatum, 1939, p. 133[32]; G. LUGLI, Mon III, pp. 597–602; id., Tecnica I, pp. 375, 409, 450 f.; II, Tavv. CVII, CVIII, 1; M. E. BLAKE I, p. 249; G. CRESSEDI, BCom LXXIII, 1949/50, p. 94 f.; J. LE GALL, Tibre, pp. 99–103; H. LYNGBY, ForBoarium, p. 70; A. VON GERKAN, Göttinger gel. Anzeigen CCIX, 1955, p. 261 f.; CCXII, 1958, p. 189 f.; id., Scritti in onore di G. Libertini, 1958, p. 153 f.; L. CREMA, ArchRom, pp. 24 f., 61; FUR, p. 81 f., Tav. XXIV (Bibl: p. 82); A. BOETHIUS, The Golden House of Nero, 1960, p. 28 f.

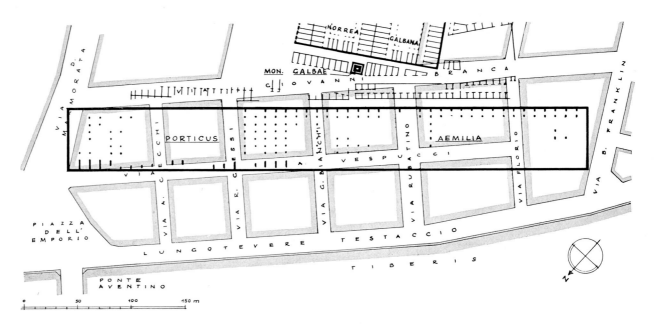

985 Site-plan of the Porticus Aemilia.

986 Remains of the south-eastern perimeter wall of the porticus on the Via Florio.

Rip X C/12

987 Partition wall inside the porticus on Via Rubattino.

Fot 3599

988  Partition wall of opus incertum on Via Rubattino, south-west side.                    Fot 3598

989  South-west end wall of the porticus on Via Beniamino Franklin.                        Fot 6205

PORTICUS DEORUM CONSENTIUM. A porticus of Corinthian columns, dedicated to the twelve Olympian gods, lies at the south-west end of the Forum, below the Tabularium. The original building dates back to the 2nd or 3rd centuries B. C. An excavation in 1834 revealed brick-built rooms, also the remains of columns, capitals and fragments of the entablature of a building of the Flavian era, which, according to an inscription found in 1835 (CIL VI, 102), was restored in 367 A. D. by the Praefectus Urbi Vettius Praetextatus. In 1858, the colonnade was restored by Pius IX, using the ancient material.

O. KELLERMANN, BullInst, 1835, pp. 33–35; C. BUNSEN, ib., pp. 75–77; id., AnnInst, 1836, p. 223; PLATNER–BUNSEN, Beschreibung III, 2, pp. 8–11; A. NIBBY, RomAnt I, pp. 545–548; L. GRIFI, DissPont Acc XIV, 1860, pp. 115–138; H. JORDAN, Top I, 2, pp. 366–368; R. LANCIANI, Ruins, p. 292; CH. HÜLSEN, FR, p. 83 f.; E. DE RUGGIERO, pp. 233–236; H. THÉDENAT, FR, pp. 162 f., 360 f.; E. B. VAN DEMAN, AJA XVI, 1912, pp. 411, 414; T. FRANK, Buildings, p. 55 f.; P-A, p. 421 f.; G. LUGLI, Centro, p. 114 f.; id., Tecnica I, pp. 437, 441, 600; M. E. BLAKE I, p. 127; II, pp. 97, 100.

990 Porticus Deorum Consentium.

Fot 184

991 The restored row of columns in front of the brick-built rooms.

Fot 6265

992 Rooms lying beneath a platform extending in front of the colonnade.                    Fot 185

PORTICUS GAI ET LUCI. A marble inscription in honour of Lucius Caesar, Augustus' grandson and adopted son (CIL VI, 36908), stands on a platform which projects south-westwards from the south-east corner of the Basilica Aemilia. It was found in 1899, broken, but apparently not far from its original place, at the south-west end of the platform on the Sacra Via, where it had fallen from the building to which it belonged. The building may thus be identified as the Porticus Gai et Luci mentioned in Suetonius (Augustus 29), and Dio Cassius (LVI, 27, 5). An excavation in April and May 1954, along the south-east side of the Basilica Aemilia, revealed the traces of a porticus, which, with two arcades, reached from the eastern entrance of the Basilica Aemilia to the Sacra Via, and then crossed the street with another arch (s. plan, Arcus Augusti I, 94). The arch over the street, on which the inscription of Lucius Caesar was presumably set, sprang on the opposite side from the foundation wall of the Porticus Iulia.

L. BORSARI, BCom XIII, 1885, p. 88; G. GATTI, NSc, 1899, p. 130; id., BCom XXVII, 1899, p. 141; R. LANCIANI, ib., pp. 190–194; D. VAGLIERI, BCom XXXI, 1903, pp. 83–87; CH. HÜLSEN, RM XX, 1905, pp. 59–62; id., FR, pp. 120, 124 f.; E. DE RUGGIERO, pp. 476–478; H. THÉDENAT, FR, pp. 141–144, 255; E. B. VAN DEMAN, AJA XVII, 1913, pp. 14–28; W. B. McDANIEL, ib., XXXII, 1928, pp. 173–177; P-A, pp. 73, 74 f.; H. MARUCCHI, Le Forum Romain et le Palatin (3), 1933, p. 79 f.; A. W. VAN BUREN, Scritti in onore di B. Nogara, 1937, pp. 507–513; G. LUGLI, Centro, p. 98 f.; id., MonMin, pp. 84–88; M. E. BLAKE I, p. 176; A. DEGRASSI, Doxa II, 1949, p. 78 f.; E. WELIN, SFR, p. 54 f.; B. ANDREAE, AA 1957, pp. 168–176.

993 The inscription in honour of L. Caesar, dating from 2 B. C. (CIL VI, 36908).                                                                 Fot 1315

994 Foundation of the south-east wall of the Porticus Gai et Luci, during the excavation in 1954.          Fot 6609

995 Segment of a column at the juncture of the Porticus of the Basilica Aemilia and the Porticus Gai et Luci.   Fot 4155

996  Steps leading into the Porticus Gai et Luci.                                          Fot 276

997 Marble sill in the façade of the Porticus Gai et Luci facing the Sacra Via, with dowel-holes for the attachment of a statue-base (s. Palladio, I Quattro Libri dell'Architettura, 1570, IV, p. 32). Fot 275

PORTICUS IULIA. The Porticus Iulia is one of the group of buildings on the south-east side of the Forum Romanum, which are named after members of the gens Iulia. The only literary evidence for its position, is in the scholia on Aulus Persius Flaccus' Satire IV, 49: "foeneratores ad puteal Scribonii Libonis, quod est in porticu Iulia ad Fabianum arcum, consistere solebant". The excavation of building foundations on the south and north sides of the Temple of Caesar in May 1952, in conjunction with the discovery of the Puteal Libonis (August 1950), and of the Fornix Fabianus (August 1953)*, confirm that the remains around the temple are those of the Porticus Iulia (s. plan, Arcus Augusti I, 94). It was an arcaded portico, surrounding the Temple of Divus Iulius on three sides, and at the back, between the temple and the Regia, it became a cryptoporticus. On the north side, it was connected by a street-arch with the Porticus Gai et Luci (q. v.).

H. JORDAN, Top I, 2, p. 210; E. B. VAN DEMAN, AJA XVII, 1913, pp. 26–28; id., JRS XII, 1922, p. 26 f.; W. B. McDANIEL, AJA XXXII, 1928, p. 175 f.; P-A, p. 73; L. DU JARDIN, Historia V, 1931, p. 393 f.; id. Roma XI, 1933, pp. 394–404; E. WISTRAND, Acta InstSueciae II, 1932, pp, 56, 61–63; G. LUGLI, Centro, p. 98; id., Mon Min, pp. 86–88; M. E. BLAKE I, p.177; E. WELIN, SFR, pp. 53–58; P. ROMANELLI, Gnomon XXVI, 1954, p. 258; B. ANDREAE, AA 1957, pp. 159–165; S. STUCCHI, Mon, pp. 61–65.

* These dates are supplied by the courtesy of the excavator, R. Gamberini Mongenet.

998 The foundations of the Porticus Iulia on the south side of the Temple of Caesar.                    Fot 279

999 Foundation walls of the porticus, on the north side of the Temple of Caesar. Fot 6610

1000 Tufa foundations on the north side of the Temple of Caesar, with cuttings for the abutments of the street-arch
leading to the Porticus Gai et Luci.                                                                    Fot 283

1001 Steps on the south edge of the Porticus Iulia, with the adjoining foundations of the Arcus Augusti.      Fot 278

PORTICUS MARGARITARIA. When the Forum Adiectum, between the Sacra Via and the Nova Via, was excavated in 1878/79, the foundations of a large rectangular building were discovered; it stretched from the Atrium Vestae, as far as the beginning of the Clivus Palatinus, near the Arch of Titus. The excavator, Rodolfo Lanciani, identified it as the Porticus Margaritaria, which is mentioned in Region VIII in the Regionary Catalogue (Cod-Top I, p. 120), basing his identification on many inscriptions in which "margaritarii de sacra via" are mentioned (CIL VI, 9545–9549, 33872; X, 6492); he dated the building to the reign of Septimius Severus. On the other hand, E. B. Van Deman recognized in the remains the porticus leading to the vestibule of Nero's Domus Aurea, the northern part of which had been built over the old Sacra Via (s. Domus Aurea I, 420). After Domitian had erected his Horrea Piperataria (q. v.), in the part of the porticus which lay to the north of the Sacra Via, the southern part also became commercialised, and the open bays of the porticus were converted into shops by the addition of cross-walls. Brickstamps of Domitia Lucilla were found during the excavations, implying that Nero's porticus was converted into the Porticus Margaritaria in the second quarter of the second century A. D. (s. H. Bloch, Bolli, p. 320[256]).

R. LANCIANI, NSc, 1878, pp. 234, 341; 1879, pp. 14, 39 f., 68, 113, Tav. VII; 1882, pp. 219 f., 228 f.; 1883, p. 470; id., Ruins, pp. 207–209; id., BCom XXVIII, 1900, p. 11, Tavv. I–II; H. JORDAN, Top I, 2, p. 476; TH. ASHBY, CR XIV, 1900, p. 238 f.; CH. HÜLSEN, RM XVII, 1902, p. 95; E. DE RUGGIERO, p. 505; H.

THÉDENAT, FR, pp. 332, 357; E. B. VAN DEMAN, AJA XXVII, 1923, pp. 384–386; id., MAARome V, 1925, pp. 115–125; P-A, p. 423; G. LUGLI, Centro, pp. 73, 218 f.; id., MonMin, p. 116; M. E. BLAKE II, p. 114; A. BOETHIUS, The Golden House of Nero, 1960, p. 110.

1002 Brick walls of the tabernae in the Porticus Margaritaria.                                    Fot 156

1003 The remains of the Porticus Margaritaria, between the Atrium Vestae and the Arch of Titus.          Fot 152

PORTICUS OCTAVIAE. The porticus surrounding the temples of Iuno Regina and Iuppiter Stator in the southern part of the Campus Martius, which was built by Q. Caecilius Metellus in 147 B. C., was replaced during the reign of Augustus by the Porticus Octaviae, named after his sister Octavia. The parts which remain mostly belong to a new building, erected by Septimius Severus in 203 A. D., after a fire had destroyed the old one. The porticus was richly decorated with works of art, and enclosed a library, as well as two temples. The whole complex is shown on the Severan marble plan (FUR, Tav. XXIX; s. Circus Flaminius I, 268; Hercules Musarum I, 578). The monumental entrance, with the inscription of Septimius Severus (CIL VI, 1034), was exposed when the houses of the Ghetto were pulled down in 1878, and at the same time several columns from the south-west wing were discovered. The south-east corner of the porticus was excavated in 1938/39.

A. NIBBY, RomAnt II, pp. 600–607; A. PELLEGRINI, BullInst, 1861, pp. 241-245; id., AnnInst, 1868, pp. 108–132; R. LANCIANI, BullInst, 1878, pp. 209–219; id., BCom XVI, 1888, pp. 132–134; G. GATTI, BCom XV, 1887, p. 331 f.; CH. HÜLSEN, RM IV, 1889, p. 264 f.; R. LANCIANI, Ruins, pp. 467–470 (Bibl: p. 470); id., Storia II, p. 107 f.; IV, pp. 15–20; H. JORDAN, Top I, 3, pp. 541–544; A. PASQUI, NSc, 1912, p. 153; C. E. BOYD, Libraries, pp. 8–10, 33 f.; P-A, p. 427; G. LUGLI, Centro, pp. 562–567 (Bibl: p. 567); id., Tecnica I, p. 612; II, Tavv. CVIII, 2, CLXX, 2; G. CRESSEDI, BCom LXXIII, 1949/50, pp. 91–93; id., Palladio, N.S. IV, 1954, p. 143 f.; G. MARCHETTI-LONGHI, RendPontAcc XX, 1943/44, pp. 101–106; A. M. COLINI, ib. XXV–XXVI, 1949/51, p. 8; M. E. BLAKE I, p. 165; II, p. 100; M. J. BOYD, BSR XXI, 1953, pp. 152–159; L. CREMA, ArchRom, p. 160; FUR, p. 92 (Bibl: p. 93) Tav. XXIX; G. GATTI, Capitolium XXXV, 1960, 7, p. 10.

1004  The Porticus Octaviae, main entrance seen from the south.                                      Fot 5656

1005  The inner row of columns of the main entrance, with late mediaeval repairs to the pediment.          Fot 5657

1006 South-east corner of
the Porticus Octa-
viae, with the en-
trance seen from the
east.          Fot 555

1007 Main entrance of the porticus and columns of the south-west side.                          Fot 6611

1008 Stylobate of the south-east side.

1009  Upright column of the Temple of Iuno Regina, in a house at Nos. 9–10, Via di S. Angelo in Pescheria.    Fot 957

PUTEAL LIBONIS. The Puteal Libonis or Scribonianum, a monument in the shape of a well-head, was built around a spot at the south-east end of the Forum where lightning had struck. It is known from coins of L. Scribonius Libo of about 60 B. C., which show a well-head decorated with lyres, tendrils and Vulcan's hammer. Its frequent mention in ancient literature is due to the fact that it stood beside the tribunal of a praetor who administered justice at a place called "ANTE ATRIA", between the Temple of Castor, the Porticus Iulia and the Fornix Fabianus. While excavations were being made in the region of the Arch of Augustus, in 1950, a rectangular pozzo made of Grottaoscura tufa was found near the south pier foundation of the Actium Arch, and its sherd content pointed to it having been struck by lightning. The excavations of the Porticus Iulia (q. v.), in the immediate neighbourhood, and the Fornix Fabianus (q. v.), at a distance of some 45 m. (s. plan, Arcus Augusti I, 94), establish the identity of this tufa foundation as the Puteal Libonis which, according to the scholia ad Persius, Sat. IV, 49, stood "in porticu Iulia ad Fabianum arcum". A half-circle of travertine, into which a metal railing was inserted, surrounded the Puteal Libonis in the imperial period (s. Arcus Augusti I, 98, 6). When the triple-gated Parthian Arch was erected, the monument was moved out of the line of the southern gateway, and placed in front of the southern pier of the centre arch.

H. JORDAN, Hermes VII, 1873, p. 285; id., Top I, 2, pp. 210 f., 403 f.; O. RICHTER, RM III, 1888, p. 100; O. BENNDORF–R. SCHÖNE, Die antiken Bildwerke des Lateranensischen Museums, 1867, p. 307 f., No. 440; CH. HÜLSEN, FR, p. 141 f.; id., Forum und Palatin, 1926, p. 41; A. PIGANIOL, Mél XXVIII, 1908, pp. 261–263; E. B. VAN DEMAN, AJA XVII, 1913, p. 27; H. THÉDENAT, FR, pp. 147 f., 278; E. DE RUGGIERO, p. 72; W. B. MCDANIEL, AJA XXXII, 1928, pp. 165–177; P-A, p. 434; L. DU JARDIN, Historia V, 1931, pp. 388–410; E. WISTRAND, ActaInstSueciae II, 1932, pp. 55–63; M. BERNHART, Deutsches Jahrbuch f. Numismatik I, 1938, p. 152; C. GIOFFREDI, Tribunali, pp. 265–267; G. LUGLI, Centro, pp. 91 f., 174 (Bibl: p. 92); id., MonMin, pp. 46–52; M. E. BLAKE I, p. 146; E. WELIN, SFR, pp. 9–37, 64–72; P. ROMANELLI, Gnomon XXVI, 1954, p. 258; B. ANDREAE, AA 1957, pp. 154–156; S. STUCCHI, Mon, pp. 62–65.

1010 The Puteal Libonis, immediately after it was excavated, on the 14th August 1950.                    Fot 6612

1011 A denarius of L. Scribonius Libo with the
Puteal (BMC, Rep I, p. 419, No. 3377).
Fot 4206

1012 Tufa blocks of the foundation of the Puteal, and the pier of the first Arch of Augustus.          Fot 6613

1013  The Puteal Libonis, with the Porticus Iulia and the Temple of Divus Iulius.                    Fot 274

QUADRIGA ARCADII ET HONORII. Fragments of an inscription in honour of Arcadius and Honorius stand in front of the north end of the Augustan Rostra. They belong to the base of a monument to both rulers, which was probably a Victory Quadriga. The inscription was excavated in 1549 and 1563 in front of the Arch of Septimius Severus, and was copied. It commemorated the victory over Gildo, the rebellious governor of Africa, in 398 A. D. (CIL VI, 1187). The six marble tablets bearing the inscription have been lost, with the exception of two fragments; the larger of these reappeared in the Naples Museum (EphEpigr IV, 1881, No. 805) and was returned to the Forum in the autumn of 1908; the smaller one was found in the Forum. The insertion of the preserved fragments into the 16th century copy of the complete text, shows that the inscription must originally have measured some 5 m. in length and 1.70 m. in height. The site of the Quadriga Arcadii et Honorii may be identified with a concrete foundation, surrounded by marble steps, which lies to the north of the inscribed fragments. This foundation, which measures 8.30 m. in length and 3.60 m. in width, has had the Decennalian Base of Diocletian's Tetrarchy mounted on it in modern times.

G. HENZEN, AnnInst, 1880, p. 172; H. JORDAN, Top I, 2, p. 214[48]; Ch. HÜLSEN, RM X, 1895, pp. 52–58; id., FR, p. 90; HÜLSEN–CARTER, p. 98 f.; CIL VI, 31256; E. DE RUGGIERO, p. 493; G. LUGLI, Centro, p. 170 f.; P. ROMANELLI, Amor di Roma, 1956, pp. 376–378; id., Storia delle province romane dell'Africa, 1959, p. 616.

1014 The concrete foundation, east of the "Rostra Vandalica", on which the marble base with the Quadriga Arcadii et Honorii probably stood.

Fot 4153

IMPERATORIBVS · INVICTISSIMIS FELICISSIMISQVE
DD·NN·ARCADIO ET HONORIO · FRATRIBVS
SENATVS POPVLVSQVE ROMANVS
VINDICATA REBELLIONE ⌾
ET AFRICAE RESTITVTIONE LAETVS

1015 Dedicatory inscription for the monument of the victory over Gildo in Africa (CIL VI, 1187).

1016 Fragments of the dedicatory inscription for the Quadriga Arcadii et Honorii.                    Fot 47

REGIA. According to tradition, Numa Pompilius, the second king of Rome, made a gift to the Pontifex Maximus of his royal abode, the Regia, which stood beside the Sacra Via. During the republic, and until the time of the emperors, the building remained the official headquarters of the Pontifex Maximus. It was orientated east-west, as were the pre-Neronian Atrium Vestae (q. v.) and the Domus Publica (q. v.). The Regia was destroyed by fire in 148 B. C., restored, and then burnt again. In 36 B. C., Cn. Domitius Calvinus replaced it with a new building of marble, of which some fragments of architectural decoration are preserved. Excavations began in the last quarter of the 19th century, and were completed in 1898/99. The eastern edge of the pronaos was found, during excavations of the Fornix Fabianus (q. v.), in July 1953 (s. plan, Arcus Augusti I, 94).

H. JORDAN, Top I, 2, pp. 298–304, 423–429; id., RM I, 1886, pp. 99–111; F. M. NICHOLS, ib., pp. 94–98; id., Archaeologia L, 1887, pp. 227–250; CH. HÜLSEN, JdI IV, 1889, pp. 228–253; id., AA, 1900, p. 7 f.; id., RM XVII, 1902, pp. 62–66; XX, 1905, pp. 77–80; id., FR, pp. 171–175; R. LANCIANI, Ruins, pp. 219–221 (Bibl: p. 221); G. BONI, NSc, 1899, pp. 220–223, 486–488; id., AttiScStor, pp. 518–525; G. GATTI, BCom XXVII, 1899, pp. 144–147; D. VAGLIERI, ib., XXXI, 1903, pp. 42–55; E. PAIS, RendLinc 5, XIX, 1910, pp. 201–205; H. THÉDENAT, FR, pp. 91–94, 274–277; E. DE RUGGIERO, pp. 249–274; Röm Gebälke I, pp. 1–12; E. TEA, BCom XLVIII, 1920, pp. 152–162; L. DEUBNER, RM XXXVI–XXXVII, 1921/22, pp. 17–23; E. B. VAN DEMAN, JRS XII, 1922, p. 28 f., T. FRANK, Buildings, pp. 81–85; P–A, pp. 440–443; L. FLAGERLIND, ActaInstSueciae II, 1932, pp. 128, 131; F. E. BROWN, MAARome XII, 1935, pp. 67–88; A. BOETHIUS, Gnomon XII, 1936, pp. 590–594; M. E. BLAKE I, pp. 117 f., 119, 121, 132 f., 150 f., 157 f., 254 f.; G. LUGLI, Centro, pp. 212–215 (Bibl: p. 215); id., MonMin, pp. 50–54; E. WELIN SFR, pp. 56 f., 59–66; B. ANDREAE, AA, 1957, p. 168; S. STUCCHI, Mon, pp. 49–60; E. GJERSTADT, ActaInstSueciae XVII, 3, 1960, pp. 295–309, 334 f.; FUR, p. 75, Tav. XXI, 17.

1017  Air photograph of the Regia.                                                                        Fot 3217

1018  The Regia, seen from west.                                              Fot 96

1019 Door with a marble sill, which
leads from the covered building
to the pronaos.          Fot 95

1020 The open courtyard of the Regia, seen from the Temple of Antoninus and Faustina.                    GFN  D/6231

1021 Corner of the entablature; the
obtuse angle corresponds with
the trapezoidal form of the pronaos.                    Fot 3693

1022 The east end of the pronaos during the excavations in July 1953, with the foundation of the Fornix Fabianus.
Fot 3517

ROMULUS DIVUS, TEMPLUM. On the basis of Maxentian coins, which show a circular temple, and of mediaeval sources, the rotunda, which stands beside the Sacra Via, between the Temple of Faustina and the Basilica of Constantine, has been accepted as the Temple of Divus Romulus, which Maxentius built in memory of his son, M. Valerius Romulus, who died in 309 A. D. A fragment of an inscription bearing the name of Constantine (CIL VI, 1147), was seen above the doorway until the 16th century. Neither the very divergent evidence of the coins, nor the mediaeval literature, (in which the title "Templum Romuli" was used indiscriminately for the Temple of Venus and Roma and for the Basilica of Constantine), furnish conclusive proof for the identification of this building. It was used as a vestibule between the Forum and the Church of SS. Cosma e Damiano, which was built into the library of the Forum Pacis under Felix IV (526–530). Soon after 1750, Benedict XIV had the eastern of the two apsed side-halls, which adjoined the rotunda, converted into the ORATORIO DELLA VIA CRUCIS; it was destroyed during the excavations of the Sacra Via in 1877/79, when everything was removed except the ancient walls.

A. NIBBY, RomAnt II, pp. 710–712; S. IVANOFF, AnnInst, 1859, pp. 105–108, Tav. F.; PLATNER–BUNSEN, Beschreibung III, 1, p. 364 f.; G. B. DE ROSSI, BACrist V, 1867, pp. 62 f., 66–69; R. LANCIANI, NSc, 1880, pp. 80, 226 f.; id., Ruins, pp. 209–211 (Bibl: pp. 211, 214); P. ADINOLFI I, p. 412 f.; L. DUCHESNE, Mél VI, 1886, pp. 25–37; M. ARMELLINI, Chiese di Roma (2), 1891, pp. 152, 155 f.; J. H. MIDDLETON, pp. 19–21; CH. HÜLSEN, FR, pp. 208–210; H. JORDAN, Top I, 3, p. 10 f.; J. MAURICE, Numismatique Constantinienne I, 1908, pp. 189, 191 f., pl. XVII, 10, 12; XIX, 1, 10; E. DE RUGGIERO, pp. 209–212; H. THÉDENAT, FR, pp. 336–338 (Bibl: p. 339); CH. HÜLSEN, Chiese, p. 242; P. B. WHITEHEAD, AJA XXXI, 1927, pp. 1–6, 13 f., 18; P-A, p. 450; J. BABELON, Mélanges Martroye, 1940, pp. 139–144; H. GRISAR, Roma alla fine del mondo antico, nuova ed. 1943, I, p. 203 f.; F. CASTAGNOLI, ArchStorPat LXX, 1947, pp. 163–169; G. LUGLI, Centro, p. 225; id., MonMin, pp. 184–190; id., Roma Aet, p. 10 f.; id., Studies pres. to D. M. Robinson II, 1953, p. 1214; P. ROMANELLI, Studi Romani I, 1953, p. 8 f.; C. C. VAN ESSEN, Mededeelingen Rome 3, VII, 1953, pp. 38–41; P. BRUUN, Arctos, Acta Philologica Fennica, N. S. I, 1954, p. 21 f.; M. WEGNER, Ornamente, pp. 68–70.

1023 The so-called Temple of Divus Romulus, with SS. Cosma e Damiano.                    Fot 507

1024, 1025  Medals of Maxentius struck in memory of "Divus Romulus" (Maurice pl. XVII, 12; XIX, 1).  Fot 4263 B, C

1026  The rotunda with the ancient door, which was moved at the time of Urban VIII, and in 1879 replaced in its original
      position.                                                                          Fot 238

1027  Right leaf of the ancient bronze door.

Fot 242

1028  The door lock.                                           Fot 241

ROSTRA. The orator's platform of the Roman Republic lay between the Comitium and the Forum Romanum. It took the name "Rostra" from the beaks of the ships, captured from the people of Antium, with which the side facing the Forum was decorated by the consul C. Maenius, in 338 B. C. Part of the excavated remains of the republican Rostra, to the east of the Lapis Niger, dates from the time of Maenius, who presumably built the first stone platform, while the part with a curved front and steps belongs to a later building of the time of Sulla. The Rostra was destroyed, when Caesar replanned the Forum, and its foundations disappeared under the raised pavement of the new Comitium. The building of a new Rostra, on the west side of the Forum, was started by Caesar and completed by Augustus (s. Rostra Augusti).

H. JORDAN, Top I, 2, pp. 353–355; E. PETERSEN, Comitium, Rostra, Grab des Romulus, 1904, pp. 14–42; G. PINZA, Il comizio romano nella età repubblicana, 1905, pp. 50–53; CH. HÜLSEN, RM XX, 1905, pp. 29–39; TH. ASHBY, CR XIX, 1905, p. 77 f.; E. PETERSEN, RM XXI, 1906, pp. 193–210; HÜLSEN–CARTER, p. 113 f., pl. V; CH. HÜLSEN, Die neuesten Ausgrabungen a. d. Forum Romanum, 1910, pp. 10–12; O. RICHTER, Beiträge IV, p. 10 f.; E. DE RUG-GIERO, pp. 347–358; H. THÉDENAT, FR, pp. 125–128; E. B. VAN DEMAN, JRS XII, 1922, pp. 7, 21–23; T. FRANK, Buildings, pp. 62–65; P–A, p. 450 f.; E. GJERSTAD, Dragma M. P. Nilsson ded., 1939, pp. 214 f., 216, 220; id., ActaInstSueciae V, 1941, pp. 97–104, 108 f., 127 f., 138–158; G. LUGLI, Centro, pp. 116–119; id., MonMin, p. 9 f.; M. E. BLAKE I, pp.122, 123, 143; G. CARETTONI, JRS L, 1960, p. 196.

1029 The remains of the republican Rostra during the excavations in 1956.                                        Fot 3343

1030 The Forum side of the Rostra, with a curved wall of tufa blocks.

Fot 3328

1031  The end of the tufa wall, seen against the Curia.                                    Fot 3313

1032 The east end of a line of straight steps, on the Comitium side of the Rostra.                    Fot 3691

ROSTRA AUGUSTI. The orator's platform was moved from the Comitium to the north-west side of the Forum, in the course of Julius Caesar's replanning of the Forum, which coincided with the building of a new Curia, while the Comitium was reduced in size and raised to a higher level. Caesar's structure, which had approximately the same measurements as the Rostra Augusti, was completed at the beginning of 44 B. C. At the festival of the Lupercalia on the 15th February, statues of Caesar and Pompey and an equestrian statue of Sulla already stood upon it. The Rostra consisted of two parts; the western, a concrete core faced with a straight brick wall on the east side, forming a stepped access to the platform. The eastern part consisted of the front wall, decorated with the beaks of ships, and the side-walls, all of opus quadratum; two rows of piers in the interior supported the platform. The straight corridor which lay between the two parts was broadened at its north side, probably when the Arch of Septimius Severus was built, by cutting out a segment of the concrete core of the western part; the remaining curved wall (Hemicyclium) was faced with slabs of Portasanta marble. The remains of the Rostra were discovered when a road was built across the Forum in 1831/34 connecting Via Bonella with Via della Consolazione. The monument was then recognized as the Rostra, but it could only be properly excavated and examined after the road, which had been built on top of it, was removed in 1882.

A. NIBBY, RomAnt II, p. 159 f.; L. CANINA, Diss PontAcc VIII, 1838, pp. 107–115; PLATNER–BUNSEN, Beschreibung III, 2, pp. 102–105; G. PELLICIONI (E. SARTI), ArchStorPat IX, 1886, pp. 438–440; H. JORDAN, AnnInst, 1883, pp. 23–58; id., Top I, 2, pp. 226-245; F. M. NICHOLS, Notizie dei rostri del Foro Romano, 1885; O. RICHTER, Rekonstruktion und Geschichte der römischen Rednerbühne, 1884; id., BullInst, 1884, pp. 113–116; id., JdI IV, 1889, pp. 1–18; id., Beiträge II, 1903; G. BONI, NSc, 1900, p. 627 f.; id., AttiScStor, pp. 556–563; CH. HÜLSEN, RM X, 1895, pp. 58–63; XVII, 1902, pp. 13–20; XX, 1905, pp. 15–26; id., FR, pp. 66–73; A. MAU, RM XX, 1905, pp. 230–266; E. PETERSEN, RM XXI, 1906, pp. 57–63; J. H. MIDDLETON I, pp. 252–262; id., Archaeologia XLIX, 1886, pp. 424–432; C. I. O'CONNOR, AJA IV, 1900, pp. 306–309; D. VAGLIERI, BCom XXXI, 1903, pp. 152–159; E. B. VAN DEMAN, AJA XIII, 1909, pp. 170–186; E. DE RUGGIERO, pp. 359–381; H. THÉDENAT, FR, pp. 128–133, 238–241; W. SCHEEL, RM XLIII, 1928, pp. 176–255; P-A, pp. 451–455; F. W. SHIPLEY, Papers in mem. J. M. Wulfing, 1930, pp. 88–102; G. LUGLI, Centro, pp. 140–144; id., MonMin, pp. 65–76 (Bibl: p. 65); M. E. BLAKE I, pp. 172–174, 295; A. VON GERKAN, Gymnasium LXII, 1955, p. 277.

1033 The Rostra Augusti.                                                                                      Fot 8

1034 The front of the Rostra, restored in 1904, showing dowel-holes for attaching the ship's beaks. Fot 29

1035 The north end of the front of the Rostra. Fot 30

1036  The south-east corner of the Rostra.                                    Fot 31

1037  The north side of the corridor under the Rostra; the bricks of the pavement bear brickstamps of the time of Cara-
      calla.                                                                              Fot 6074

1038  The corridor under the Rostra with traces of an impluvium.

1039  The south end of the corridor.

Fot 6077

1040 "Rostra Vandalica", an enlargement of the platform added in the 5th century.                    Fot 32

1041 The "Hemicyclium" with slabs of Portasanta marble.                                              Fot 34

1042 Traces of an earlier straight flight of steps; behind, the curved steps which correspond to the Hemicyclium.   Fot 5778

SACRA VIA. The oldest street in Rome, the name of which has not ben satisfactorily explained either in ancient literature or by modern research. It follows the course of a stream, which was later canalised and covered over. According to tradition, it started in the valley where the Colosseum now stands, crossed the Velia, and, after passing along the north side of the Forum Adiectum, it entered the Forum through the Fornix Fabianus, and approached the Arch of Augustus between the Regia and the Temple of Vesta. At this point the stream, flowing below the Sacra Via, joined the Cloaca Maxima; and according to ancient official accounts the Sacra Via ends here. However, it continued as a processional way, past the Temple of Castor and the Basilica Iulia, until, at the entrance of the Vicus Iugarius into the Forum, it merged into the Clivus Capitolinus. After the Temple of Caesar was built, a new branch of the street passed on the north side of the Regia and the Temple of Caesar, turning south-west in front of the Rostra Aedis Divi Iuli, and joining the original Sacra Via opposite the Vicus Tuscus.

s. a. Domus Aurea I, 420.

A. NIBBY, RomAnt I, pp. 49–53; J. H. PARKER, The Via Sacra in Rome, 1876; R. LANCIANI, NSc, 1878, p. 341; 1882, pp. 219–222; H. JORDAN, Capitol, Forum u. Sacra Via in Rom, 1881, pp. 39–45; id., Top I, 2, pp. 274–289, 415 f.; O. GILBERT, Rom I, pp. 214–220, 236–238, 300–334; R. LANCIANI, Ruins, p. 188 f. (Bibl: p. 190); G. BONI, NSc, 1899, pp. 265–267; id., AttiScStor, pp. 514–518; TH. ASHBY, CR XIII, 1899, pp. 322, 467; XIV, 1900, p. 239 f.; XVI, 1902, pp. 96, 286; CH. HÜLSEN, AA, 1900, p. 9; id., RM XVII, 1902, p. 94 f.; id., FR, pp. 195–197; H. JORDAN, Top I, 3, p. 14 f.; D. VAGLIERI, BCom XXX, 1902, p. 34; XXXI, 1903, pp. 19–25; A. PIGANIOL, Mél XXVIII, 1908, pp. 233–253; E. DE RUGGIERO, pp. 498–506; H. THÉDENAT, FR, pp. 167–173, 265, 355–357; E. B. VAN DEMAN, JRS XII, 1922, p. 13 f.; id., AJA XXVII, 1923, pp. 283–424; id., MAARome V, 1925, pp. 115–126; P-A, pp. 456–459; G. SÄFLUND, Acta InstSueciae II, 1932, p. 70 f.; G. COZZO, Il luogo primitivo di Roma, 1935, pp. 115–117, 127–133; G. LUGLI, Centro, pp. 75–77 (Bibl: p. 77); B. ANDREAE, AA, 1957, p. 139 f.; E. GJERSTAD, ActaInstSueciae XVII, 3, 1960, pp. 321–358; L. A. HOLLAND, Janus and the bridge, 1961, pp. 36 f., 119 f.

1043 The Sacra Via in front of the Basilica of Constantine, late imperial level.                                    Anderson 560

1044 The Sacra Via, north of the Arch of Titus, at the time of Augustus.
Fot 136

1045 The "Clivus Sacer" of the Sacra Via, Augustan level.                           Fot 130

1046 The Sacra Via beside the "Temple of Romulus", showing the bifurcation in front of the Regia.     GFN D/6144

1047 The Sacra Via, between the Temple of Vesta and the Regia.                    Fot 5044

1048  The new branch of the Sacra Via, between the Regia and the Temple of Antoninus and Faustina.          Fot 5045

1049 The Sacra Via in front of the Basilica Iulia. Fot 5046

1050 The junction of the branch
     leading round the Temple of
     Caesar with the original Sacra
     Via.                  Fot 131

1051 A row of "pozzi" under the Sacra Via, from the middle as far as the west end of the Basilica Iulia (H. Thédenat,
     FR, p. 265).                                                                                    Foro E/206

SAEPTA IULIA ET DIRIBITORIUM. The great voting precinct in the Campus Martius, for the elections of the comitia tributa, was started by Julius Caesar. The work was continued by the triumvir Lepidus and, in 26 B.C., it was dedicated by Agrippa. Until 1934, the remains of the Saepta Iulia were thought to lie along the Via Lata, on the west side of the Via del Corso; but Guglielmo Gatti's researches have ascertained, on the evidence of the Severan marble plan, that the building lay between the Pantheon and the Temple of Isis, in the Campus Martius. The central structure was about 300 m. long and 95 m. wide, and was bounded on the east by the PORTICUS MELEAGRI and on the west by the PORTICUS ARGONAUTARUM. The perimeter wall of the latter, decorated with niches, may be seen on the east side of the Pantheon. Across the south end of the Saepta Iulia lay the DIRIBITORIUM where, after the elections, the votes were counted. Its south wall was discovered, over a length of some 105 m., between Piazza del Gesù and Via di S. Nicola de' Cesarini, while sewers were being built under the new Corso Vittorio Emanuele in 1884.

s. a. Basilica Neptuni I, p. 196.

R. LANCIANI, NSc, 1884, p. 103 f.; id., MALinc I, 1889, p. 471 f.; id., FUR, 21; id., Ruins, p. 47 f.; G. B. DE ROSSI – G. GATTI, BCom XXI, 1893, pp. 189–191; CH. HÜLSEN, ib., pp. 119–142; id., RM XVIII, 1903, pp. 47–54; H. JORDAN, Top I, 3, pp. 558–564; P–A, p. 460 f.; V. LUNDSTRÖM, pp. 86–88, 120–124; F. W. SHIPLEY, MAARome IX, 1931, p. 18; id., Agrippa, pp. 37–43; G. GATTI, BCom LXII, 1934, pp. 126–128; LXVI, 1938, p. 263 f.; id., L'Urbe II, 1937, 9, pp. 8–23; VII, 1942, 1, p. 9; G. LUGLI, Mon III, pp. 96–102, 103–105, 120 f.; F. CASTAGNOLI, CM, p. 139², 186–188; id., BCom LXXIV, 1951/52, p. 53; E. SJÖQVIST, ActaInstSueciae XVIII, 1954, p. 105; M. E. BLAKE I, p. 154, 161 f.; II, p. 104; L. CREMA, ArchRom, p. 170 f.; FUR, pp. 97–101 (Bibl: p. 102); Tav. XXXI.

1052 Outer wall of the Porticus Argonautarum of the Saepta Iulia, on the east side of the Pantheon.          Fot 671

1053 Outer wall of the Porticus Argonautarum, with niches on the inner side.                Fot 668

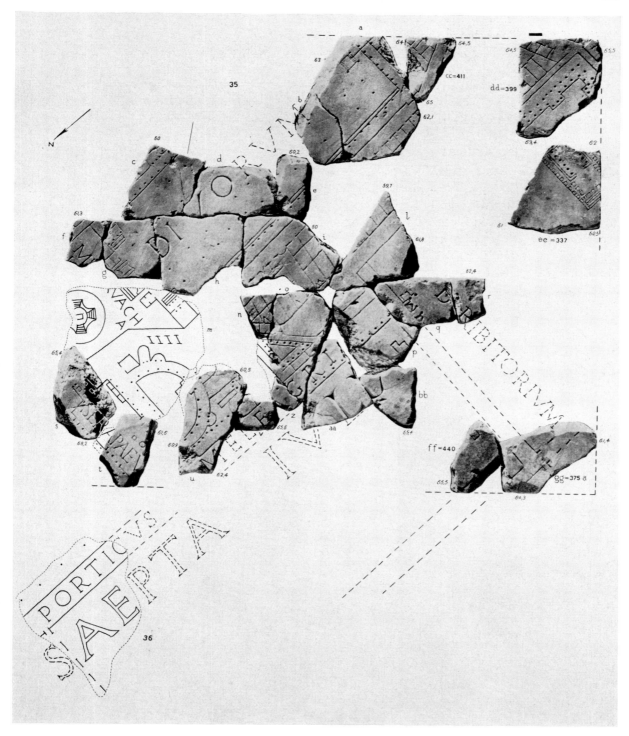

1054 Plate XXXI FUR showing the Saepta Iulia and Diribitorium.

Fot 4729

SATURNUS, TEMPLUM. According to tradition, the Temple of Saturn was consecrated in 498 B. C. The existing remains of the podium belong to a rebuilding by L. Munatius Plancus in 42 B.C. From the inscription on the architrave (CIL VI, 937), we know that the temple was again rebuilt, after being destroyed by fire, presumably at the beginning of the 4th century A. D. From republican times it was the repository of the State Treasury: AERARIUM POPULI ROMANI, or AERARIUM SATURNI. The room, which has been indentified as the Aerarium, lies to the east of the narrow stairway of the temple (FUR, Tav. XXI), and was accessible from the Clivus Capitolinus, through a door which could be locked. The temple is represented on one of the Plutei Traiani (q. v. II, 905).

H. JORDAN, Top I, 2, pp. 360–363; O. GILBERT, Rom III, pp. 401–404; G. GATTI, NSc, 1899, p. 49 f.; TH. ASHBY, CR XIII, 1899, p. 234; D. VAGLIERI, BCom XXX, 1902, p. 26; XXXI, 1903, p. 162 f.; CH. HÜL-SEN, RM XVII, 1902, p. 9; id., FR, p. 74 f.; O. RICHTER, Beiträge IV, 1910, p. 14 f.; E. B. VAN DEMAN, AJA XVI, 1912, p. 391 f.; H. THÉDENAT, FR, pp. 113–115, 227–229; E. DE RUGGIERO, pp. 151–160; M. MARCHETTI, BCom XLII, 1914, pp. 87 f., 102; L. G. ROBERTS, MAARome II, 1918, p. 58 f.; Röm Gebälke I, pp. 5, 65 f.; T. FRANK, Buildings, pp. 51–53; P-A, pp. 463–465; F. W. SHIPLEY, MAARome IX, 1931, p. 15 f.; M. E. BLAKE I, pp. 156, 334; G. LUGLI, Centro, pp. 149–151 (Bibl: p. 151); id., Mon Min, pp. 29–38; id., Tecnica II, Tav. XXXIX, 2; L. CREMA, ArchRom, p. 584 f.; FUR, p. 75, Tav. XXI.

1055 The Temple of Saturn.

1056  Side view of the pronaos.                                                            Fot 3341

1057 Rear view of the columns of the pronaos; the palmette frieze over the capitals comes from the Forum of Trajan.
Fot 198

1058 Late-antique Roman-Ionic capitals and frieze from the Forum of Trajan.                    Fot 4335

1059 The door sill of the Aerarium, with holes for the lock.
Fot 203

1060 The site of the Aerarium, east of the stairway to the pronaos, with its double marble threshold.
Fot 201

SCALAE CACI. Immediately east of the "casa Romuli" (s. Palatinus Mons II, p. 163) a narrow and steep path, enclosed by walls on both sides, descended from the Palatine to the valley of the Circus Maximus. At the upper end are the remains of a gate of the early imperial period, with a travertine sill and piers. Only a short stretch of the path is preserved, and buildings of the imperial epoch cover its lower part. This entrance to the Palatine was called the Scalae Caci because, according to the legend, the giant Cacus had his den in the region of the Forum Boarium, at the foot of the steps, and was slain there by Hercules. No steps are visible in the preserved part of the Scalae Caci.

O. RICHTER, AnnInst, 1884, pp. 191–199; H. JORDAN, Top I, 2, p. 482; R. LANCIANI, Ruins, p. 129 f. (Bibl: p. 130); H. JORDAN, Top I, 3, p. 41; TH. ASHBY, The Classical Quarterly II, 1908, pp. 145–147; T. FRANK, BUILDINGS, p. 107; CH. HÜLSEN, Forum und Palatin, 1926, p. 69; V. GROH, Athenaeum, NS VII, 1929, pp. 329 f., 347–350, 361; P–A, p. 465 f.; G. SÄFLUND, Mura, pp. 11–15; G. LUGLI, Centro, pp. 405 f., 453; P. ROMANELLI, Bullettino di Paletnologia Italiana N. S. IX, vol. 64, 1954/55, p. 258.

1061  The Scalae Caci with the remains of a gateway in the foreground.                    Fot 416

1062  The Scalae Caci seen from the west.

Fot 415

SCHOLA XANTHI. An office of the "scribae, librarii et praecones aedilium curulium", which was restored by the curatores: one, the freedman Bebryx Drusianus and one, Aulus Fabius Xanthus. This fact is known from an inscription (CIL VI, 103 == 30692), which was found in 1539 during an excavation beneath the Temple of Saturn (which at that time was called the Temple of Concordia), together with other remains of a small building, richly decorated with marble. The upper structure no longer exists, but the small trapezoidal room with the remains of a marble floor, which lies between the Arch of Tiberius and the Rostra, is attributed to the Schola Xanthi.

B. MARLIANUS, Urbis Romae Topographia, 1544, II, cap. X, p. 29; H. JORDAN, Top I, 2, p. 366 f.; CH. HÜLSEN, RM III, 1888, pp. 208–232; IV, 1889, p. 240; XVII, 1902, p. 12 f.; id., FR, pp. 63–65; O. GILBERT, Rom III, p. 161 f.; D. VAGLIERI, BCom XXXI, 1903, p. 164; R. LANCIANI, Storia II, p. 185 f.; O. RICHTER, Beiträge II, 1903, p. 8; E. B. VAN DEMAN, AJA XVI, 1912, p. 398; E. DE RUGGIERO, pp. 385–387; H. THÉDENAT, FR, pp. 162, 265; W. SCHEEL, RM XLIII, 1928, pp. 244–248; P-A, p. 468; G. LUGLI, Centro, pp. 95 f., 152; M. E. BLAKE II, p. 11.

1063 The remains of the Schola Xanthi between the Arch of Tiberius (left) and the Rostra (right).                Fot 62

SEPTIZODIUM. Septimius Severus built a monumental façade to his palace on the Palatine facing the Via Appia, which in ancient literature was called the Septizonium or Septizodium. A new arrangement of the fragments of the Severan marble plan, in which the inscription belonging to the building is completed, shows that its official title was "Septizodium" (FUR, p. 67). The name is thought to refer to the seven planets. The Septizodium was dedicated in 203 A. D., according to an inscription (CIL VI, 1032, 31229) which once ran the whole length of the façade. The eastern corner of the building, which was still standing at the time of Sixtus V, is known from countless drawings and paintings of the 15th and 16th centuries. It was pulled down in 1588/89 and the material, about which a detailed account was drawn up by the architect Domenico Fontana, was used for other papal buildings.

s. a. Obeliscus Constantii II, 861.

H. JORDAN, BullInst, 1872, pp. 145–152; id., Forma Urbis Romae, 1874, pp. 37–41; CH. HÜLSEN, 46. Berliner Winckelmannsprogramm, 1886; E. STEVENSON, BCom XVI, 1888, pp. 269–298; R. LANCIANI, RM IX, 1894, p. 4 f.; id., Ruins, pp. 181–183 (Bibl: p. 183); id., Storia II, pp. 51–54; IV, pp. 137–139; E. PETERSEN, RM II, 1887, p. 295; XXV, 1910, pp. 56–73; H. JORDAN, Top I, 3, pp. 100–103; A. BARTOLI, BArte III, 1909, pp. 253–269; id., RendLinc 5, XVIII, 1909, pp. 540–551; E. MAASS, Die Tagesgötter in Rom und den Provinzen, 1902, pp. 3–45, 97–153; CH. HÜLSEN, Zeitschrift f. Geschichte d. Architektur V, 1911/12, pp. 1–24; id., Heemskerck II, p. 55 (Text); TH. ASHBY Top 1581, p. 112 f.; Th. DOMBART, Das Palatinische Septizonium zu Rom, 1922; id., RE, Septizonium, 1923, pp. 1578–1586; G. RODENWALDT, AA, 1923/24, pp. 39–44; P-A, pp. 473–475; G. GULLINI, BCom LXXI, 1943/45, Appendice, XIV, pp. 32–34; J. GUEY, Mélanges de la Société Toulousaine d'Études Classiques I, 1946, pp. 147–166; G. LUGLI, Centro, pp. 519–521 (Bibl: p. 521); G. SPANO, MemLinc 8, III, 1951, pp. 178–199; id., RendLinc 8, VII, 1952, pp. 158–163; L. CREMA, ArchRom, pp. 545–548; FUR, p. 67, Tav. XVII.

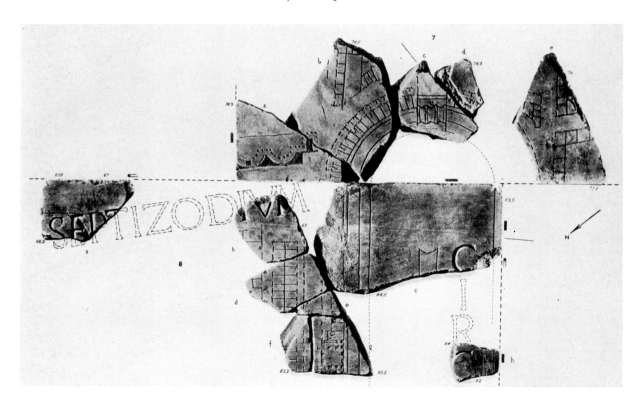

1064 The Septizodium and the Circus Maximus on the Severan marble plan (FUR, Tav. XVII).           Fot 5927

1065 Remains of the cavea of the Circus Maximus, and the back of the Septizodium, a drawing by Marten van Heemskerck (Skizzenbücher II, fol. 14 r.). Fot 4758

1066 The Septizodium in a drawing by Jan Brueghels (Egger, Röm. Veduten I, 95) with the entrance to S. Gregorio Magno on the right and the Arch of Constantine in the background. Fot 6627

1067 The east corner of the
      Septizodium, front view
      (Heemskerck, Gabinet-
      to Nazionale delle Stam-
      pe, Roma No. F. N.
      3382).          Fot 4756

MARTIN · HEMSKE RCK DE[LG]

1068 The east corner of the
     Septizodium, seen from
     the right (Heemskerck,
     Gabinetto Nazionale
     delle Stampe, Roma F.
     N. 3381).      Fot 4757

SEPULCRETUM. In April 1902, an archaic necropolis was discovered beside the Sacra Via, south-east of the Temple of Antoninus and Faustina, which was given the name "Sepulcretum" by the excavator Giacomo Boni (NSc, 1903, p. 123[1]). The cemetery contained both cremations and inhumations from the 8th to the 6th centuries B. C. During the excavations which began in 1950, near the Arch of Augustus and the Temple of Divus Iulius, more urn burials were discovered in what was apparently an extension of the Sepulcretum along the Sacra Via. A tomb, discovered in 1951 on the south side of the Temple of Divus Iulius, dated from the 9th century, and the following year three tombs of a later period (about the middle of the 7th century) were found in the immediate neighbourhood. Four cremations of the same period were excavated in 1959, below the pronaos of the Temple of Divus Iulius.

G. BONI, NSc, 1902, pp. 96–111; 1903, pp. 123–170, 375–427; 1905, pp. 145–193; 1906, pp. 5–46, 253–294; 1911, pp. 157–190; id., AttiScStor, pp. 499–514; G. PINZA, BCom XXX, 1902, pp. 37–55; id., MALinc XV, 1905, pp. 273–314; D. VAGLIERI, BCom XXXI, 1903, pp. 33–42, 252–271; CH. HÜLSEN, RM XVII, 1902, pp. 92–94; XX, 1905, pp. 95–115; id., FR, pp. 199–205; E. DE RUGGIERO, pp. 9–11 (Bibl: p. 10[1]); D. RANDALL-MACIVER, Villanovans and early Etruscans, 1924, pp. 73–78; F. K. VON DUHN, Italische Gräberkunde I, 1924, pp. 417–428; P-A, p. 475 f.; G. LUGLI, Centro, pp. 221–224; E. GJERSTAD, BCom LXXIII, 1949/50, pp. 16–18; id., ActaInstSueciae XVII, 1, 1953, p. 129 f.; XVII, 2, 1956, pp. 13–161; id., Festschrift B. Schweitzer, 1954, pp. 291–296; S. M. PUGLISI, Rivista di scienze preistoriche VII, 1952, pp. 113–115; id., Bullettino di Paletnologia Italiana N. S. VIII, pt IV, 1951/52, pp. 45–59; N. S. IX, 1954/55, pp. 299–322; E. GJERSTAD, ib., p. 296; P. ROMANELLI, ib., p. 257 f.; B. ANDREAE, AA, 1957, pp. 133–134, 137–140; R. GAMBERINI MONGENET, Rivista di scienze preistoriche XIV, 1959, p. 318 f.; G. CARETTONI, JRS L, 1960, p. 195; R. PERONI in Civiltà del Ferro, studi pubbl. nella ricorrenza centenaria della scoperta di Villanova, 1960, pp. 463–499.

1069 The site of the Sepulcretum, south-east of the Temple of Antoninus and Faustina.                                        Fot 63

1070  The excavated Sepulcretum before it was filled in; the Sacra Via is on the right.                      Fot 4326

SEPULCRUM P. AELII GUTTAE CALPURNIANI. The famous charioteer, whose name and whose 1127 victories are known from an inscription (CIL VI, 10047) copied in the 8th century by the Anonymous Einsidlensis, had his tomb built during his life time on the Via Flaminia, beyond the gate. Remains of the reliefs which decorated it, showing three quadrigas racing, were found in the fill of the eastern tower of the Porta Flaminia (q. v. II, 952), when it was demolished in 1877. The fragments of these reliefs, which have been dated to the middle of the 2nd century A. D., are now in the garden of the Museo Nuovo Capitolino (Inv. 2243–2244).

R. LANCIANI, NSc, 1877, p. 270, Ni. 6, 7; 1878, p. 138; C. L. VISCONTI – V. VESPIGNANI, BCom V, 1877, pp. 200 f., 271, Ni. 7–14; VI, 1878, p. 285, Ni 8, 9; IX, 1881, pp. 176–179, Tav. VI–VII; H. JORDAN, Top I, 3, p. 463 f.; G. GATTI, BCom XXXIX, 1911, pp. 187–192; L. FRIEDLAENDER, Sittengeschichte Roms (9) IV, 1921, pp. 179–185; P-A, p. 476; I. A. RICHMOND, Wall, p. 197; D. MUSTILLI, p. 182.

1071 Marble decoration of the tomb of P. Aelius Mari Rogati Fil. Gutta Calpurnianus from outside the Porta Flaminia, now in the Museo Nuovo Capitolino.                                                                      Fot 1151

SEPULCRUM ARRUNTIORUM. A columbarium on the ancient Via Praenestina which was built by L. Arruntius, consul in 6 A. D., for his family, freedmen, and slaves. It was discovered in 1733, about 100 m. north-west of the Porta Maggiore, between the modern Via Giolitti and Via di Porta Maggiore (s. plan, Sepulcrum Statiliorum II, 1136). The interior of the tomb, with its walls of opus reticulatum, and the barrel-vaulted ceiling with its stucco decoration, is only known to us from the drawings and engravings of three 18th century artists, Pier Leone Ghezzi, Giovanni Battista Piranesi, and Jean Barbault. By 1838, it was in such a state of decay as to be hardly recognizable (Nibby).

C. FEA, Miscellanea filologica critica antiquaria I, 1790, p. 143, No. 52 (Notizie Ficoroni); G. B. PIRANESI, Le Antichità Romane II, 1784, Tavv. 7–15; A. NIBBY, RomAnt II, p. 518 f.; CIL VI, 5931–5960; R. LANCIANI, BCom IX, 1882, p. 209 (P. L. GHEZZI, Bibl. Vaticana, Cod. Ottoboni No. 3108, fol. 189–198); G. B. DE ROSSI, Note per la pianta di G. B. Nolli, 1884, p. 25 f.; K. RONCZEWSKI, Gewölbeschmuck im römischen Altertum, 1903, p. 27 f., Taf. XIV; H. JORDAN, Top I, 3, p. 362; E. STRONG, Apotheosis and After Life, 1915, p. 209 f.; E. L. WADSWORTH, MAA Rome IV, 1924, p. 36 f.; P-A, p. 477; P. GRIMAL, Mél LIII, 1936, p. 273; G. LUGLI, Mon III, p. 426 f.; F. L. BASTET, De Datum van het grote Hypogaeum by de Porta Maggiore te Rome, 1958, p. 20 f.; M. E. BLAKE, II, p. 59 f.

1072 Sepulcrum Arruntiorum – drawing by Jean Barbault (Vues des plus beaux restes des antiquités romaines, 1775, pl. 21).                                                                                     Fot 2990

1073 Stucco decoration of a
     vaulted ceiling; cf. Basilica
     Sotterranea I, 186 (G. B.
     Piranesi, Le antichità Ro-
     mane II, tav. XII).
                    Fot 2992

1074 Chamber of the columbarium with a vaulted ceiling and stucco decoration (J. Barbault, pl. 22).          Fot 2994

SEPULCRUM AURELIORUM. The burial place of a Christian sect, of the first half of the 3rd century, was discovered in 1919, on the corner of Viale Manzoni and Via Luigi Luzzatti. The upper burial chamber is to a great extent destroyed, but both chambers of the lower level (A – the northern and B – the southern), together with a vestibule V, between room B and the stairway, are preserved with all their wall-paintings. The rooms of the lower storey have stairs leading down to a catacomb, which apparently did not extend very far; after the Aurelian Wall was built (270–282 A. D.), the Sepulcrum Aureliorum lay inside the city and could no longer be used for burials.

G. BENDINELLI, NSc, 1920, pp. 123–141; 1921, pp. 230–234; R. PARIBENI, BArte I, 1921/22, pp. 97–104; F. VON DUHN, AA, 1921, pp. 111–114; O. MARUCCHI, NBACrist XXVI, 1920, pp. 53–55; XXVII, 1921, pp. 44–47, 83–93; XXVIII, 1922, pp. 128–131; G. BENDINELLI, MALinc XXVIII, 1922, pp. 289–520; G. WILPERT, MemPontAcc 3, I, parte II, 1924, pp. 1–43; K. LEHMANN-HARTLEBEN, AA, 1926, p. 97 f.; M. I. ROSTOVTZEFF, Mystic Italy, 1927, pp. 148–155; M. H. SWINDLER, Ancient Painting, 1929, pp. 401–403; P. MARCONI, La pittura dei Romani, 1929, pp. 109–111; P-A, p. 346; F. WIRTH, pp. 177 f., 185–189; G. LUGLI, Mon III, pp. 435–455; id., Tecnica I, p. 578; II, Tav. CLXXV, 4; P. MINGAZZINI, RendPont Acc 3, XIX, 1942/43, pp. 355–369; C. CECCHELLI, Monumenti cristiano-eretici di Roma, 1944, pp. 1–119 (Bibl: p. 103); CH. PICARD, CRAI, 1945, pp. 26–51; M. BORDA, La Pittura Romana, 1958, pp. 316–319.

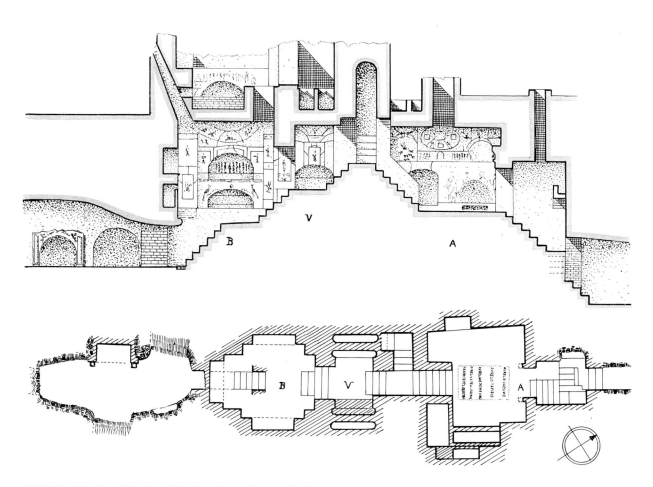

1075 The Tomb of the Aurelii; elevation and ground plan.

1076 Stairway from the upper storey to the two lower rooms.

1077 Mosaic inscription on the floor of room A with the dedication of Aurelius Felicissimus to his "Fratres" and "Coliberti".

GFN E/5032

1078 Funeral inscription of Aurelia Myr-
     sina, a 5½ year old child, which was
     found in room A.   Pont Com 9138

1079 South-west corner of tomb-chamber B.

1080 South wall of tomb-chamber B. Alinari 41220

1081  View from room B to the north wall of room A.                                                Fot 5243

1082  A monumental door leading to the catacomb, a later addition to room A.                    GFN  E/5020

1083  East wall of room A with paintings of the Apostles.                     GFN E/5021

1084  Wall paintings in the lunette of the north wall, which was partially destroyed when an entrance was made into the
      catacomb.                                                            Pont Com 9104

SEPULCRUM BIBULI. The tomb of C. Poplicius Bibulus stands on the east side of the Victor-Emanuel Monument; according to the inscription (CIL VI, 1319, 31599), it was erected by the Senate "honoris virtutisque caussa". It stood outside the Servian Wall, on the street which led from the PORTA FONTINALIS to the Via Flaminia. The south-west façade is preserved and has an opening like a window in the centre, which was presumably a niche for the statue of the deceased. The tomb dates from the first half of the 1st century B. C. The podium, which is 4.75 m. high, was excavated in 1907. The inscription is on the upper register.

R. VENUTI, Descrizione topografica delle antichità di Roma (3), 1826, pp. 129–131; A. NIBBY, RomAnt II, pp. 532–534; R. BERGAU, Philologus XXVI, 1867, pp. 82–91; H. JORDAN, Top I, 1, p. 207 f.; G. BONI, NSc, 1907, pp. 410–414; R. DELBRÜCK, HB II, pp. 37–41; T. FRANK, Buildings, p. 144; id., ClPhil XIX, 1924, p. 78; Röm Gebälke I, pp. 6, 9, 10; P-A, p. 477; C. RICCI, VdI, p. 32 f.; G. SÄFLUND, Mura, p. 207; G. LUGLI, Mon III, pp. 262–264; M. E. BLAKE I, p. 147; T. R. S. BROUGHTON, The magistrates of the Roman Republic I, 1951, pp. 286, 289[4]; A. E. and J. S. GORDON, Album of dated Latin inscriptions I, 1958, p. 15 f.; L. CREMA, ArchRom, p. 129 f.

1085 Sepulcrum C. Poplicii Bibuli.

Fot 1130

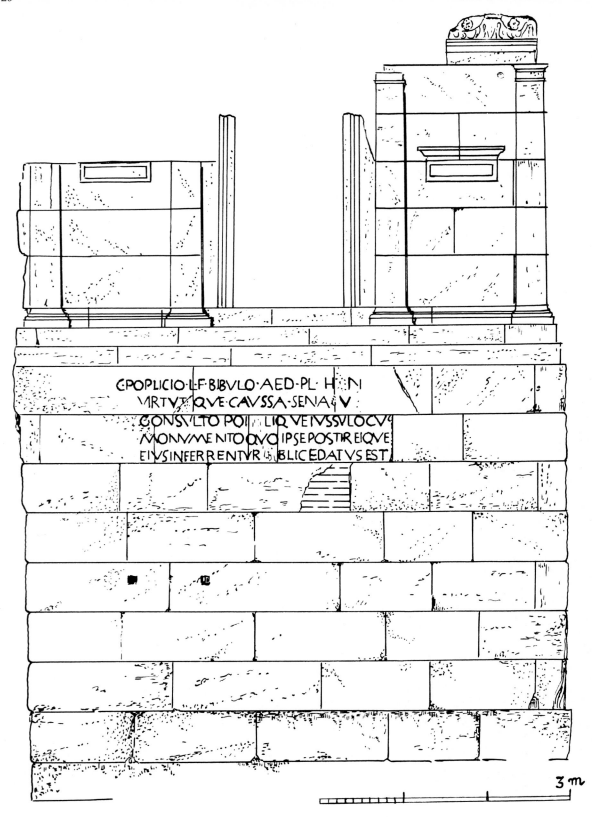

1086 A drawing of the tomb based on the 1907 excavation.

SEPULCRUM C. CESTII. C. Cestius, a contemporary of Augustus, had his tomb on the Via Ostiensis built in the form of a pyramid. The inscriptions on the east and west sides of the pyramid name his official position as Praetor, Tribunus Plebis, and Septemvir Epulonum (CIL VI, 1374). Two statue bases, which were found in front of the monument in 1662, give the names of his heirs (CIL VI, 1375) among whom was M. Agrippa, the son-in-law of Augustus. The date of the death of C. Cestius is not known; we only know that he died before Agrippa in 12 B. C. The pyramid is incorporated in the Aurelian city fortifications, next to the Porta Ostiensis. In the middle ages it was known as the Meta Remi (CodTop IV, p. 73), as distinct from the Meta Romuli (q. v. II, p. 59) in the Borgo. In 1663 it was restored by Alexander VII and a new entrance to the burial chamber was made, with a door on the west side.

P. S. BARTOLI, Gli antichi sepolcri Romani, 1697, Tavv. 60–70; O. FALCONIERI, Discorso intorno alla piramide di C. Cestio, in Nardini-Nibby IV, pp. 1–43; G. A. GUATTANI, Roma Antica (2), 1805, pp. 59–61; A. NIBBY, RomAnt II, pp. 534–540; PLATNER-BUNSEN, Beschreibung III, 1, pp. 435–439; F. REBER, Ruinen, pp. 540–542; J. H. MIDDLETON II, pp. 284–287; H. JORDAN, Top I, 3, p. 179 f.; E. CAETANI LOVATELLI, Aurea Roma, 1915, pp. 59–82; TH. ASHBY, Top 1581, pp. 137–139; G. LUGLI, Architettura ed Arti Decorative I, 1921/22, p. 236 f.; G. T. RIVOIRA, RomArch, p. 15 f.; P. MARCONI, La pittura dei Romani, 1929, p. 111, fig. 152; P-A, p. 478; M. P. PIERMATTEI, Capitolium VI, 1930, pp. 292–301; R. HERBIG, RM XLVIII, 1933, pp. 313–316; G. LUGLI, Mon III, pp. 612–615; M. E. BLAKE I, pp. 181, 294; A. E. and J. C. GORDON, Greece and Rome XX, 1951, pp. 79 f., 95; id., Album of dated Latin inscriptions, 1958, p. 34 f.; M. BORDA, La pittura Romana, 1958, pp. 56, 202; L. CREMA, ArchRom, p. 247 f.

1087 The Pyramid of Cestius, the inscriptions on the west side.                                         Fot 6637

1088 The Pyramid of Cestius in the Aurelian Wall with the doorway made in 1663, leading to the burial chamber.
Fot 1146

1089  An inscription on a statue base. It was found in front of the Pyramid in 1662 and gives the names of Cestius' heirs
(CIL VI, 1375 b).                                                                                Fot 5938

SEPULCRUM TI. CLAUDII VITALIS. This columbarium, of the middle of the 1st century A. D., was discovered in 1866 in the Villa Wolkonsky, on an ancient road which ran parallel with the Arcus Caelimontani of the Aqua Claudia (q. v. I, p. 37). The three-storeyed structure was built for Tiberius Claudius Vitalis by members of his family, of whom two were called "architectus" (CIL VI, 9151).

R. BERGAU, BullInst, 1866, pp. 112–117; J. H. PARKER, The archaeology of Rome, IX, 1877, p. 6 f.; P. MINGAZZINI, BCom L, 1922, p. 73 f.; G. LUGLI, Mon III, pp. 431–433; A. M. COLINI, Celio, pp. 389–391; M. E. BLAKE II, p. 61 f.; L. CREMA, ArchRom, p. 264.

1090 Marble inscription on the outside of the tomb of Tiberius Claudius Vitalis.

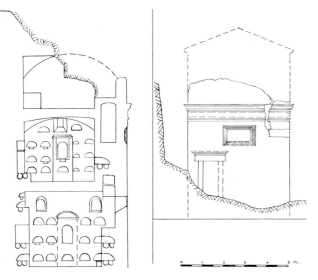

1091 Section through the columbarium and an elevation with the reconstructed third storey (Gismondi).

1092 Interior of the second storey.

Fot 3638

1093 Exterior view of the façade.                                                                  Fot 3637

SEPULCRUM CORNELIAE. When the Porta Salaria of the Aurelian Wall was pulled down in 1871, the remains of a tomb were found under the west tower. It consisted of a square travertine base, supporting a circular building faced with marble. According to fragments of an inscription (CIL VI, 1296), it was the grave of Cornelia, daughter of L. Scipio and wife of Vatienus. When the new Porta Salaria (q. v. II, p. 229) was removed for traffic reasons, the remains of the tomb were reassembled west of the new opening in the wall. Since 1950, the Tomb of Cornelia has stood outside the wall, between the Porta Salaria and Porta Pinciana.

s. a. Porta Salaria II, 976.

G. HENZEN, BullInst, 1871, p. 115; P-A, p. 478 f.; I. A. RICHMOND, Wall, pp. 12, 185; G. LUGLI, Mon II, p. 173 f.; III, p. 340; M. E. BLAKE I, p. 170 f.; G. GATTI, Fasti Archaeologici V, 1950, p. 34, No. 311.

1094 The remains of the Tomb of Cornelia in its original position, in front of the new Porta Salaria which was built in 1873.

GFN C/9010

1095 The Tomb of Cornelia in front of the Aurelian Wall, where it has stood since 1950.

Fot 1128

SEPULCRUM EURYSACIS. The tomb of the baker M. Vergileus Eurysaces stands outside the Porta Maggiore, in the angle where the ancient Via Labicana (now Casilina) branched off the Via Praenestina. It dates from the second half of the 1st century B. C. The sanctity of the tomb was respected during the subsequent building of the monumental arches of the Aqua Claudia and the Anio Novus (Porta Maggiore); but when the Porta Praenestina was rebuilt by Honorius, the tomb was covered by the central tower of the gateway. In 1838, under Gregory XVI, the double-gateway was pulled down (s. Porta Praenestina II, p. 225) and the tomb of Eurysaces came to light. Its inscription (CIL VI, 1958) was already known from Renaissance drawings. The tomb was decorated with rows of vertical and horizontal corn-measures, and a frieze representing the various operations of bread-making, weighing and delivering; it was called a "panarium" by its owner (funeral inscription of Atistia, CIL VI, 1958; fig. 1100). The base of the monument was uncovered, down to its ancient level, during the 1955/57 excavations.

L. GRIFI, Brevi cenni di un monumento scoperto a Porta Maggiore, 1838; G. MELCHIORRI, Intorno al monumento di M. Virgilio Eurisace, 1838; E. BRAUN, BullInst, 1838, pp. 165–169; L. CANINA, AnnInst, 1838, pp. 202–230; O. JAHN, ib., pp. 231–248; G. ABEKEN, ib., 1841, p. 123, Tav. G; L. CANINA, Bull Inst, 1840, p. 19 f.; E. PLATNER – L. URLICHS, Beschreibung Roms (Auszug), 1845, pp. 332–334; A. MAU, RM I, 1886, p. 47 f.; TH. ASHBY, BSR I, 1902, p. 150; R. LANCIANI, Storia III, p. 158; E. CAETANI LOVATELLI, Passegiate nella Roma antica, 1909, pp. 151–176; A. BARTOLI, Disegni IV, Tav. 384, fig. 672 (Sallustio Peruzzi); E. STRONG, Art in Ancient Rome I, 1928, p. 94; P-A, p. 479; I. A. RICHMOND, Wall, p. 207 f.; G. LUGLI, Mon III, pp. 493–495; id., Tecnica I, pp. 326, 430; M. E. BLAKE I, p. 181 f.; L. CREMA, ArchRom, p. 256; H. KÄHLER, Rom und seine Welt II, 1960, pp. 161–165.

1096 The funerary inscription of M. Vergileus Eurysaces on the north side of the monument.     Fot 5614

1097 The frieze on the south side. From the left: sifting and grinding the corn, sorting the grain.          Alinari 6736 A

1098 The frieze on the north side. From the right: a kneading machine, rolling the bread, the oven. Alinari 6736 B

1099 The Tomb of Eurysaces, south and west sides during the excavation in 1957.                              Fot 3646

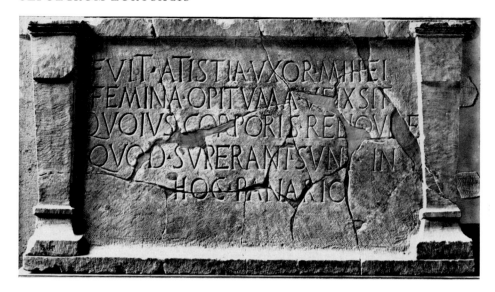

1100 Funerary inscription of Atistia, wife of Eurysaces (CIL VI, 1958).    Fot 6636

1101 The north side of the monument.                                              Fot 5615

1102 The portraits of Eurysaces and Atistia, found near the tomb in 1838 and, until 1955, placed beside Via Labicana.
Inst Neg 33.749

SEPULCRA FAMILIAE MARCELLAE ET ALIORUM. Since the middle of the 15th century countless columbaria with hundreds of niches for urns have been discovered in the area between the Via Appia and Via Latina, and bounded on the south by the Aurelian Wall. Apart from the Sepulcrum Pomponii Hylae (q. v.), only the three COLUMBARI DI VIGNA CODINI are preserved. They served as burial places for the freedmen of the Julian-Claudian dynasty, and for relations of the imperial family. In 1847, the second columbarium to be excavated contained an overwhelming number of burial places of the freedmen of Marcella, who was the first wife of Agrippa, and of her daughter, Marcella the younger. The first columbarium was excavated in 1840 and the third in 1852.

COLUMBARIUM I: P. CAMPANA, DissPontAcc XI, 1852, pp. 317–403; E. BRAUN, BullInst, 1840, pp. 136–139; CIL VI, 4881–5178 (forma parietum p. 927); R. LANCIANI, Ruins, p. 330 f.; id., FUR 46; H. JORDAN, Top I, 3, p. 211 f.; G. LUGLI, Mon I, pp. 447–450; M. E. BLAKE I, p. 273; II, p. 60; L. CREMA, ArchRom, p. 261. COLUMBARIUM II: W. HENZEN, BullInst, 1847, pp. 49–51; id., AnnInst, 1856, pp. 9–18; CIL VI, 4414-4880 (forma parietum p. 910); R. LANCIANI, Ruins, p. 331; G. LUGLI, Mon I, pp. 450–452; M. E. BLAKE I, p. 272 f.; COLUMBARIUM III: E. BRAUN, Bull Inst, 1852, pp. 81–83; G. HENZEN, Monumenti ed annali pubblicati dall'Instituto nel 1856, pp. 8–24; CIL VI, 5179–5538 (forma parietum p. 940); R. LANCIANI, Ruins, p. 332 f.; G. LUGLI, Mon I, pp. 452–457; M. E. BLAKE I, p. 273; II, p. 60.

1103 Columbarium I, central pier and west side.                                      Alinari 6232

1104 Columbarium I, west wing.                                            Fot 4742

1105 The first columbarium of Vigna Codini excavated in 1840 (right), with the columbarium of Pomponius Hylas, excavated in 1831 (left). From P. Campana, DissPontAcc XI, 1852, p. 316.                                       Fot 5278

1106 Columbarium II, east and south sides.                                       Arch Vat XVIII–8.–2

1107  Columbarium II, west and north sides.                                    Anderson 264

1108 Columbarium III, east wing.

Arch Vat XVIII–8–1

1109 Columbarium III, stairway in the west wing.                    Arch Vat XVIII–7–30

1110 Columbarium III, west wing seen from the south.                          Anderson 265

SEPULCRUM Q. HATERII. Early in 1826, the south tower of the Porta Nomentana (q. v. II, p. 217), which had been closed since 1564, was pulled down in order to expose the tomb beneath it. Pieces of travertine facing and marble decoration were found, as well as the rectangular concrete core. It was in the form of a large altar with two volutes. On the front was the funerary inscription of Q. Haterius (CIL VI, 1426), presumably the celebrated orator who died in 26 A. D. (Tacitus, Ann. IV, 61).

A. NIBBY, Memorie Romane d'antichità e di belle arti III, 1826, pp. 456–458; id., RomAnt II, p. 519 f.; H. JORDAN, Top I, 1, p. 344 f.; L. HOMO, Essai sur le règne de l'empereur Aurélien, 1904, p. 243 f.; P-A, p. 480; I. A. RICHMOND, Wall, p. 93 f.; G. LUGLI, Mon II, p. 177 f.; M. E. BLAKE II, p. 59.

1111 The Tomb of Q. Haterius in the Aurelian Wall, south of the walled-up Porta Nomentana.                    Fot 1131

SEPULCRUM A. HIRTII. The consuls C. Vibius Pansa and A. Hirtius, who were killed in the battle of Mutina in 43 B. C., were awarded a state funeral in the Campus Martius by the Senate. The tomb of Hirtius was discovered in July 1938, during building operations under the Palazzo della Cancelleria. The perimeter wall, in brick-faced concrete, was cut through by the foundation wall of the Palazzo della Cancelleria, so that only the east wall and parts of the north and south walls are preserved. The tombstones set into the corners of the brick walls, with the name of A. Hirtius A F, establish the identity of the tomb.

P-A, p. 480; A. M. COLINI, BCom LXVI, 1938, p. 269 f.; F. MAGI, ib. LXVII, 1939, p. 205; H. FUHRMANN, AA, 1940, pp. 461–463; G. LUGLI, Mon IV, 3, p. 19 f.; B. NOGARA, Monumenti romani scoperti negli anni 1938/39 nell'area del Palazzo della Cancelleria (Quaderni di Studi Romani IX, 1941) pp. 12–15; A. DEGRASSI, RendPontAcc 3, XIX, 1942/43, pp. 389–396; F. MAGI, I rilievi flavi del Palazzo della Cancelleria, 1945, pp. 37–50; M. E. BLAKE I, p. 155; II, p. 161; G. LUGLI, Tecnica I, p. 533 f.; II, Tav. CLXVI, 3; L. CREMA, ArchRom, p. 261.

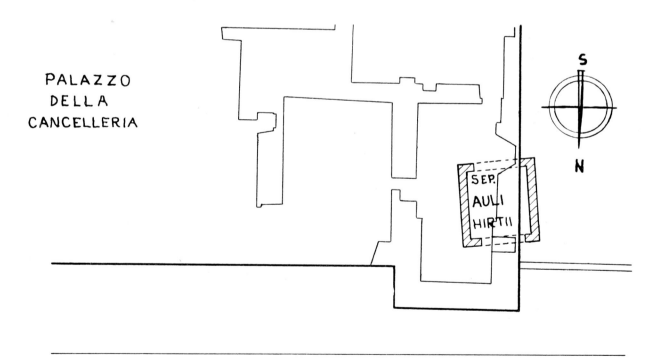

1112 Site-plan of the Hirtius tomb under the Palazzo della Cancelleria (after Nogara).

1113 Tombstone with the name of Hirtius in the north-east
corner of the perimeter wall.          Arch Vat XVIII–17–22

1114 The preserved east wall of the precinct surrounding the tomb.                    Arch Vat XVIII–17–18

1115 Two cippi of the Hirtius tomb, now in the Galleria Lapidaria of the Vatican Museum.          Arch Vat XI–31–18

1116 The east wall of the tomb as seen from the south.                                Arch Vat XVIII–17–23

SEPULCRUM LUCILII PAETI. The tomb of M. Lucilius Paetus, who held the office of tribunus militum, praefectus fabrum, and praefectus equitum, was discovered in 1885. It lies about 300 m. outside the Porta Salaria, in the grounds of No 125, Via Salaria. He built it during his lifetime, for himself and his sister Lucilia Polla (CIL VI, 32932). This circular tomb, built in the style of an Etruscan tumulus, measures 34.90 m. in diameter, and the original height of the mound was about 16 m. At the back, a corridor led to the burial chamber, which measured 1.70 × 1.55 m., and was roofed by a low crossvault. This tomb dates from the end of the 1st century B. C., and at the time of Trajan it was already covered over with earth. In the 4th century A. D., it was reopened and the walls of the corridor were hollowed out for burial places (loculi). In addition, a catacomb was excavated in the tufa below the burial chamber, starting from the original entrance of the tomb.

R. LANCIANI, NSc, 1885, p. 190; E. LE BLANT, CRAI, 1885, p. 175 f.; 1886, p. 374 f.; G. GATTI, BCom XIV, 1886, pp. 200 f., 226–231; R. LANCIANI, Pagan and Christian Rome, 1893, pp. 283–286; J. H. MIDDLETON II, p. 282 f.; H. JORDAN, Top I, 3, p. 437 f.; Capitolium I, 1925/26, p. 31; P-A, p. 480 f.; O. MARUCCHI, Le catacombe romane, 1933, p. 426; G. LUGLI, Mon III, p. 341 f.; C. PIETRANGELI, L'Urbe V, 1940, 11, pp. 20–28; M. E. BLAKE I, pp. 170, 339 f.; L. CREMA, ArchRom, pp. 139, 242.

1117 The funerary inscription of the Lucilii Paeti.

Rip X C/3228

1118  The circular tomb on the Via Salaria.                    Rip X  C/3227

1119  The burial chamber.                                      Rip X  C/3895

SEPULCRUM POMPONII HYLAE. The columbarium of Pomponius Hylas lies immediately inside the Porta Latina of the Aurelian Wall (R. Lanciani, FUR, 46); it was discovered and excavated in 1831 by Pietro Campana. The name of its founder and his wife Pomponia Vitalinis are recorded in an inscription in coloured mosaic (CIL VI, 5552) at the entrance to the tomb, over the stairway of 28 steps which lead down to the burial chamber. The other funerary inscriptions belonging to the columbarium (CIL VI, 5539–5557), which can be dated up to the second half of the 2nd century A. D., show no family connection with Pomponius Hylas.

A. NIBBY, RomAnt II, p. 556 f.; P. CAMPANA, Diss PontAcc XI, 1852, pp. 259–313; TH. ASHBY – F. G. NEWTON, BSR V, 1910, pp. 463–471, pls. XXXVII–XLVII; E. B. VAN DEMAN, AJA XVI, 1912, p. 398; G. LUGLI, Architettura ed Arti Decorative I, 1921/22, p. 225, figg. 2–4; G. T. RIVOIRA, RomArch, p. 4 f.; C. VALLE, Capitolium II, 1926/27, p. 29 f.; P. MARCONI, La pittura dei romani, 1929, p. 100; P-A, p. 482; G. LUGLI, Mon I, pp. 439–446; id., Tecnica I, p. 590; A. VON GERKAN, Göttingische gelehrte Anzeigen CCXII, 1958, p. 192; M. PALLOTTINO, BCom LXII, 1934, p. 51; M. BORDA, MemLinc 8, I, 1948, pp. 357–383; id., La Pittura Romana, 1958, pp. 225–228; F. L. BASTET, De Datum van het grote Hypogaeum bij de Porta Maggiore te Rome, 1958, p. 17 f.; H. STERN, Études d'archéologie classique (Université de Nancy) II, 1959, p. 112; M. E. BLAKE II, p. 61.

1120 The columbarium of Pomponius Hylas during the excavation in 1831 (DissPontAcc XI, 1852, p. 259).   Fot 5277

1121  The inscription of CN POMPONIUS HYLAS in the well of the stairway of the columbarium.     Fot 5007

1122  The apse of the burial chamber.

SEPULCRUM QUINCTIORUM ET ALIORUM. When the Via di S. Croce in Gerusalemme was widened in 1916/18, a row of tombs was uncovered at its intersection with Via Statilia. Of these, the ones at the north-east corner of the Villa Wolkonsky have been preserved. The tomb of P. Quinctius was nearest to Via di S. Croce in Gerusalemme; he built it for himself, his wife Quinctia, and the freedwoman Quinctia Agatea whom he took as his common-law wife after the death of the first. Next came a double tomb, the travertine façade of which is decorated with portraits of the deceased, freedmen of the families Clodia, Marcia, and Annia. Two other tombs stood at the west end of the row, of which the furthest to the west was built for one A. Caesonius. The tombs date from the end of the Republic; they flanked an ancient road which left the city by the Porta Caelimontana (s. Arcus Dolabellae et Silani I, p. 113), and reached the Porta Maggiore by way of Via di S. Stefano Rotondo, Piazza S. Giovanni in Laterano, Via Domenico Fontana, Villa Wolkonsky, and Via Statilia.

F. FORNARI, NSc, 1917, pp. 174–179, 274; L. CANTA-RELLI, BCom XLV, 1917, pp. 237–242; E. GATTI, NSc, 1919, p. 38; G. LUGLI, Mon III, p. 433; A. M. COLINI, Capitolium XVIII, 1943, pp. 268–279; id., Celio, pp. 393–396; L. CREMA, ArchRom, p. 126.

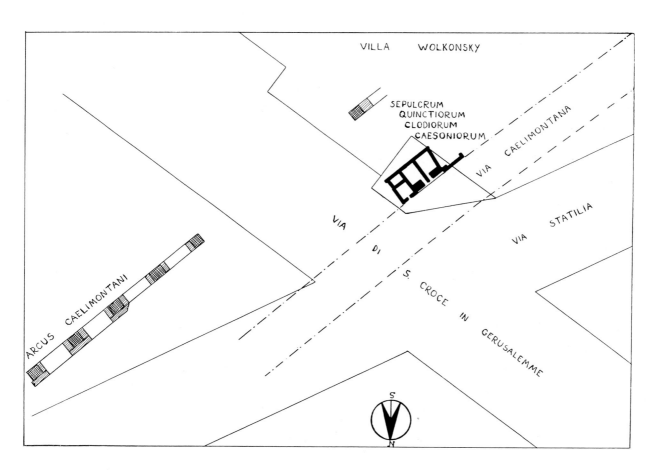

1123 Site-plan of the tombs on the Via di S. Croce in Gerusalemme (after Colini).

1124 Portraits of the
      freedmen of the fa-
      milies Clodia, Mar-
      cia, and Annia, on
      the east façade of
      the double-tomb.
        Inst Neg 30.582

1125 The interior of the double tomb.                                      Fot 3268

1126  The façades of the double tomb and of the tomb of P. Quinctius.                        Fot 3267

SEPULCRUM SCIPIONUM. The tomb of the Cornelii Scipiones lay on the Via Appia, about 380 m. inside the Porta Appia of the Aurelian Wall. It was first discovered in 1614, when the funerary inscription of Lucius Scipio, son of L. Cornelius Scipio Barbatus (CIL VI, 1287) came to light. The site of the tomb was forgotten, then in May 1780 it was rediscovered, and in the course of three years work it was excavated. The funerary inscriptions of the members of the family of the Cornelii Scipiones are preserved (CIL VI, 1284–1294); they were buried in sarcophagi, of which only that of Scipio Barbatus, consul in 298 B. C., is decorated. It was discovered in 1782 and taken to the Vatican. The tomb, which had been defaced by unsystematic excavations, was restored as far as possible to its original condition, in 1926.

G. B. PIRANESI – E. Q. VISCONTI, Monumenti degli Scipioni, 1785; A. NIBBY, RomAnt II, pp. 561-575; E. WÖLFFLIN, Sitzungsberichte der Bayrischen Akademie, 1892, pp. 188–219; R. LANCIANI, Ruins, pp. 321–326 (Bibl: p. 326 f.); H. JORDAN, Top I, 3, p. 210 f.; G. TOMASSETTI, La Campagna Romana II, 1910, p. 30 f.; CIL I², 1918, pp. 373–382; P. NICORESCU, Ephemeris Dacoromana I, 1923, pp. 1–56; C. VALLE, Capitolium II, 1926/27, pp. 24–29; A. M. COLINI, ib. III, 1927/28, pp. 27–32; id., ib. V, 1929, pp. 182–195; E. STRONG, Art in ancient Rome, 1928, p. 45 f.; P-A, pp. 484–486; W. AMELUNG, VatCat II, pp. 4–9 (Bibl: pp. 7, 9); G. LUGLI, Mon I, pp. 432–438; G. DE ANGELIS D'OSSAT, BCom LXIV, 1936, pp. 37–53; C. PIETRANGELI, Scavi, p. 16 f.; U. SCAMUZZI, Rivista di studi classici V, 1957, pp. 248–268.

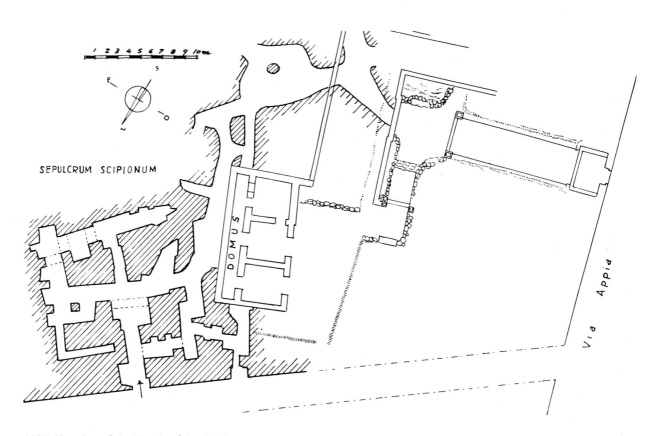

1127 Site-plan of the Tomb of the Scipiones.

1128 The east gallery of the tomb, with the substructures of the 3rd century house which was built over it. Rip X A/90

1129  The gallery at the back of the tomb, with the sarcophagus of L. Cornelius Scipio Barbatus (cast).    Rip X  A/76

1130 The funerary inscription of Lucius Scipio, which was found in 1614 and taken to the Barberini Palace. Since 1912 it has been in the Vatican Museum.                                                    Fot 5261

1131 The sarcophagus of L. Cornelius Scipio Barbatus (CIL VI, 1284, 1285).                    Arch Vat XVIII–19–12

1132  The north-east gallery, with an arched opening to the street.                                  Rip X  C/222

SEPULCRUM SEMPRONIORUM. In 1863, a tomb dating from the late republican era was excavated on the slope of the Quirinal, in Via Dataria. The inscription over the arch of the entrance, which gives the name of one CN. SEMPRONIUS, his sister SEMPRONIA and their mother LARCIA, had been known since the 17th century (CIL VI, 26152). The travertine façade faced south-west, standing beside a street which led from the Campus Martius to the gate in the Servian Wall, at the north-west side of the Quirinal Hill.

G. HENZEN, BullInst, 1864, p. 6; R. BERGAU, Archäologische Zeitung XXV, 1867, pp. 20–22, Taf. CCXIX; R. LANCIANI, BCom IV, 1876, p. 126 f., Tav. XII; id., FUR, 16; J. H. MIDDLETON II, p. 284; H. JOR-DAN, Top I, 3, p. 403; P-A, p. 486; G. LUGLI, Mon III, p. 318; M. SANTANGELO, Quirinale, p. 113 f.; M. E. BLAKE I, p. 148; L. CREMA, ArchRom, p. 126.

1133 The Tomb of the Sempronii in the Palazzo S. Felice, 21 Via della Dataria.

Fot 3239

1134 Part of the travertine façade with the funerary inscription (CIL VI, 26152).                    Fot 3238

SEPULCRUM STATILIORUM ET ALIORUM. In 1875, the Compagnia Fondiaria Italiana conducted a systematic excavation in the cemetery which stretched from the Nymphaeum in the Licinian Gardens to the Porta Maggiore; it led to the discovery of the Columbarium of the family of Statilius Taurus which contained more than 700 loculi (CIL VI, 6213–6640). Not far off, a small tomb 2.90 × 1.95 m. and 4.20 m. in height, was excavated, the fresco decoration of which is of especial artistic and historic interest. A frieze of the time of Augustus with illustrations of the Aeneid and the early history of Rome, occupied the middle zone of the walls; the upper half and the vaulted ceiling was decorated with paintings of the early 3rd century. The frieze was removed, and is now in the Museo Nazionale Romano. The remaining ceiling and wall frescoes were reburied or destroyed, after they had been photographed in 1875 (Parker Catalogue, 3312–3316).*

E. BRIZIO, Pitture e sepolcri scoperti sull'Esquilino, 1876; R. LANCIANI, NSc, 1877, pp. 314–327; id., BCom VIII, 1880, pp. 51–75; F. GORI, ArchStor I, 1875, pp. 55–59, 122 f.; C. ROBERT, AnnInst, 1878, pp. 234–274; J. H. PARKER, The Archaeology of Rome IX, 1877, pls. XVII–XX; id., A catalogue of 3391 historical photographs of antiquities in Rome and Italy, 1879, 3301–3318; W. H. ROSCHER II, 2, pp. 2946–2948 (Mezentius); H. JORDAN, Top I, 3, p. 363; W. HELBIG, Führer II, pp. 190–196; K. LEH-MANN-HARTLEBEN, Die Trajanssäule, 1925, pp. 40, 44, 91; E. STRONG, Art in ancient Rome I, 1928, p. 109; P. MARCONI, La pittura dei Romani, 1929, p. 48 f.; M. SWINDLER, Ancient Painting, 1929, pp. 364–366; P-A, p. 486; R. PARIBENI, MusNaz, p. 257 f.; G. LUGLI, Mon III, pp. 427–431; M. BORDA, La pittura romana, 1958, pp. 172–175; id., CAPITOLIUM XXXIV, 1959, 5, pp. 3–10 (Bibl: p. 10); V. LEON, Römische Historische Mitteilungen III, 1958/1960, pp. 279–287.

* Of the flashlight photographs taken in 1875 Gori writes: "Per timore che tali pitture non deperissero sotto l'azione dell'aria, della luce e del salnitro, abbiamo indotto il sig. I. H. Parker vice-presidente della Società Archeologica Britannica ed Americana a farle ritrarre in fotografia colla luce del magnesio dal suo valente fotografo sig. G. B. Colamedici, l'unico che sia riuscito a fotografare gli affreschi delle Catacombe di Roma e di Napoli. Il lavoro è riuscito perfetto, non ostante l'angustia del luogo ed il colorito che ogni giorno si rende più smorto; ciascuno dunque può ora acquistare dal sullodato sig. Parker l'esatta riproduzione di queste pitture in via della Panetteria n. 15 (ArchStor I, 1875, p. 122 f.).

1135 Inscription of the "FAMILIA T. STATILI TAURI" which stood over the entrance to the Columbarium (CIL VI, 6213).

Fot 5903

1136 Site-plan of the Columbaria
     Statiliorum, Arruntiorum and
     the tomb with the fresco de-
     coration.

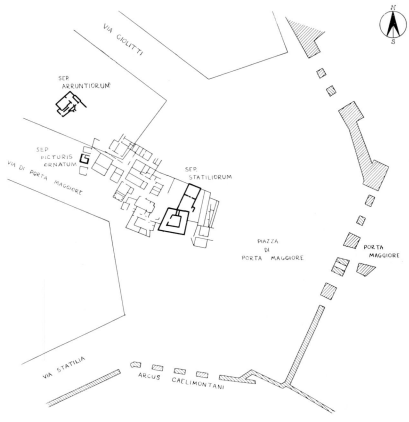

1137 The Columbarium with the fresco decorations during the excavation in 1875.                    Parker 3301

1138 The excavated Columbarium before it was filled up again. Fot 3572

1139 The building of Lavinium from the frieze of the south wall, photographed in the Columbarium in 1875. Parker 3304

1140  Left side of the south wall frieze.                                    Fot 6643

1141  Left side of the east wall frieze.                                     Fot 5282

1142  Left side of the north wall frieze.                                    Fot 6644

1143  Right side of the south wall frieze.                    Fot 6643

1144  Right side of the east wall frieze.                     Fot 5282

1145  Right side of the north wall frieze.                    Fot 6644

1146  The preserved remains of the west wall frieze.                              Fot 6645

1147  Scene of the Battle of Numicus, from the frieze of the south wall.         Parker 3309

1148  Romulus as a shepherd, from the north wall frieze.                    Parker 3318

1149 Painting of the vaulted ceiling, photographed after the excavation. Fortuna with a cornucopia in the centre, in
     the lower field Apollo with a female figure.                                              Parker 3316

1150 A section of the ceiling painting, Hercules with a female figure. Parker 3315

1151 Section of the ceiling painting, Hippolytos and Phaidra (AnnInst, 1878, p. 237).                    Parker 3314

1152 Wall painting with a picture of a funeral banquet.          Parker 3312

SEPULCRUM SER. SULPICII GALBAE. The tomb of Sergius Sulpicius Galba, consul in 108 B. C., was discovered in 1885 on Via Giovanni Branca. It lay between the Porticus Aemilia and the Horrea Galbae (q. v. I, 589, 590), where it is shown on a fragment of the Severan marble plan (FUR, tav. XXIV). The remains of the tomb, of Monte-Verde tufa, with an inscription on a travertine tablet (CIL VI, 31617) have been reassembled in the Antiquarium of the City of Rome, on the Caelian.

R. LANCIANI, NSc, 1885, p. 527; id., BCom XIII, 1885, p. 165 f.; id., FUR, 40; G. GATTI, RM I, 1886, pp. 62, 71; H. JORDAN, Top I, 3, p. 175; T. FRANK, Buildings, p. 143; P-A, pp. 261, 480; Ant, p. 24; G. LUGLI, Mon III, p. 605; M. E. BLAKE I, pp, 31, 135; L. CREMA, ArchRom, p. 126; FUR, p. 81, Tav. XXIV.

1153 Tomb of Sergius Sulpicius Galba.

SEPULCRUM Q. SULPICII MAXIMI. The tomb of Q. Sulpicius Maximus, an eleven year old boy, was discovered under the east tower of the Porta Salaria, when it was pulled down in 1871 (s. Porta Salaria II, 977). The tomb-stone has a statue of Q. Sulpicius in a niche; he is wearing a toga, and on either side is the Greek poem (CIL VI, 33976), with which the boy won distinction at the third Capitoline contest, under Domitian, in 94 A. D. (s. Suetonius, Domitian, IV, 4). The stone is now in the Museo Nuovo Capitolino. The remains of the tomb were left where they had been found, in front of Vespignani's new Porta Salaria (q. v. II, 976), until 1921, when the gate was removed to ease the flow of traffic. The tomb was then re-erected to the east of the new opening in the wall.

G. HENZEN, BullInst, 1871, pp. 98–114; C. L. VI-SCONTI, Il sepolcro del fanciullo Quinto Sulpicio Maximo, 1871; R. LANCIANI, Pagan and Christian Rome, 1893, pp. 280–282; H. St. JONES, Cons, p. 149 f. (Bibl: p. 150); G. LUGLI, Architettura ed Arti Decorative V, 1925/26, p. 404 f.; P-A, p. 486 f.; G. LUGLI, Mon II, p. 173; III, p. 340 f.; D. MUSTILLI, p. 97 (Bibl: p. 97); F. POULSEN, Römische Kultur-bilder, 1949, p. 235 f.; H. KÄHLER, Rom und seine Welt II, 1960, p. 242 f.

1154 The tomb of Q. Sulpicius Maximus, in front of the Porta Salaria, where it was found in 1871.     GFN C/9011

1155  The tombstone of Q. Sulpicius Maximus in the Museo Nuovo Capitolino.

1156  The tomb in the position which it has occupied since 1921.                    Fot 1139

SEPULCRUM C. SULPICII PLATORINI. When the Tiber embankment was being built in 1880, the family tomb of the Sulpicii Platorini was discovered on the right bank, between the Pons Agrippae and the Aurelian Wall (s. plan, Pons Agrippae II, 915). The marble tablet over the entrance gives the owner's name as C. Sulpicius Platorinus (CIL VI, 31761), who was triumvir monetalis in 18 B. C. The other inscriptions found in the tomb (CIL VI, 31762–31768a) date from the time of Augustus to the Flavians. When the Aurelian Wall was built, the upper part of the tomb had been covered over, and the urns and statues which it contained were thus preserved. They could not be left in situ, because of the depth at which they were situated in the Tiber bank. Accordingly, they were removed to the Baths of Diocletian, together with the architectural remains, and the tomb was reassembled, and its façade restored, on the occasion of the Archaeological Exhibition in 1911.

F. GORI, ArchStor IV, 1880, p. 171 f.; R. LANCIANI, NSc, 1880, pp. 129–138, Tavv. IV, V; 1883, p. 372; C. L. VISCONTI, BCom VIII, 1880, pp. 136–138; F. BARNABEI, NSc, 1896, pp. 467–469; W. ALTMANN, Die römischen Grabaltäre der Kaiserzeit, 1905, pp. 44–48; H. JORDAN, Top I, 3, p. 650 f.; R. PARIBENI – A.

BERETTI, BArte V, 1911, pp. 365–372; Catalogo della mostra archeologica nelle Terme di Diocleziano, 1911, pp. 171–173; P-A, p. 487; R. PARIBENI, MusNaz, p. 59; G. LUGLI, Mon III, pp. 654–657; id., Tecnica I, pp. 533, 588; M. E. BLAKE I, pp. 182, 294, 339.

1157  The restored tomb of C. Sulpicius Platorinus in the Museo Nazionale Romano.                    Fot 1138

1158 The tomb after its discovery below the Aurelian Wall; watercolour by the painter E. Roesler Franz in the Museo
di Roma.                                                                                        Fot 5270

SERAPIS, TEMPLUM. The ruins of a building on the west slope of the Quirinal have been identified as the Temple of Serapis (CIL VI, 570), which was built by Caracalla in the VI Region (CodTop I, p. 107). Part of the ruins lies in the gardens of the Palazzo Colonna, and part in the Università Gregoriana Pontificia. Until early in the 17th century, part of the rear wall of the temple cella was still standing, and it is known to us from numerous 16th century drawings as "Torre Mesa", "Torre di Mecenate", or "Frontispizio di Nerone" (s. Egger, Römische Veduten II, 86–88). A corner-piece of the marble pediment of the rear wall, and a fragment of the marble frieze, have lain in the gardens of the Palazzo Colonna since about 1630 when the wall was destroyed. A monumental double-stairway led down from the temple on the Quirinal to the Campus Martius; part of its enclosure walls and sections of four partition walls are still preserved.

A. PALLADIO, I quattro libri dell'architettura, 1570, I, pp. 64, 66; IV, pp. 41–47; A. NIBBY, RomAnt II, p. 715 f.; R. LANCIANI, NSc, 1878, pp. 92, 369; L. URLICHS, RM III, 1888, p. 98; CH. HÜLSEN, RhM XLIX, 1894, pp. 392–396; id., BCom XXIII, 1895, pp. 39–59; R. LANCIANI, BCom XXII, 1894, pp. 297–307; XXIII, 1895, pp. 94–101; id., Ruins, pp. 428–432 (Bibl: p. 432); id., Storia II, pp. 154 f., 249 f.; III, pp. 203–205; IV, pp. 97 f., 155 f.; H. JORDAN, Top I, 3, pp. 421–423; M. MARCHETTI, BCom XLII, 1914, p. 374; G. CULTRERA, MemLinc 5, XVIII, 1923, p. 528 f.; Röm Gebälke I, pp. 73–84; TH. ASHBY, The years work in class. studies XX, 1926/27, p. 103; P-A, pp. 487, 491 f; H. KÄHLER, RM LII, 1937, p. 94 f.; G. LUGLI, Mon III, pp. 279, 304–307; M. SANTANGELO, Quirinale, pp. 154–177; L. CREMA, ArchRom, p. 521.

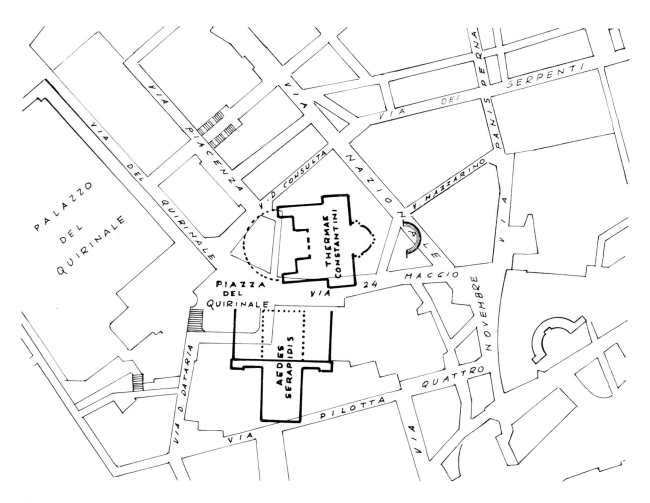

1159 Site-plan of the Temple of Serapis and the Baths of Constantine.

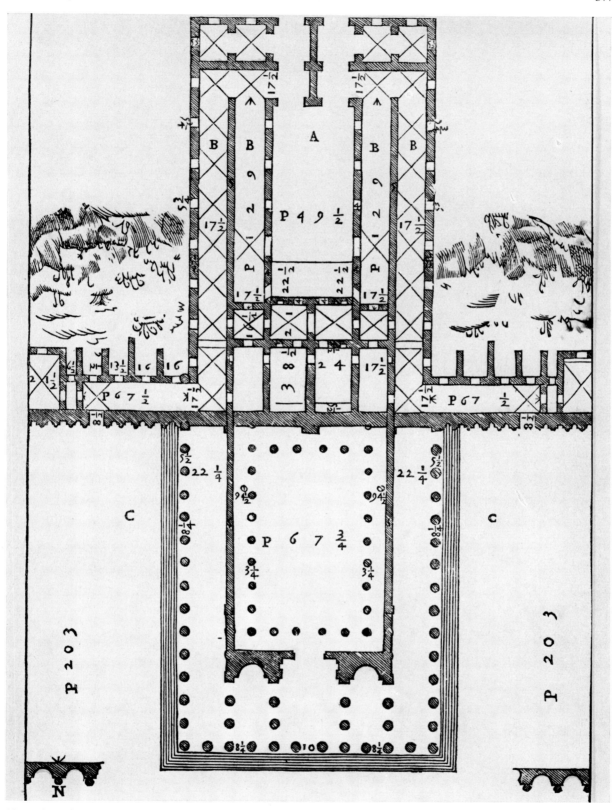

1160 Plan of the temple and the stairway leading down to the Campus Martius (Palladio, I Quattro Libri, IV, p. 42).
Fot 3050

1161 Walls of the well of the stairway: northern outer wall and partition wall.                                    Fot 973

1162 Northern outer wall of the well of the stairway.                                Fot 974

1163 Substructure of the stairways in the Università Gregoriana.                              Fot 975

1164 Southern outer wall of the well of the stairway, and terraces in the gardens of the Palazzo Colonna.      Fot 978

1165 Rear wall of the temple and outer wall of the well of the stairway (Heemskerck II, fol. 81 v. and 82 r.).      Fot 4767

1166 Garden of the Palazzo Colonna, with part of the southern outer wall of the well of the stairway (s. fig. 1164); drawing by Pannini at the beginning of the 18th century.      Fot 3051

1167 The entablature of the pediment, and part of the frieze in the garden of Palazzo Colonna.　　　Fot 6638

1168 "Torre Mesa", the remains of the rear wall of the temple and wall of the well of the stairway (S. Du Pérac, I vestigi dell'Antichità di Roma, 1575, fol. 3).　　　Fot 3049

SESSORIUM. The residence of the empress Helena, which was known as the Sessorium, or the PALATIUM SESSO-
RIANUM (CIL VI, 1134) was situated in the HORTI SPEI VETERIS. In the preceding century, Heliogabalus (218–
222 A. D.) had a villa there, which in size and character was comparable with Nero's Domus Aurea, or Hadrian's
Villa at Tivoli. The Amphitheatrum Castrense (q. v. I, 1–4), the Circus Varianus (q. v. I, 280–282) and the
Thermae Helenae (q. v. II, 1257–1262) all formed part of it. An atrium of the palace, measuring 39.25 m. ×
24.80 m. and 22 m. in height, with five arched entrances on the side and rectangular windows above, was
converted by Constantine into the church of S. Croce in Gerusalemme. A covered corridor, more than 300 m.
long, led down the south side of the building, from the Amphitheatrum Castrense to the Circus Varianus (s.
plan, Circus Varianus I, 280). The grounds of the villa were cut in half when the Aurelian Wall was built (270–272
A. D.), and the part outside the wall was apparently abandoned. The rear wall and apse of a building which
stands north of the church, is referred to in Renaissance drawings as the "Tempio di Venere e Cupido", for
no apparent reason. This hall does not belong to the original complex of the Sessorium, but dates from the beginning of the 4th century. The excavations, which started in 1958 and are not yet completed, have discovered
further rooms of the palace with fresco decorations, to the east of the church.

s. a. Thermae Helenae II, 1258, 1259

NARDINI–NIBBY II, pp. 12–14; A. NIBBY, RomAnt II,
pp. 370–372; R. LANCIANI, MALinc I, 1889, pp. 490–
492; id., Ruins, pp. 397–400 (Bibl: p. 400); id., Storia
III, p. 163 f.; CH. HÜLSEN, RM VII, 1892. p. 300;
P. CROSTAROSA, NBACrist VII, 1901, pp. 119–144;
H. JORDAN, Top I, 3, p. 249 f.; M. MARCHETTI,
BCom XLII, 1914, p. 356 f.; R. LANCIANI, Wander-
ings through ancient Roman churches, 1924, pp. 215–
220, 225 f., 252 f.; E. GATTI, BCom LIII, 1925, p. 278;
G. T. RIVOIRA, RomArch, p. 147 f., figs. 177–179;
CH. HÜLSEN, Chiese, p. 243; P-A, p. 487 f.; G. LUGLI,
Horti Variani, DizEpigr III, 1922, p. 1004 f.; id.,
Mon III, pp. 486–490; R. KRAUTHEIMER, Corp, pp.
171–177; A. M. COLINI, MemPontAcc 3, VIII, 1955,
pp. 137–140, 154–168, 170–177.

Ecclesia Sanctæ Crucis in Hierusalem          S. CROCE IN GIERVSALEM .          L'Eglise de saincte Croix de Hierusalem
vna ex ijs quæ Romæ visitantur .                                                Vne des stations de Rome .

*Israel excudit .*

1169 The buildings of the Sessorium in 1642, an engraving by Israel Silvestre.                    Fot 2970

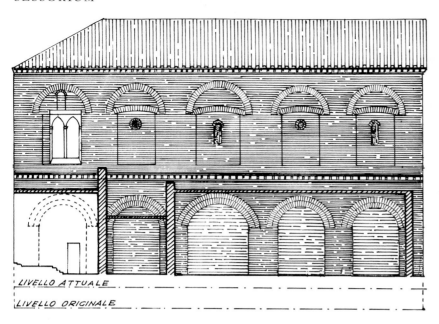

1170 Elevation of the ancient atrium, before it was converted into the church of S. Croce in Gerusalemme (after Krautheimer).

LIVELLO ATTUALE

LIVELLO ORIGINALE

1171 The ancient north wall of S. Croce in Gerusalemme.                                Fot 2968

1172  The ancient hall of the Sessorium behind the façade of S. Croce in Gerusalemme.                    Fot 672

1173  The 4th century apse in the Sessorium complex, known as "Tempio di Venere e Cupido".                Anderson 2354

SPES, TEMPLUM, s. Forum Holitorium.

SOL INVICTUS ELAGABALUS, s. Iuppiter Ultor.

STADIUM DOMITIANI. The Piazza Navona now occupies the site of the stadium, which was built by Domitian in 92/96 A. D., and restored in 228 A. D. by Alexander Severus. It was used for athletics, and gladiator contests were also held there, when the Colosseum was out of use after a fire at the time of Macrinus in 217 A. D. The stadium differed from the circus in having neither spina nor carceres. In mediaeval times, it was known as the "Circus Flaminius" (CodTop II, pp. 176, 180, 195), "Theatrum Alexandri" (CodTop III, p. 23), and "Circus Alexandri" (CodTop III, p. 219) and, until the 19th century, antiquarians and topographers unanimously identified it as the Circus of Alexander Severus. It was first recognized as the Stadium of Domitian by Urlichs in 1842. Its form and dimensions were established by excavations in 1868 (north side), 1869 (south perimeter), 1933/34 (east side, in the Corsia Agonale), and 1936/37 (the north curve). The remains of the north curve with the entrance gate, which were discovered in 1936, can be seen below the newly built houses to the west of Via Agonale.

F. CANCELLIERI, Mercato, pp. 23–31; A. NIBBY, RomAnt I, pp. 599–603; PLATNER-BUNSEN, Beschreibung III, 3, pp. 70–74; R. LANCIANI, BullInst, 1869, p. 228 f.; E. SARTI, ArchStorPat IX, 1886, p. 478; R. LANCIANI, Ruins, pp. 496–498 (Bibl: p. 498); id., Storia II, pp. 228–231; III, p. 224 f.; H. JORDAN, Top I, 3, pp. 592–594; L. DE GREGORI, Roma IV, 1926, pp. 14–25; P-A, p. 495 f.; G. GATTI, NSc, 1934, p. 151 f.; id., BCom LXII, 1934, pp. 172–174; A. M. COLINI, BCom LXVI, 1938, p. 266 f.; id., Bull. Mus. Imp. Rom X, 1939 (BCom LXVII) p. 182 f.; id., Palladio III, 1939, p. 186 f.; id., Capitolium XVI, 1941, pp. 209–223; id., Stadium Domitiani, 1943 (Bibl: p. 15 f.); G. LUGLI, Mon III, pp. 218–223; F. CASTAGNOLI, Roma XXI, 1943, p. 166 f.; P. ROMANO – P. PARTINI, Piazza Navona, s. d. (1953), pp. 7–38; L. CREMA, ArchRom, p. 302 f.; M. E. BLAKE II, p. 107 f.

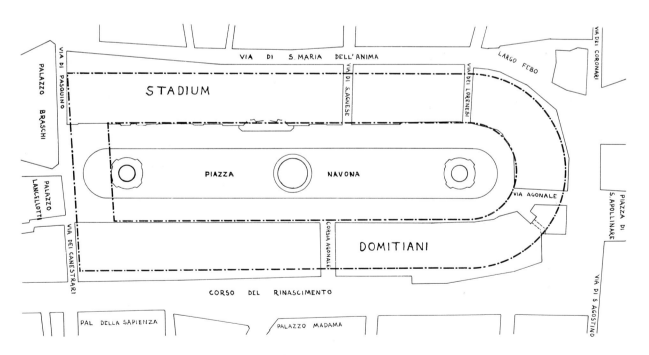

1174 The Stadium of Domitian and the Piazza Navona (Colini).

1175  Aureus of Septimius Severus with the Stadium
      Domitiani (Mattingly-Sydenham, Roman Imp.
      Coinage IV, 1936, p. 124, No. 260).

                                          MCR  A/789

1176  Air photograph of the Piazza Navona.                          Fot 3031

1177 Excavation of the north side of the stadium in 1936.     Rip X C/3517

1178 The north curve of the stadium, with the main entrance.     Rip X C/3530

1179  Travertine pier of the east side, discovered in 1933, in the Corsia Agonale.                    Fot 778

STATIO ANNONAE. The headquarters of the Praefectus Annonae, who was responsible for supplying the population of Rome with food, was situated in the Forum Boarium, near the Temple of Ceres (q. v. I, 261). In the 4th century A. D., a portico was built for the Statio Annonae, separated from the temple by a brick wall; its remains can be seen in the church of S. Maria in Cosmedin. Apparently it was part of this pagan building, and not the nearby Temple of Ceres, which was used as the foundation of the Diaconia in the 6th century. The identification of the building depends on inscriptions, which were found nearby and give the names of praefecti annonae (CIL VI, 1151, 31856).

G. B. DE ROSSI, AnnInst, 1885, pp. 223–231; L. DU-
CHESNE, Mél VII, 1887, p. 242 f.; G. B. DE ROSSI –
G. GATTI, BCom XVII, 1889, pp. 358–360; E. STE-
VENSON, RömQuart VII, 1893, pp. 11–31; CH. HÜL-
SEN, DissPontAcc 2, VI, 1896, pp. 231–236; R. LAN-
CIANI, Ruins, pp. 519–522 (Bibl: p. 522); id., Storia
III, p. 43; H. JORDAN, Top I, 3, p. 146 f.; TH. ASHBY,
JRS IX, 1919, p. 183; M. DE DOMINICIS, BCom LII,
1924, pp. 135–149; CH. HÜLSEN, Chiese, p. 327 f.;
G. B. GIOVENALE, La basilica di S. Maria in Cosme-
din, 1927, pp. 334–350; P-A, p. 496 f.; D. VAN BER-
CHEM, BCom LXIII, 1935, pp. 91–95; J. LESTORQUOY,
RACrist VII, 1930, pp. 274, 294 f., 298; G. LUGLI,
Centro, pp. 585–587 (Bibl: p. 587).

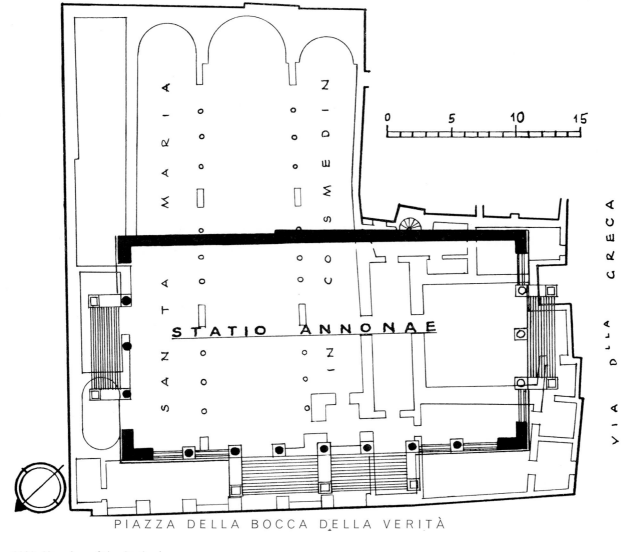

1180 Site-plan of the Statio Annonae.

1181 Columns and arches of the Statio Annonae in the front wall of S. Maria in Cosmedin.                    Fot 2972

1182 A composite capital from the front of the Statio
Annonae.                              GFN C/292

1183 North-east aisle of the church, with the columns of the front and the east side of the Statio Annonae.     Fot 2971

1184 Plaster ornament of the arches over the columns at the front.                      GFN E/133

STATIO AQUARUM. At the south and east sides of the Lacus Iuturnae (q. v.) are rooms which were possibly used for the care of the sick, who sought relief from their sufferings through the health giving waters of the spring of Iuturna. Statues of healing deities, such as the Dioscuri, Apollo, Serapis and Aesculapius, were found in the rooms and in the lacus itself, and give rise to the belief that the rooms were used for healing sleep, the "incubatio". In the 4th century A. D., these rooms became the headquarters of the curatores aquarum, who administered Rome's water supply. On the occasion of the dedication of the Statio Aquarum on 1st March 328 A. D., the curator aquarum, Fl. Maesius Egnatius Lollianus, erected a statue to the emperor Constantine.

G. BONI, NSc, 1900, p. 293; 1901, pp. 129–131; D. VAGLIERI, BCom XXVIII, 1900, pp. 71–73; XXXI, 1903, p. 174; CH. HÜLSEN, RM XVII, 1902, p. 72 f.; id., Klio II, 1902, pp. 235, 244, 271 f.; id., FR, p. 149; L. DEUBNER, Neue Jahrbücher f. d. klass. Altertum IX, 1902, pp. 384–388; H. THÉDENAT, FR, p. 311 f.; E. DE RUGGIERO, p. 242; P-A, p. 313; G. LUGLI, Centro, p. 194 f.

1185 The rooms round the Lacus Iuturnae, behind the Lacus the hall with the statue of Aesculapius.                    Fot 87

1186 An inscription dedicated to the Genius Stationis Aquarum, found in situ (CIL VI, 36781).
Fot 93

1187 The rooms of the Statio Aquarum below the ramp leading to the Nova Via.                    Fot 4680

1188 The base for a statue of Constantine, erected on the occasion of the dedication of the Statio Aquarum by Fl. Maesius
Egnatius Lollianus (CIL VI, 36951). Fot 4678

STATIONES MUNICIPORUM. In the Forum Romanum, near the Volcanal (Pliny, Nat. Hist. XVI, 236), and flanking the Sacra Via between the Regia and the Arch of Titus, were certain small offices, similar to tabernae. They were maintained by representatives of cities of the Roman Empire, and were administered by a "stationarius" (CIL VI, 250). Among the cities mentioned in the inscriptions are: Noricum, Tivoli, Vienne, Caesarea, Tiberias (Claudiopolis) and Tarsus (Athenaeum 1958, pp. 106–116). A fragment of the architrave of the statio of Tarsus (Inscriptiones Graecae XIV, 1006 a) has been set up beside the Sacra Via, near its place of origin opposite the Templum Divi Romuli.

NARDINI–NIBBY II, p. 226 f.; PLATNER–BUNSEN, Beschreibung III, 1, p. 68; R. LANCIANI, BCom VI, 1878, p. 257; VIII, 1880, p. 80 f.; id., NSc, 1879, p. 113; G. GATTI, NSc, 1899, pp. 289, 386, 435; id., BCom XXVII, 1899, pp. 237–239, 242 f.; L. CANTARELLI, BCom XXVIII, 1900, pp. 124–134; CH. HÜL-SEN, RM XVII, 1902, p. 11; XX, 1905, p. 9 f.; id., Klio II, 1902, pp. 238, 280; W. KUBITSCHEK, ÖJh VI, 1903, Beiblatt, pp. 80–82; W. H. ROSCHER V, p. 936; H. THÉDENAT, FR, pp. 164, 269; P-A, p. 497; G. LUGLI, MonMin, pp. 111-120; L. MORETTI, Athenaeum, NS XXXVI, 1958, pp. 106–116.

1189 Fragment of the architrave of the statio municipii of Tarsus beside the Sacra Via.                              Fot 70

STATUA MARSYAE. In the centre of the Forum stood a fig-tree, an olive and a vine (s. Ficus Olea Vitis I, 485), and a statue of the satyr Marsyas, carrying a full wine-skin on his left shoulder. The statue with the fig-tree appears on the two Plutei Traiani reliefs (q. v. II, 902, 905), and on coins of L. Marcius Censorinus, which were struck between 86 and 81 B. C. (BMC, Rep I, p. 338, pl. XL, 3, 4). Copies of the statue of Marsyas, which stood near a praetor's tribunal in Rome, were set up as symbols of liberty in the fora of those provincial towns which possessed the ius Italicum.

H. JORDAN, Top I, 2, pp. 264–266, 322; id., Marsyas auf dem Forum in Rom, 1883; O. GILBERT, Rom III, p. 155 f.; G. LÖSCHKE, AA, 1891, p. 14 f.; B. HEISTERBERGK, Philologus L, 1891, pp. 639–647; CH. HÜLSEN, RM VII, 1892, p. 287 f.; id., Die neuesten Ausgrabungen auf dem Forum Romanum, 1910, p. 19; A. REINACH, Klio XIV, 1914, pp. 321–337; H. THÉDENAT, FR, p. 134 f.; W. SESTON, Mél XLIV, 1927, pp. 175–183; P-A, p. 499; C. GIOFFREDI, Studia et documenta historiae et iuris IX, 2, 1943, pp. 256–262, 275–282; A. PIGANIOL, RA 6, XXII, 1944, pp. 118–126; J. PAOLI, Revue des études latines XXIII, 1945, pp. 150–167; G. LUGLI, Centro, p. 89 f. (Bibl: p. 90).

1190  The statue of Marsyas, beneath the fig-tree, on the left Pluteus Traiani.                                      Fot 6458

1191  The unpaved square in the centre of the Forum, where the statue of Marsyas stood.                    Fot 123

STATUA STILICHONIS. Three monuments were erected in the Forum to Flavius Stilicho, who was Honorius' commander-in-chief. Their dedicatory inscriptions are preserved (CIL VI, 1730, 1731, 31987), although only one, which was found in 1880, is still in situ. This upright block of marble, (which in its original horizontal position supported an equestrian statue), is dedicated to the armies of the emperors Honorius, Arcadius and Theodosius, which in 403 A. D., under the command of Stilicho, conquered Alaric's Goths at Pollentia and Verona, thus rescuing the city for the last time from the onslaught of the barbarians. After his murder in 408 A. D., the name of Stilicho was erased from the inscription.

G. HENZEN, BullInst, 1880, pp. 169–174; R. LANCIANI, NSc, 1880, p. 53; id., BCom VIII, 1880, p. 135, No. 384; F. GORI, ArchStor IV, 1880, pp. 164–166; CH. HÜLSEN, FR, p. 91; H. THÉDENAT, FR, pp. 131 f., 262; E. DE RUGGIERO, p. 493 f.; G. LUGLI, Centro, p. 171.

1192 The monument to Stilicho for the victory over the Goths (CIL VI, 31987). Lines 10 and 11, with the name and titles of Stilicho, have been chiselled out.

Fot 46

TABULARIUM. The repository of the state archives of the Roman Republic was built in 78 B. C. by Q. Lutatius Catulus, between the two summits of the Capitoline Hill, facing the Forum. The identification of the building as the Tabularium, which is not mentioned in ancient literature, rests on two inscriptions which were found in the building, and give its name and that of its builder (CIL VI, 1314, 1315). At the beginning of the 19th century, this, the best preserved building of the Republic (on top of which stands the mediaeval Palazzo Senatorio), was thoroughly cleared, both inside and out, and the building rubble of a thousand years removed from it. In 1811/13, the substructures on the Forum side were exposed, and further excavations took place in 1830/31, 1844/45 and in 1851. Two arcades of the great hall in the upper storey were reopened in 1939 and, in the same year, the discovery of the Templum Veiovis (q. v.) made the general plan of the Tabularium clear.

A. NIBBY, RomAnt I, pp. 551–555; PLATNER-BUNSEN, Beschreibung III, 1, pp. 40–44; L. CANINA, Ann Inst, 1851, pp. 268–278; H. JORDAN, ib., 1881, pp. 60–73; id., Top I, 2, pp. 135–154; J. H. MIDDLETON I, pp. 372–377; R. LANCIANI, Ruins, pp. 293–296 (Bibl: p. 294 f.); id., Storia II, p. 70; R. DELBRÜCK, HB, I, pp. 23–46, Taf. 3–9; II, Taf. 3 (Bibl: p. 26); E. RODOCANACHI, Le Capitole Romain (3), 1912, pp. 22–25, 96–102; TH. ASHBY, JRS IX, 1919, p. 192 (88 r); G. CULTRERA, MemLinc 5, XVII, 1923, p. 505; T. FRANK, Buildings, pp. 49–51; P-A, pp. 506–508; A. M. COLINI, BCom LXVII, 1939, p. 201; ib., Bull. Mus. Imp. X, 1939, p. 185; id., BCom LXX, 1942, pp. 5–8, 32–37; G. LUGLI, Centro, pp. 42–46 (Bibl: p. 46); id., Tecnica II, Tavv. LXXX, 1, LXXXVI, 1, M. E. BLAKE I, pp. 143 f., 331; L. CREMA, ArchRom, p. 58; C. C. VAN ESSEN, Précis d'histoire de l'art (coll. Latomus XLII), 1960, pp. 60–62.

1193 Entrance to the Tabularium on the south side.                                              Fot 5662

1194 The façade of the Tabularium facing the Forum.                    Fot 141

1195  The façade of the Tabularium, seen from the south.

Rip X  C/3920

1196  The arcaded hall of the upper storey.                                            Fot 5263

1197  The entrance from the Forum which was blocked by the podium of the Temple of Vespasian.          Fot 142

1198  Stairway leading to the upper storey from the Forum.                    Fot 3271

1199 The inscription of Lutatius Catulus (CIL VI, 1313) found inside the building by Canina in 1845, and set up on ancient door-posts on the northern outer wall.                                                                Fot 145

TARPEIUS MONS. The earliest name of the Capitoline Hill, which is possibly derived from the name of an Italic god. After the building of the Temple of Iuppiter, during which, according to tradition, a man's head (caput) was found, from which the name Capitolium was derived, the ancient names of saxum Tarpeium or rupes Tarpeia continued to be used for the Tarpeian Rock proper. From this precipice it was customary to cast down such criminals as traitors, perjurers, slaves caught in the act of stealing and, under the Empire, those guilty of sacrilege against the emperor. The name of the rock, thus used as a place of execution for traitors, came to be connected with the legend of Tarpeia, the daughter of the officer in command of the arx who, in the days of Romulus, threw open the gates to the Sabines, and was rewarded for her treachery by being crushed beneath their shields (s. Basilica Aemilia I, 197, 199). The Tarpeian Rock rises on the south-east flank of the Capitoline, overhanging the present-day Piazza della Consolazione. It was excavated in 1931/33, after the houses which formerly covered it had been removed.

DUREAU DE LA MALLE, Mémoire sur la position de la Roche Tarpéienne, 1819; PLATNER-BUNSEN, Beschreibung III, 1, pp. 26–30; H. JORDAN, Capitol, Forum and Sacra Via, 1881, p. 60; id., Top I, 2, pp. 127–131; II, p. 463 f.; CH. HÜLSEN, Festschrift f. H. KIEPERT, 1898, p. 215; R. LANCIANI, BCom XXIX, 1901, pp. 245–269; H. A. SANDERS, The myth about Tarpeia, Univ. of Michigan Studies I, 1904, pp. 1–47; E. PAIS, Ancient legends of Roman history, 1905, pp. 96–127; S. REINACH, RA 4, XI, 1908, pp. 43–74; W. H. ROSCHER V, pp. 111–116; L. PASCHETTO, Diss PontAcc 2, X, parte II a, 1912, p. 50; P-A, p. 509 f.; A. W. VAN BUREN, Ancient Rome as revealed by recent discoveries, 1936, p. 43; H. LYNGBY, Eranos XXXVI, 1938, pp. 95–98; id., ForBoarium, pp. 77–86; A. MUÑOZ, L'isolamento del Colle Capitolino, 1943, pp. 11–20; G. LUGLI, Centro, p. 18 f.; (Bibl: p. 19).

1200 The Tarpeian Rock, seen from the south-west, on the right is S. Maria della Consolazione.                    Fot 651

1201  The Tarpeian Rock, seen from north-east.                                    Fot 652

TESTACEUS MONS. In the ancient warehouse quarter by the Tiber, to the south of the Horrea Galbae (q. v.), and east of the modern slaughter-house (mattatoio), rises an artificial hill some 50 m. high, made entirely from the broken sherds of amphorae which once contained wine, oil, grain and other goods. It was a dump of useless pottery, cast out from the boats tied up in the Tiber, and it grew to its present height over a period of some one hundred and fifty years, from the beginning of the Empire to the middle of the 2nd century. Many of the sherds have potters' stamps or painted inscriptions, from which the date and origin of the amphorae can be determined; the most recent belong to the middle of the 3rd century A. D. The hill is not mentioned in literature, and its name "Testacius" appears for the first time in an 8th century inscription at S. Maria in Cosmedin. Nevertheless, it may well have been known as Mons Testaceus in antiquity.

G. M. CRESCIMBENI, L'Istoria della Basilica di S. Maria in Cosmedin, 1715, pp. 63, 79; A. NIBBY, Rom-Ant I, pp. 31–34; H. DRESSEL, AnnInst, 1878, pp. 118–192; id., BCom XX, 1892, pp. 48–53; id., CIL XV, p. 491 f., Ni. 2558–3374; pp. 560–565, Ni. 3636–4528; G. B. DE ROSSI, AnnInst, 1885, pp. 232–234; R. LANCIANI, Ruins, p. 529 f.; H. JORDAN, Top I, 3, p. 177 f.; G. MANCINI, BCom XXXIX, 1911, pp. 246–260; R. LANCIANI, ib. XLII, 1914, pp. 241–250; L. CANTARELLI, ib. XLIII, 1915, pp. 41–46, 279–288; P-A, p. 512 f.; T. FRANK, AJP LVII, 1936, pp. 87–90; id., JRS XVII, 1937, pp. 72–79; C. PIETRANGELI, BCom LXXII, 1946/48, p. 214; R. ÉTIENNE, Mél LXI, 1949, pp. 151–181; P. ÅSTRÖM, ActaInstSueciae XVI, 1952, pp. 166–171.

1202 Testaceus Mons.                                                                                    Fot 629

1203  Broken amphorae on the south slope of the hill.                                              Fot 631

1204  The overgrown hillside and exposed potsherds near the top of the hill which is crowned with a cross.      Fot 632

THEATRUM BALBI. In the year 19 B. C., L. Cornelius Balbus celebrated his triumph for the victory over the Garmantes and erected in the southern part of the Campus Martius a theatre, which was dedicated in 13 B. C. According to the Constantinian Regionary Catalogue (CodTop I, p. 122), it had 11510 loca, that is to say accomodation for 6000–7000 spectators. Until recently, it was believed that the remains of the theatre lay beneath the elevation of Monte Cenci, upon which the Palazzo Cenci and the church of S. Tommaso stand; however, it was not possible to insert the fragments of the Severan marble plan which bear the inscription "Theatrum Balbi" (FUR, Tav. XXXII) in this position. A new arrangement of those fragments which relate to the Circus Flaminius (q. v. I, 266–268) and the Theatre of Balbus (published by Guglielmo Gatti in July 1960) transfers the theatre to Piazza Paganica. The architectural remains beneath the Palazzo Mattei di Paganica, which were formerly thought to be the curve of the Circus Flaminius, are now recognized as part of the cavea of the Theatre of Balbus. On the other hand, the ancient walls of opus quadratum, east of Via Michelangelo Caetani, in the cellars of Via delle Botteghe Oscure, belong to the CRYPTA BALBI.

CodTop IV, p. 474 (Francesco Albertini, Opusculum de mirabilibus, 1510); A. NIBBY, RomAnt II, pp. 586–588; CH. HÜLSEN, BCom XXII, 1894, p. 319 f.; R. LANCIANI, Ruins, pp. 493–495; id., BCom XXVII, 1899, p. 21, Tav. I–II, 23; H. JORDAN, Top I, 3, pp. 519–521; G. MARCHETTI-LONGHI, MemLinc 5, XVI, 1922, pp. 733-761; P–A, p. 513; F. W. SHIPLEY, MAA Rome IX, 1931, pp. 37 f., 50; G. MARCHETTI-LONGHI, Capitolium VIII, 1932, pp. 313–319; id., RendPont Acc 3, XVI, 1940, pp. 225–307; G. LUGLI, Mon III, pp. 85–87; id., Dioniso IX, 1942, p. 62 f.; M. E. BLAKE I, p. 222; FUR, p. 228; G. GATTI, Capitolium XXXV, 1960, 7, pp. 3–12; id., Palatino V, 1961, 1–2, pp. 17–20; G. MARCHETTI-LONGHI, ib. IV, 1960, 11–12, pp. 162–165.

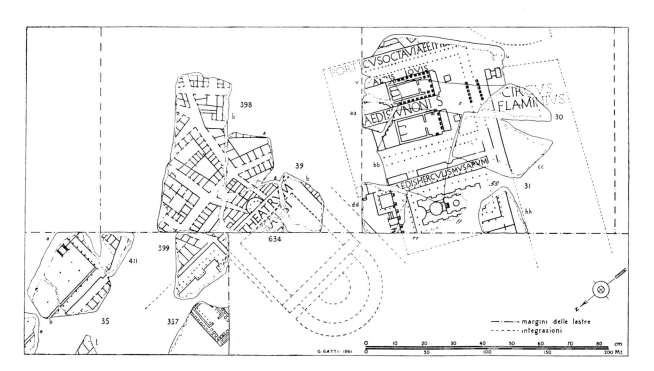

1205 The position of the Theatrum Balbi on the Severan marble plan (G. Gatti).

1206  A travertine pilaster at the west end of the cavea, under the Palazzo Mattei di Paganica.                    Fot 3256

1207  Corridor around the cavea and a wall of opus reticulatum beneath Palazzo Mattei di Paganica.          Fot 3255

1208 Remains of the reticulate walls of the cavea of the theatre under the Casa Mattei, at No. 19 Piazza Mattei.

Fot 3259

1209 Remains of the travertine north wall of the Crypta Balbi, under No. 19, Via Botteghe Oscure.      Fot 3258

THEATRUM MARCELLI. Julius Caesar began to buy land in the northern part of the Forum Holitorium for the construction of a permanent theatre and razed the buildings on the acquired property, among others a TEMPLE OF PIETAS. Augustus acquired further ground, and built the theatre, which he dedicated in 13 or 11 B. C., to the memory of his nephew and son-in-law Marcellus, destined to be his successor, who had died in 23 B. C. (s. Mausoleum Augusti, II, 720). The theatre accomodated from 10.000 to 14.000 spectators (20500 loca; CodTop I, p. 123). Apparently it was already in a state of ruin by the end of the 4th century, since at that time it furnished building material for the reconstruction of the Pons Cestius (q. v. II, p. 187). In the middle ages, the ruins served as a residence and fortress for the Roman families of the Pierleoni, Savelli and Orsini. When the work of excavation and isolation was begun in 1926, the arcades of the lower storey were found to be buried in four metres of accumulated debris. The task of restoring the exterior and exploring the interior was completed in 1932.

A. NIBBY, RomAnt II, pp. 593–600; CH. HÜLSEN, BCom XXII, 1894, p. 319 f.; R. LANCIANI, Ruins, pp. 490–492 (Bibl: p. 493); id., Storia III, p. 7 f.; L. PERNIER, BCom XXIX, 1901, pp. 52–70; LV, 1927, pp. 5–40; H. JORDAN, Top I, 3, pp. 515–519; E. CAETANI LOVATELLI, Passeggiate nella Roma Antica, 1909, pp. 51–88; TH. ASHBY, Top 1581, pp. 134–136; M. MARCHETTI, BCom XLII, 1914, p. 109; E. B. VAN DEMAN, AJA XVI, 1912, p. 392 f.; CH. HÜLSEN, RendPontAcc 3, I, 1921/23, pp. 169–174; G. MAR-CHETTI-LONGHI, Capitolium I, 1925/26, pp. 529–534; P. FIDENZONI, ib. II, 1926/27, pp. 594–600; P-A, pp. 513–515; R. PACINI, Capitolium IX, 1933, pp. 356–364; G. MARCHETTI-LONGHI, RendPontAcc 3, XX, 1943/44, pp. 93–99; id., Dioniso IX, 1942, p. 22 f.; G. LUGLI, ib., pp. 55–64; id., Centro, pp. 568–572 (Bibl: p. 572); id., Tecnica II, Tav. LXXIX, 2; M. E. BLAKE I, pp. 154 f., 265; A. CALZA BINI, Il Teatro di Marcello, Boll. del centro di studi per la storia dell'architettura 7, 1953 (Bibl: p. 5 f.); L. CRE-MA, ArchRom, pp. 187–190; FUR, p. 91 f., Tav. XXIX.

1210 The exterior of the Theatre of Marcellus.

1211 The eastern part of the exterior.

1212 Arcades with engaged columns, Doric below and Ionic in the upper storey.

Fot 540

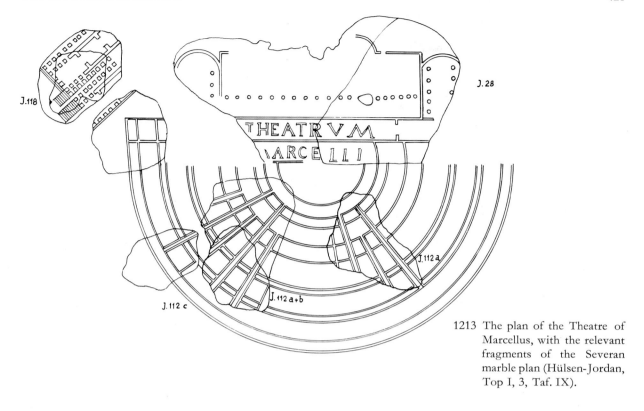

J.118

J.28

THEATRVM
MARCELLI

J.112 a

J.112 a+b

J.112 c

1213 The plan of the Theatre of
Marcellus, with the relevant
fragments of the Severan
marble plan (Hülsen-Jordan,
Top I, 3, Taf. IX).

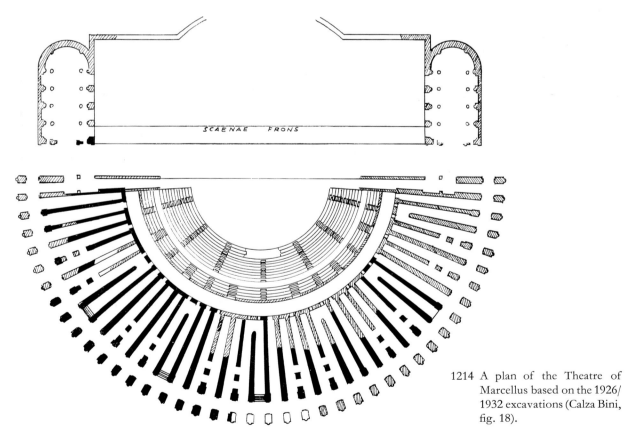

SCAENAE FRONS

1214 A plan of the Theatre of
Marcellus based on the 1926/
1932 excavations (Calza Bini,
fig. 18).

1215 A pilaster and column at the entrance to the eastern "Aula Regia", beside the scaena.                    Fot 546

THEATRUM POMPEI. The first permanent theatre in the Campus Martius was built by Pompey in 55 B. C. To overcome the opposition of those who maintained the ancient prejudice against a permanent place of entertainment, he built the Temple of VENUS VICTRIX at the top of the cavea, so that the tiers of seats lay in front of it, as though they were its podium stairs. The theatre could accomodate some 10000 spectators (17580 loca; CodTop I, p. 122 f.). Even after the Theatres of Marcellus and Balbus had been built, the Theatre of Pompey remained the most important in Rome. It was sometimes known as Theatrum Magnum or Marmoreum, and as late as 357 A. D., it was extolled by Ammianus Marcellinus (XVI, 10, 14), as one of the principal ornaments of the city.

A. NIBBY, RomAnt II, pp. 609–623; O. GILBERT, Rom III, pp. 322–327; CH. HÜLSEN, BCom XXII, 1894, pp. 319–321; H. JORDAN, Top I, 3, pp. 524–530; R. LANCIANI, Storia II, p. 244; III, pp. 123 f., 234; G. CASCIOLI, DissPontAcc 2, XV, 1921, p. 371; G. CULTRERA, MemLinc 5, XVII, 1923, p. 505; G. MARCHETTI-LONGHI, Capitolium II, 1926/27, pp. 531–544; P-A, pp. 515–517, 555; G. MARCHETTI-LONGHI, RendPontAcc 3, XII, 1936, pp. 233–297; A. M. COLINI, Capitolium XII, 1937, pp. 118–122; G. LUGLI, Mon III, pp. 70–78; id., Dioniso IX, 1942, pp. 55–64; G. MARCHETTI-LONGHI, ib., p. 22 f.; D. K. HILL, ClJ XXXIX, 1943/44, pp. 360–365; M. E. BLAKE I, pp. 149, 254, 265, 332; F. CASTAGNOLI, CM, p. 167; A. RUMPF, Mitt. Deutsches Arch. Inst. III, 1950, pp. 40–50; G. CAPUTO, Dioniso XVII, 1954, pp. 171–177; C. PIETRANGELI, Scavi, p. 71 f.; J. A. HANSON, Roman Theater-Temples, 1959, pp. 43–55; L. CREMA, ArchRom, pp. 93–95; FUR, p. 104 f. (Bibl: p. 106), Tav. XXXII; M. BIEBER, The history of the Greek and Roman theatre (2), 1961, p. 181 f.

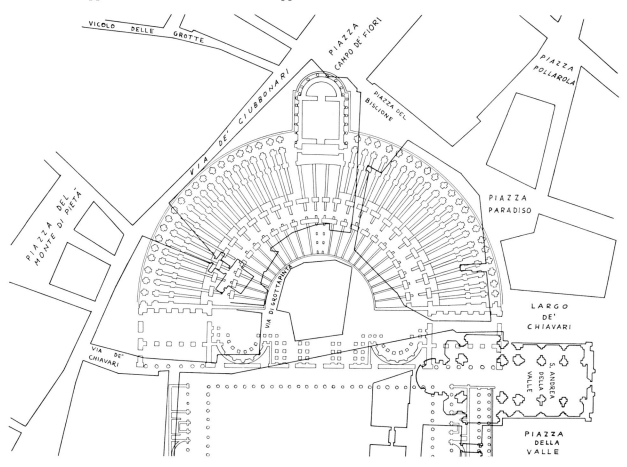

1216 Site-plan of the Theatre of Pompey.

1217 The area of Pompey's Theatre, in the Campus Martius, where the outline of the modern buildings indicates the
plan of the theatre.
                                                                                              Fot 5796

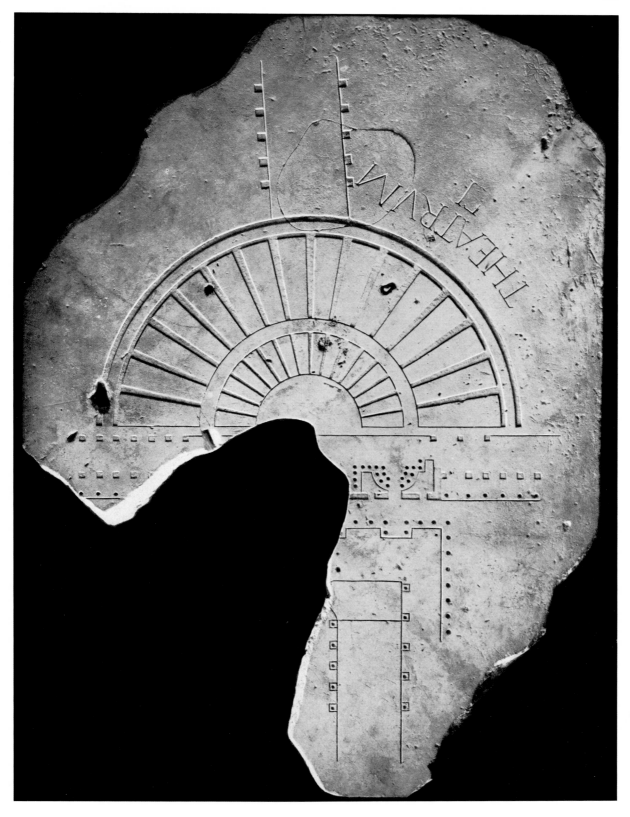

1218 A fragment of the Severan marble plan (FUR, Tav. XXXII, 38), depicting the Theatre of Pompey.  Rip X  G/31

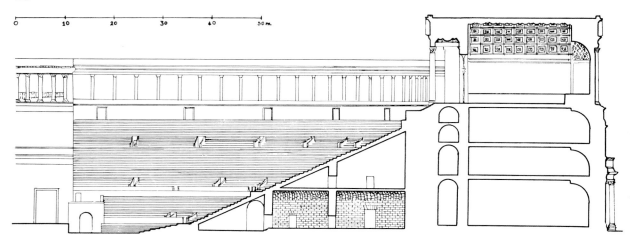

1219 Cross-Section on the axis of the cavea and the Temple of Venus Victrix (after Baltard, Mon. antiques II, pl. 142).

1220 Tufa foundations for the steps which led up to the Temple of Venus Victrix, seen in the Palazzo Pio-Righetti.
Rip X C/3290

1221 Walls of opus caementicium and opus reticulatum on Via di Grotta Pinta.                    Rip X  C/3291

1222 A barrel-vault of opus cae-
     menticium on Via di Grotta
     Pinta.        Rip X C/3295

1223 A chamber beneath the central part of the cavea, seen in the house at Nos. 92–94 Piazza del Biscione.

Rip X C/3298

THERMAE AGRIPPAE. As well as the Pantheon and the Basilica Neptuni, Agrippa initiated the construction of his thermae by building a laconicum, or hot air bath, in 25 B. C. (Dio Cassius LIII, 27, 1); but it was not transformed into a complete bathing establishment until the Aqua Virgo (q. v. I, p. 55) was finished, in 19 B. C. The Thermae of Agrippa were damaged and partly destroyed by fire, on several occasions; they were restored, first by Domitian, again by Hadrian and finally, under Constantius and Constans, in 344/45 A. D. (CIL VI, 1165). The circular hall, the remains of which can be seen in Via dell'Arco della Ciambella, may be attributed to the time of Alexander Severus (222/236 A. D.); its dome is constructed with longitudinal brick ribs.

B. d'OVERBEKE II, pl. b 35, p. 61 f.; A. NIBBY, RomAnt II, pp. 760–766; R. LANCIANI, NSc, 1881, pp. 276–281; 1882, pp. 347–352, 357 f.; H. DE GEYMÜLLER, Documents inédits sur les Thermes d'Agrippa, le Panthéon et les Thermes de Dioclétien, 1883, pp. 9–24; G. BONI, NSc, 1900, p. 633 f.; R. LANCIANI, BCom XXIX, 1901, pp. 3–19; id., Storia II, p. 209; CH. HÜLSEN, RM XX, 1905, p. 75; H. JORDAN, Top I, 3, pp. 576–580; CH. HÜLSEN, Die Thermen des Agrippa, 1910; G. T. RIVOIRA, RomArch, pp. 128, 175 f.; A. VON GERKAN, Gnomon V, 1929, p. 277; D. KRENCKER, Kaiserthermen, p. 263; P-A, pp. 518–520; F. W. SHIPLEY, Agrippa, pp. 47–53; G. LUGLI, Mon III, pp. 151–157; id., Tecnica I, p. 668; H. BLOCH, Bolli, p. 103[91]; id., Harvard studies in class. philology LVI–LVII, 1947, No. 330; M. E. BLAKE I, pp. 162, 298; A. M. COLINI, Capitolium XXXII, 1957, pp. 6–14; L. CREMA, ArchRom, p. 404; C. C. VAN ESSEN, Précis d'histoire de l'art (coll. Latomus XLII), 1960, p. 108; FUR, p. 106 f., Tav. XXXII.

1224 The surviving portion of the rotunda of the Baths of Agrippa, on the north side of Via dell'Arco della Ciambella.
Fot 4261

1225 The "Arco della Ciambella", seen from Via dei Cestari.

Fot 797

1226  The dome of the rotunda, showing its longitudinal brick ribs.                Fot 796

*Thermæ M· Agrippæ, uulgo Arcus Ciambellæ· Vergit ad Orientem Corpus S· Eustachij, et Sociorum, in Ecclesiam ei dicatam inferuntur·* Foa
*Terme di ·M·Agrippa, hora detto Arco della Ciambella· Verso Leuante· Alla Chiesa di S· Eustachio si porta il suo Corpo, è de Compagni·* 74

1227 The circular hall, with an adjacent vestibule on the east side, seen from Via dei Cestari (Alò Giovannoli, 1616).
Inst Neg 53.385

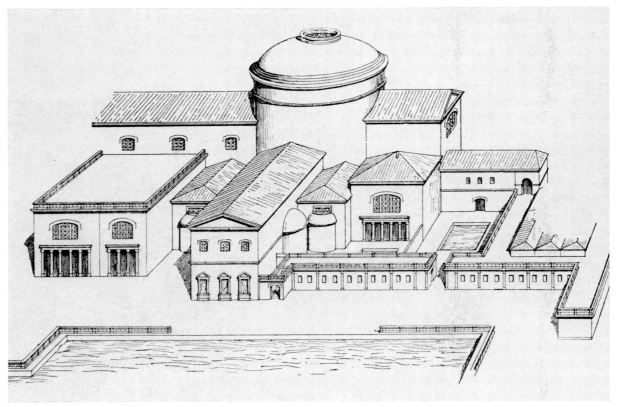

1228 Reconstruction of the Baths of Agrippa, seen from the west. In the foreground the "stagnum" (Hülsen). Fot 2963

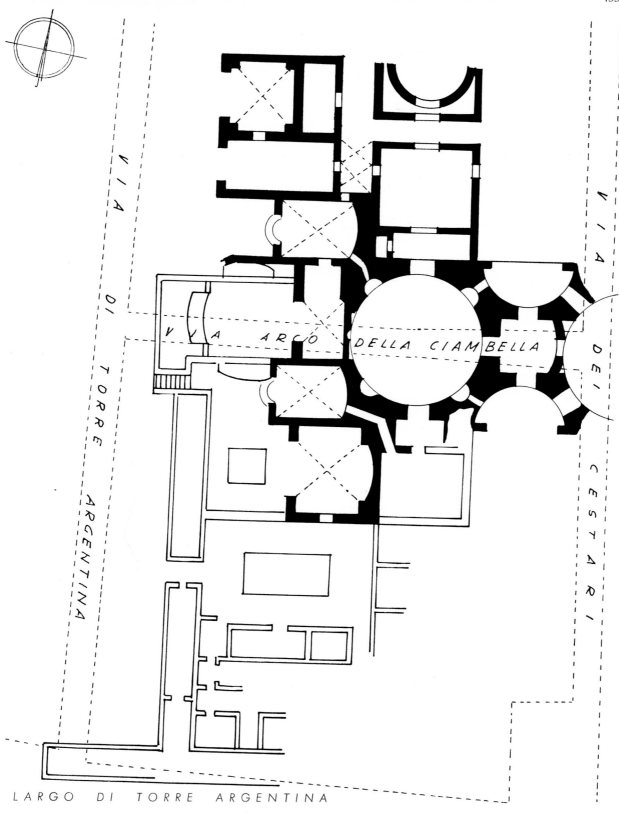

1229 Plan of the Baths of Agrippa (after Hülsen).

THERMAE ANTONINIANAE (CARACALLAE). The construction of the Baths of Caracalla started in 212 A. D., and they were dedicated in 216, when the main building containing the actual baths was ready for use. The surrounding peribolus was built under Elagabalus and Alexander Severus. The baths continued to operate until the 5th century; and only fell into disuse when the aqueducts were broken, during the Gothic Wars, in 537 A. D. Exploration and excavation of the ruins began in the middle of the 16th century, under Paul III, but systematic work was not started until the 19th century. The most important excavations of the main structure began in 1824, and were continued in the years 1867/73 and 1878/80. The underground service corridors were first opened up in 1901, the work continued in 1912 and was finally completed in 1938/39.

s. a. Mithraeum Thermarum Antoniniarum II, p. 85

A. NIBBY, RomAnt II, pp. 777–793; G. A. BLOUET, Restauration des thermes d'Antonin Caracalla à Rome, 1828; A. PELLEGRINI, BullInst, 1867, pp. 109–119; P. ROSA, Relazione, pp. 83–85; R. LANCIANI, Ruins, pp. 533–540 (Bibl: p. 540); S. A. IWANOFF – CH. HÜLSEN, Architektonische Studien III, 1898; G. DE ANGELIS, Relazione degli lavori eseguiti dall'ufficio 1899–1902, 1903, pp. 108–114, Tavv. I, II; H. JORDAN, Top I, 3, pp. 189–196; L. SAVIGNONI, NSc, 1901, pp. 248–253; E. GHISLANZONI, ib., 1912, pp. 305–325; La Zona Monumentale di Roma, 1914, pp. 55–63; W. HELBIG, Führer II, p. 53 f., No. 1240; TH. ASHBY, Top 1581, pp. 123–125; Röm Gebälke I, pp. 100–107; G. T. RIVOIRA, RomArch, pp. 167–177; P-A, pp. 520–524; D. KRENCKER, Kaiserthermen, pp. 269–279; A. VON GERKAN, Gnomon VIII, 1932, pp. 44–46; G. LUGLI, Mon I, pp. 414–428; Mon IV, 1, p. 159 f.; id., Tecnica I, p. 612; II, Tavv. CLXV, 3, CCX, 1; Soprint. Mon. Lazio, Capitolium XIII, 1938, pp. 275–278; A. TERENZIO, BCom LXVI, 1938, p. 285 f.; A. M. COLINI, ib. LXVII, 1939, p. 210 f.; DE GREGORI, pp. 16–18; C. Callmer, ActaInstSueciae X, 1944, p. 164 f.; H. BLOCH, Bolli, pp. 19 f., 283–303; F. CASTAGNOLI, BCom LXXIII, 1949/50, pp. 167–173; E. BRÖDNER, Untersuchungen an den Caracallathermen, 1951 (Bibl: p. 2 f.); A. VON GERKAN, Bonner Jahrbücher CLI, 1951, pp. 132–135; L. CREMA, Palladio N. S. II, 1952, p. 94 f.; id., ArchRom, pp. 531–539.

1230 Aerial view of the Baths of Caracalla.                                                          Fot 5214

1231 The outer wall of the swimming pool (natatio).          Fot 812

1232 The north-east wall of the main building.                               Fot 813

1233  The so-called Frigidarium (natatio).                              Anderson 41301

1234  The central hall (so-called Tepidarium).                              Brogi 3405

1235 Composite capital with figures, in the central hall.                     GFN C/6783

1236 The Calidarium.                                                    Alinari 6749

1237 The Library.                                                      GFN C/6919

1238 The south-east court of the main building (so-called Palaestra). Inst Neg 59.2054

1239 The north-east corner of the court, with the passage through to the Apodyterium; on the left in the pavement, traces of bases for columns or pilasters. Anderson 579

1240  The north-east corner of the court with fragments of the pavement of the surrounding terrace.                    Fot 820

1241 Vaulting in the north-east corner of the court, which formerly supported the terraces.          Fot 819

THERMAE CONSTANTINIANAE. The Baths of Constantine appear to have been built towards the beginning of his reign, about 315 A. D. They stood on the south-west promontory of the Quirinal Hill, close to the Temple of Serapis (q. v. II, 1159). The restricted site causes the ground plan to differ in certain respects from the other imperial bath buildings. A large part of the structure was still erect, at the beginning of the 16th century (BCom XXIII, 1895, Tavv. X–XIII), but the northern part was destroyed in about 1570 to make way for new dwellings and warehouses, where the Palazzo della Consulta now stands. The southern part disappeared in 1611/12, under Paul V, when Cardinal Scipio Borghese began to build the palace, which now bears the name of Palla-vicini-Rospigliosi. Elements of the original bath structure are still conserved in the foundations of the palace. Among the sculpture which adorned the baths, were the horse-tamers of Piazza del Quirinale, the statues of Constantine and his son which are now on the balustrade of the Piazza del Campidoglio, and the two river gods which recline at the base of the steps to the Palazzo Senatorio, on the Capitol.

A. Palladio, Le Terme dei Romani, 1797, Tavv. XIV, XV; A. Nibby, RomAnt II, pp. 793–799; F. Reber, Ruinen, pp. 496–500; H. Jordan, Top II, pp. 526–529; R. Lanciani, NSc, 1877, pp. 204, 267; 1878, pp. 233, 340; O. Gilbert, Rom III, p. 300; Ch. Hül-sen, RhM XLIX, 1894, pp. 389–392; A. Michaelis, RM XIII, 1898, pp. 248–274; E. Petersen, RM XV, 1900, pp. 309–338; R. Lanciani, BCom XXIII, 1895, pp. 103–107; id., Storia III, p. 196 f.; H. Jordan, Top I, 3, pp. 438–441; E. Rodocanachi, Le Capitol Romain (3) 1912, pp. 121, 142 f.; Th. Ashby, Top 1581, pp. 140–142; id., BSR VII, 1914, pp. 40–45, pl. XVIII; G. Bendinelli, BArte V, 1925/26, pp. 147–163; G. Cultrera, MemLinc 5, XVII, 1923, p. 534 f.; D. Krencker, Kaiserthermen, p. 282 f.; P-A, p. 525 f.; J. Mandl, Festschrift f. H. Egger, 1933, pp. 63–68, Abb. 1; G. Lugli, Mon III, pp. 307–312; H. Bloch, Bolli, p. 314; M. Santangelo, Quirinale, pp. 203–208; P. Pecchiai, Il Campidoglio nel Cinquecento, 1950, pp. 65 f., 70; H. Siebenhüner, Das Kapitol in Rom, 1954, pp. 48–51, 78 f., 88, 91, 107; L. Crema, ArchRom, pp. 587, 589, 592; G. Zorzi, Palladio, p. 64 f., figg. 84–88.

1242 The Calidarium and adjoining halls of the Baths of Constantine, seen from the south (S. Du Pérac, I vestigi dell'Antichità di Roma, 1575, fol. 32).                                                          Fot 4769

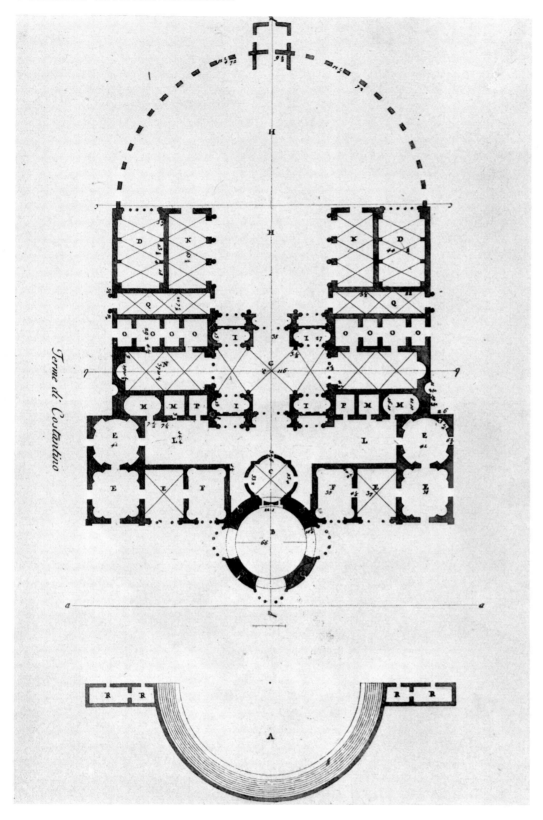

*Terme di Costantino*

1243 Palladio's plan of the baths.

1244  The horse-tamers from the Baths of Constantine, now in Piazza del Quirinale.                    Fot 1353

1245  The horse-tamers and statues of Constantine, recovered from the baths, in a painting by Marten van Heemskerck,
      dated 1546 (private collection).                                                                Fot 6653

1246  The statue of Constantinus Augustus on the left hand
      side of the Capitol balustrade, where it has been since
      1653.                                         Inst Neg 7192

1247  The statue of Constantinus Caesar on the right hand
      side of the Capitol balustrade.               Inst Neg 7196

1248 The effigy of the Nile by the left hand stairway to the Palazzo Senatorio, where it has been since 1565. Together
     with the effigy of the Tigris, it was brought from the Baths of Constantine in 1518.                          Fot 3687

1249 The effigy of the Tigris from the Baths of Constantine. When it was set up by the steps to the Palazzo Senatorio in 1565/66, the tiger, which originally lay beneath the river-god's right arm, was replaced by the Roman she-wolf with Romulus and Remus.
Fot 3686

THERMAE DIOCLETIANI. The construction of these baths was initiated by Maximinian, Diocletian's co-emperor, after his return from Africa in A. D. 298. They were dedicated in the names of both emperors, between May 1st, 305, and July 25th, 306; the former being the day when both emperors went into retirement, and the latter being the death of Constantius Chlorus, who is mentioned in the dedicatory inscription (CIL VI, 1130). Very little is known of the history of these baths in ancient times, but in the Renaissance, considerable use was made of the buildings, parts of which were well preserved. In 1561, Pius IV handed over the surrounding land to the Carthusian monks of S. Croce in Gerusalemme, and in 1563/66 the central hall of the baths was converted, by Michelangelo, into the church of S. Maria degli Angeli. In 1575, the north-western part of the complex was used by Gregory XIII for the construction of the Horrea Ecclesiae, or granaries. These were extended by Paul V in 1609, by Urban VIII in 1630 and by Clement XI in 1705. They were demolished in 1936, during the excavation of this part of the baths. In 1889, the Museo Nazionale Romano was established in the cloisters of the monastery, and was extended to include the greater part of the main building, after its isolation in 1908/11.

A. NIBBY, RomAnt II, pp. 799–807; E. PAULIN, Restauration des Thermes de Dioclétien, 1890; CH. HÜLSEN, RM VII, 1892, pp. 308–311; id., RhM XLIX 1894, p. 388 f.; R. LANCIANI, NSc, 1890, p. 184 f.; id., BCom XX, 1892, p. 275; id., Ruins, pp. 432–435 (Bibl: p. 435); id., Storia II, pp. 135–149; H. JORDAN, Top I, 3, pp. 377–382; C. RICCI, BArte III, 1909, pp. 361–372, 401–405; P. GUIDI – R. PARIBENI, ib. V, 1911, pp. 347–361; TH. ASHBY, Top 1581, pp. 125–128; Röm Gebälke I, pp. 113–116; G. CULTRERA, MemLinc 5, XVII, 1923, p. 533 f.; G. T. RIVOIRA, RomArch, pp. 204–210; I. GISMONDI, Architettura ed Arti Decorative VIII, 1928/29, pp. 385–394; D. KRENCKER, Kaiserthermen, pp. 279–282; P-A, pp. 527–530; R. PARIBENI, MusNaz, pp. 9–49; G. LUGLI, Mon III, pp. 359–371; id., Tecnica I, p. 618 f.; II, Tav. CLXXI, 3; H. BLOCH, Bolli, pp. 303–316; V. INVERNIZZI, Le Arti II, 1939/40, p. 398; M. SANTANGELO, Quirinale, pp. 192–203; G. CARAFFA, L'ampliamento della piazza dei Cinquecento e le Terme di Diocleziano, 1943; L. CREMA, BCom LXXI, 1943/45, pp. 141–143; id., ArchRom, p. 586 f.; E. BRÖDNER, Untersuchungen an den Caracallathermen, 1951, pp. 9, 35–37, 44; B. M. FELLETTI MAJ, NSc, 1952, pp. 33–41.

1250 Air photograph of the Baths of Diocletian.                                                                      Fot 5209

1251 The central hall of the baths, converted into the church of S. Maria degli Angeli. GFN E/25136

1252  The Frigidarium.

1253  The south-east court ("Palaestra"), and a hall with apses in the background.                    Fot 830

1254  The south-east wall of the chambers which lie between the court and the central hall of the baths, now the church
      of S. Maria degli Angeli.                                                                              Fot 832

1255  An exedra in the north-east
wall of the outer peribolus.
Fot 834

1256  The north-west part of the main building, between Via Cernaia and Via Parigi. The Horrea Ecclesiae of Gregory
XIII and Paul V stood here until 1936.
Fot 831

THERMAE HELENAE. The baths, which were restored by the Empress Helena between 323 and 326 A. D., after a fire (CIL VI, 1136), belonged to the complex of buildings of the Villa of Heliogabalus in the Horti Spei Veteris (s. Sessorium II, p. 384). The remains, which could still be seen in the 16th century, have now completely disappeared under modern buildings. Only the water-reservoir of the baths is to any extent preserved; it was supplied by the AQUA ALEXANDRINA, which was built by Alexander Severus (222/235 A. D.), and stands at the intersection of Via Eleniana and Via Sommeiller. It consisted of 12 communicating chambers, one of which was turned into a chapel of S. Angeli in the middle ages.

A. PALLADIO, Le Terme dei Romani, 1797, Tav.XIV; R. LANCIANI, Frontino, Tav. VIII, fig. 5 a; id., FUR, 31, 32; id., BCom XXIV, 1896, p. 238 f.; id., Ruins, pp. 398–400; G. B. DE ROSSI, Note per la pianta di G. B. NOLLI, 1884, p. 29 f., No. 1083; G. GATTI, BCom XXXV, 1907, pp. 114–121; H. JORDAN, Top I, 3, p. 247 f.; G. LUGLI, DizEpigr II, p. 2167; CH. HÜLSEN, Chiese, p. 586 f.; P-A, pp. 391, 530; E. B. VAN DEMAN, Aqueducts, p. 342; W. AMELUNG, Vat Cat III, 1, p. 190 f.; G. LUGLI, Mon III, p. 492 f.; A. M. COLINI, MemPontAcc 3, VIII, 1955, pp. 140–147; G. ZORZI, Palladio, p. 72, fig. 144.

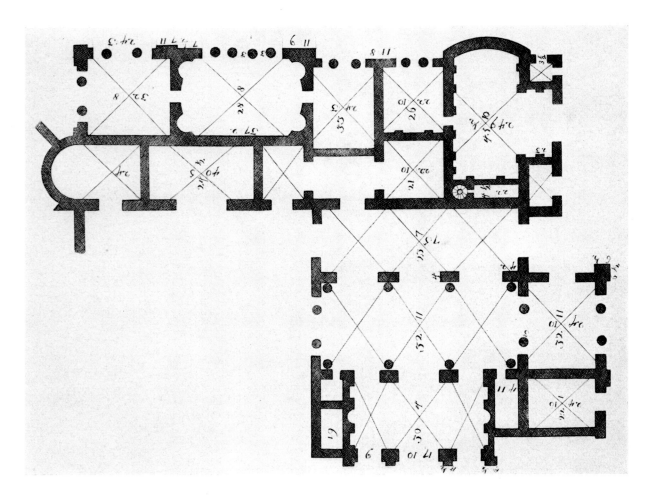

1257 Andrea Palladio's plan of the Baths of Helena.

Fot 2988

1258  The ruins of the baths, from the plan of Du Pérac-Lafréry of 1577.                    Fot 5264

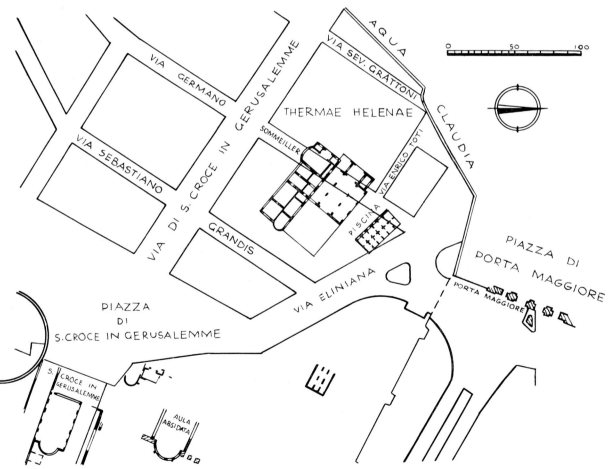

1259  The position of the baths and the water-reservoir in the modern street plan.

1260 The inscription in the Vatican Museum, recording the restoration of the baths by Helena (CIL VI, 1136).
Arch Vat XXI–24–17

1261 Front view of the water-reservoir in Via Eleniana.                                    Fot 6257

1262  The water-reservoir, side view.                                      Fot 886

THERMAE LATERANENSES. At the point where Via Amba Aradam (formerly Via della Ferratella) enters Piazza di S. Giovanni in Laterano, there stands a rectangular, cross-vaulted brick building, 10 × 12.50 m. in plan, and some 13.50 m. high. This was the frigidarium of a bathing establishment which dates from the beginning of the 3rd century. Its north-east front flanked the ancient Via Tusculana. The ground on which the baths stood was first explored by Corvisieri in 1873, yielding a great quantity of sculptured fragments and brick-stamps. After the removal of the Casa Parrocchiale di S. Giovanni, in 1936, it was possible to establish the complete plan of the baths (Colini, Celio, p. 335, fig. 273). At the same time, the frigidarium was isolated, and its arched openings freed from obstructing walls.

E. STEVENSON, AnnInst, 1877, pp. 358-367, Tav. T; A. M. COLINI, Roma XV, 1937, p. 165 f. (= Atti 4 CStR II, pp. 170–172); M. S., Palladio I, 1937, p. 74; B. NOGARA, Atti 5 CStR II, p. 34 f.; G. LUGLI, Mon III, p. 523 f.; A. M. COLINI, Celio, pp. 334–339.

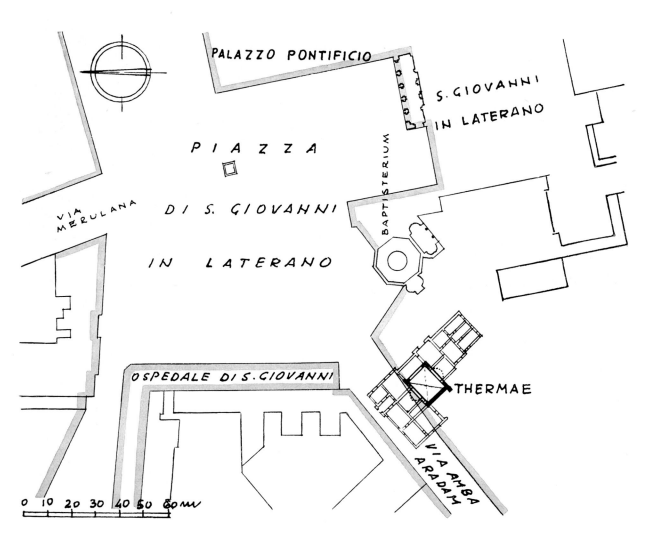

1263 Site-plan of the baths (after Colini and Gismondi).

1264 The remains of the baths at the beginning of the 17th century (Alò Giovannoli, Vedute degli antichi vestigj di
     Roma, 1619, fol. 13).                                                                Inst Neg 53.384

1265 The Frigidarium beside Via Amba Aradam.                                              Fot 827

THERMAE NERONIANAE. Following Agrippa's precedent, Nero built Rome's second public baths in 62 or 64 A. D., to the north-west of the Pantheon, in the Campus Martius. They were repaired and enlarged in 227 A. D., by Alexander Severus, and from then on were known as Thermae Alexandrinae. Fragments of walls, columns and capitals are discovered whenever excavations are made for foundations of buildings, in the area of the baths. Certain ruined walls were visible in the courtyard of the Palazzo Madama until the 18th century; they were removed in the time of Benedict XIV (1740–58).

B. d'OVERBEKE II, p. 65 f., pl. b 43; A. PALLADIO, Le Terme dei Romani, 1797, Tav. III; A. NIBBY, Rom-Ant II, pp. 766–777; Rosa, Relazione, p. 73; P. ADINOLFI II, pp. 423–426; R. LANCIANI, NSc, 1881, pp. 270–273; 1882, p. 412 f., Tav. XXI; 1883, pp. 81,130; id., FUR, 15; id., Ruins, p. 498 f. (Bibl: p. 499); G. GATTI, NSc, 1892, p. 265; id., BCom XXXV, 1907, p. 330; J. H. MIDDLETON II, p. 144 f.; H. JORDAN, Top I, 3, pp. 590–592; E. B. VAN DEMAN, AJA XVI, 1912, p. 406 f.; TH. ASHBY, JRS IX, 1919, p. 183 f.; CH. HÜLSEN, Chiese, pp. 183 f., 268 f., 455 f.; D. KRENCKER, Kaiserthermen, pp. 263–265; P-A, p. 531 f.; A. M. COLINI, BCom LXI, 1933, p. 274; G. GATTI, BCom LXII, 1934, p. 171 f.; H. G. RAMSAY, AntC IV, 1935, pp. 430–436; G. DE ANGELIS D'OSSAT, Tecnica costruttiva e impiante delle terme, 1943, p. 13; F. CASTAGNOLI, BCom LXXI, 1943/45, pp. 3–20 (Bibl: p.3[1]); G. GATTI, Fasti Archaeologici V, 1950, 311; M. E. BLAKE II, p. 34; L. CREMA, Arch Rom, p. 539.

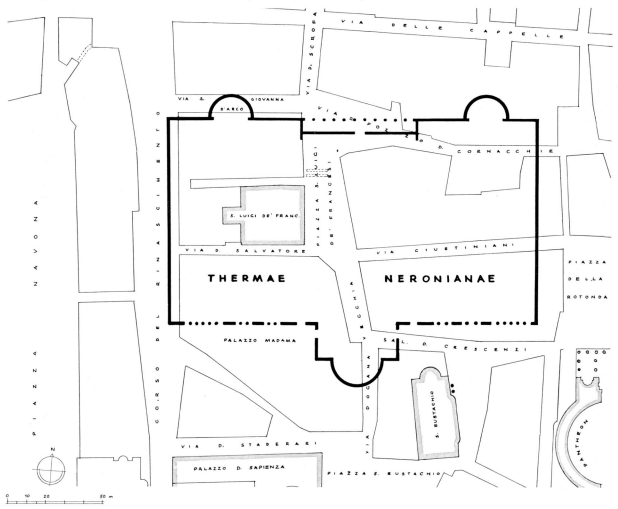

1266 Site-plan of the Thermae Neronianae.

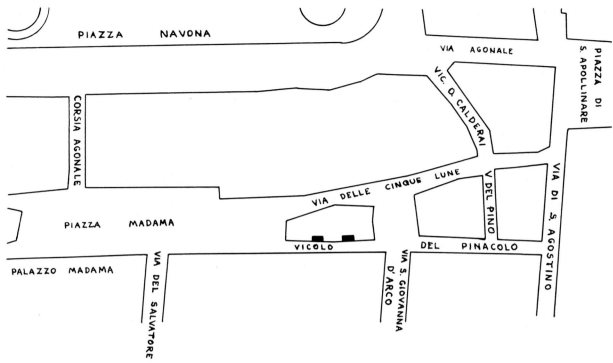

1267 Via delle Cinque Lune and Vicolo del Pinacolo, before the construction of Corso del Rinascimento.

1268 Two brick piers, belonging to the western perimeter wall of the Baths of Nero, isolated and subsequently removed, during the construction of the Corso del Rinascimento.
Rip X C/2188

1269 Two columns from the Frigidarium of the Baths of Nero, found in 1934 under the Piazza S. Luigi dei Francesi.
Rip X  C/2521

1270 The two columns which remained in Via Giovanna d'Arco from the time of their discovery, until they were re-
erected in Via di S. Eustachio in 1950.                                                                Fot 799

*Thermæ Neronianæ è conspectu ædium Cardinalis Iustiniani Pars I Vergit ad Orientem S. Agnes ad Circum Agonalem proftituenda ducitur*
*Terme Neroniane incontro al Palaggio del Cardinal Giustiniano Parte I Riguarda ìs Leuante S. Agnese e menata al Cerchio Agonale, perche fia violata*

1271  The ruins of the Thermae Neronianae opposite the Salita de'Crescenzi (Alò Giovannoli, Vedute degli Antichi
      Vestigj di Roma, 1619, fol. 76).                                                          Inst Neg 53.381

1272  The ruins of the baths, seen in the Palazzo Madama in the last quarter of the 17th century (B. d'Overbeke II, pl.
      b 43).                                                                                         Fot 2954

THERMAE NOVATIANAE SIVE TIMOTHEANAE. According to Christian tradition, a certain senator named Pudens, of the family of the Acilii Glabriones, received Saint Peter at his house in the VICUS PATRICIUS, which corresponds with the present Via Urbana. Subsequently, his two sons, brothers of the maidens Pudentiana and Praxedes, are supposed to have constructed a bath building on the site of their father's house. Excavations underneath the church of S. Pudenziana in the years 1928–33, disclosed mosaics and walls dating from the end of the Republic, at a depth of 9 m. below the present floor level. Above these stood a house, parallel to the Vicus Patricius, having brick-stamps of the time of Hadrian in its walls. The baths date from the middle of the 2nd century A. D., and are built over the preceding house, on a series of high barrel-vaulted substructures. In the 4th century, the most north-easterly hall of the baths was converted into the church of S. Pudenziana. Part of the bath building which stands above and behind the apse of the church, is distinguishable in Via Balbo.

NARDINI–NIBBY II, p. 43 f.; R. LANCIANI, Ruins, p. 390 f.; H. MARUCCHI, Basiliques et églises de Rome, 1902, pp. 364–367; H. JORDAN, Top I, 3, p. 340; P-A, p. 532; A. TERENZIO, BArte XXV, 1931/32, pp. 188–191; G. MANCINI, Atti III Congresso Intern. di Archeologia Cristiana, 1934, pp. 193–197; A. PETRIGNANI, La Basilica di S. Pudenziana, 1934, pp. 23– 44; A. M. COLINI, BCom LXIII, 1935, pp. 183–186; R. KRAUTHEIMER, RACrist XII, 1935, pp. 184–186; G. LUGLI, Mon III, p. 354; M. ARMELLINI, Le chiese di Roma (nuova ed. Cecchelli) II, 1942, pp. 1420–1422; C. CECCHELLI, Monumenti cristiano-eretici di Roma, 1944, pp. 224–228; H. BLOCH, Bolli, p. 244[182].

1273 The remains of baths and nymphaea, uncovered in the nave of S. Pudenziana.                    Sopr Lazio 4968

1274 The hall of the baths, now converted into the nave of the church (Petrignani).

1275 The north-west end of the bath hall, exposed in Via Balbo in 1931. The floor of the chamber is 6 m. below road
     level.
                                                                                                        Fot 828

THERMAE SURANAE. Licinius Sura, friend and fellow-countryman of Trajan, owned a palace on the slope of the Aventine which lay towards the Circus Maximus. On this property he, or possibly after his death Trajan, built a bath which appears on a fragment of the Severan marble plan as BALneum SURAE (FUR, Tav. XXIII). In design, it resembles the Forum Baths of Pompeii, rather than the contemporary Baths of Trajan. If it is correct to suppose that the street flanked by shops, which is seen on the marble plan, is the present Via di S. Prisca, it follows that the baths must have occupied the site of the present Accademia Nazionale di Danza, in Largo Arrigo VII (formerly No. 7, Via di S. Prisca). An inscription (CIL VI, 1703) found there in 1725, in the Vigna Cavaletti, records the restoration of a "cella tepidaria" by the Praefect of the City, in 414 A. D. Another inscription, discovered at S. Sabina in 1919 (NSc, 1920, p. 141), refers to a restoration of the "Balneum Surae" under Gordian III (238–244 A. D.). The last remains of the Thermae Suranae, in the form of walls and hypocausts (suspensurae), came to light during the construction of the Accademia di Danza in 1943, and were destroyed.

A. PELLEGRINI, BullInst, 1868, pp. 177–179; G. B. DE ROSSI, Note per la pianta di G. B. NOLLI, 1884, p. 35 f., Ni. 1386, 1385, 1383, 1393, 1382, 1380; A. MERLIN, L'Aventin dans l'antiquité, 1906, p. 315 f.; H. JORDAN, Top I, 3, p. 156 f.; R. PARIBENI, NSc, 1920, p. 141 f.; id., OP II, pp. 52–54; P-A, p. 532 f.; A. M. COLINI, BCom LXVI, 1938, p. 286; G. LUGLI, Mon III, pp. 561–563; H. FUHRMANN, AA, 1940, p. 476; CodTop I, pp. 141, 154, 181, 185, 191, 245, 254, 308; K. CAPRINO, BCom LXXII, 1946/48, p. 217; R. A. STACCIOLI, Amor di Roma, 1956, pp. 393–401; L. CREMA, ArchRom, p. 404; FUR, p. 79, Tav.XXIII.

1276 Fragment of the Severan marble plan, showing the Balneum Surae.                    Rip X C/3189

1277 A corner of the baths, showing the
     "suspensurae", before destruction
     in 1943.                    Fot 3584

1278 A north wall of the bath building during excavation in 1943, with the Domus Augustiana on the Palatine in the
     background.                                                                                              Fot 3583

THERMAE TITI. In 80 A. D., at the same time as he inaugurated the Amphitheatrum Flavium (Colosseum), which he had enlarged, Titus also dedicated his baths on the Oppian Hill. They lay in the area of Nero's Golden House, immediately to the west, and adjacent to the part which was later built over by the Baths of Trajan. The baths, of which the ground plan and parts of the architecture are known from Palladio's drawings, disappeared without trace in the 16th century. A porticus opposite the main entrance of the Colosseum, from which a monumental stairway led to the bathing establishment on the hill, was excavated in 1895, and parts of it can still be seen on the north side of the Piazza del Colosseo.

A. PALLADIO, Le Terme dei Romani, 1797, Tavv. V, VI; ST. PIALE, Delle Terme Traiane, della Domus Aurea di Nerone e della Titi Domus, Dissertazioni I, 1832, I; A. NIBBY, RomAnt II, pp. 807–810; CH. HÜLSEN, RM IV, 1889, p. 78 f.; VII, 1892, pp. 302–304; G. GATTI, NSc, 1895, pp. 201–203; id., BCom XXIII, 1895, pp. 118–121; R. LANCIANI, ib., pp. 110–115; id., Ruins, pp. 363–365; id., Storia III, p. 248; H. JORDAN, Top I, 3, pp. 307–310; R. PARIBENI, OP II, pp. 43–45; D. KRENCKER, Kaiserthermen, p. 265 f.; G. T. RIVOIRA, RomArch, pp. 97–101; P–A, p. 533 f.; G. LUGLI, Centro, p. 353 f. (Bibl: p. 374); E. BRÖDNER, Untersuchungen an den Caracallathermen, 1951, p. 8; M. E. BLAKE II, p. 98; L. CREMA, ArchRom, p. 287; G. ZORZI, Palladio, p. 65 f., figg. 89–95 a.

1279 The porticus of the Baths of Titus, opposite the Colosseum, from which a stairway led to the bathing establishment on the Oppian Hill.

Fot 840

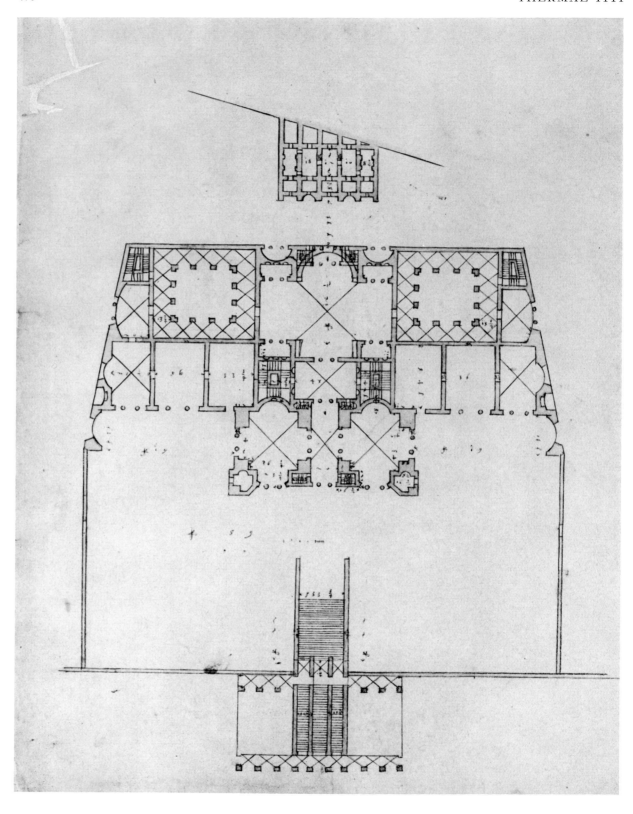

1280  Plan of the Baths of Titus, by Andrea Palladio (Royal Inst. of British Architects, vol. II, fol. 1).     GFN F/3130

1281 The porticus in the Piazza del Colosseo, during the excavation in 1895.          GFN B/203

1282 The excavation of the porticus; the brick pilasters with half columns in the third row have survived, those in the
     front rows were destroyed.                                                        GFN B/200

THERMAE TRAIANI. When Nero's Golden House was burned down in 104 A. D., Trajan had thermae built over the ruins; the architect being Apollodorus of Damascus. They were opened on the 22nd June 109 A. D.; and two days later, the emperor dedicated the Aqua Traiana (q. v. I, 49, 50) which supplemented the water supply to the baths. The "Sette Sale", a building of nine intercommunicating water chambers, to the east of the north-east corner of the baths, served as a reservoir. In early mediaeval sources (CodTop I, pp. 97 f., 274 f.; II, pp. 230, 232), the Baths of Trajan are said to have been built by Domitian, an attribution which is refuted by the brick-stamps, which are exclusively Trajanic, together with the homogeneity of construction.

A. PALLADIO, Le Terme dei Romani, 1797, Tavv.VII, VIII; A. DE ROMANIS, Le antiche camere esquiline, 1822, p. 48 f.; A. NIBBY, RomAnt II, pp. 810–815; G. B. DE ROSSI – G. GATTI, BCom XIV, 1886, p. 245 f.; R. LANCIANI, Ruins, pp. 365–367 (Bibl: p. 367); H. JORDAN, Top I, 3, pp. 310–314; G. T. RIVOIRA, RomArch, p. 117; R. PARIBENI, OP II, pp. 40–52; D. KRENCKER, Kaiserthermen, pp. 266–269; P-A, pp. 534–536; G. CALZA, NSc, 1932, p.194; CH. HÜLSEN, RhM LXXXII, 1933, p. 370; A. MUÑOZ, Il Parco di Traiano, 1936; DE GREGORI, p. 18 f.; C. CALLMER, ActaInstSueciae X, 1944, p. 164; G. LUGLI, Centro, pp. 355–358, 369–373; H. BLOCH, Bolli, pp. 36–49; id., AJA XLVIII, 1944, pp. 339–341; E. BRÖDNER, Untersuchungen an den Caracallethermen, 1951, pp. 8, 37 f., 42; C. C. VAN ESSEN, Mededeelingen Nederl. Akad. v. Wetenschappen, N R Deel 17, No. 12, 1954, p. 388 f.; F. CASTAGNOLI, AC VIII. 1956, pp. 53–55; L. CREMA, ArchRom, p. 403 f.; FUR p. 69, Tav. XVIII.

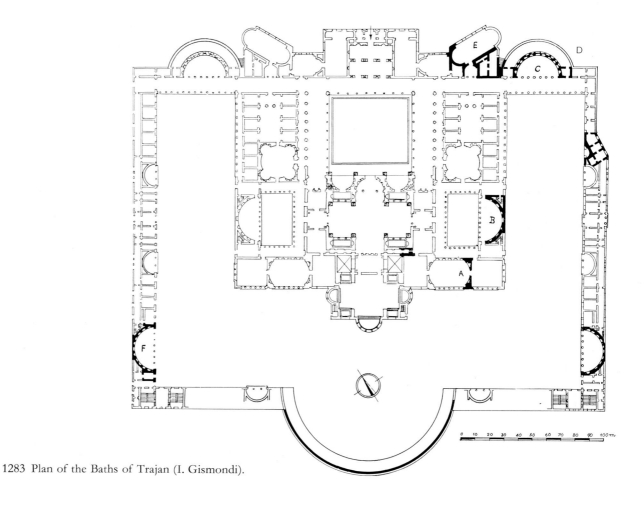

1283 Plan of the Baths of Trajan (I. Gismondi).

1284  The southern exedra of the Baths of Trajan.                                    Fot 809

1285  Air photograph of the Baths of Trajan.                                         Fot 4725

1286  East wall of the second chamber, east of the Calidarium; plan A.                          Fot 806

1287  Exedra to the east of the colonaded courtyard (Palaestra); plan B.                        Fot 805

1288  North-eastern exedra of the perimeter wall; plan C.                                      Fot 803

1289  Exterior, showing the corridor which lies behind the exedra; plan D.                     Fot 804

1290  Library of the baths; plan F.                                              Fot 801

1291  Hall with two apses, between the entrance and the north-eastern exedra; plan E.          Fot 808

1292  A water-chamber of the "Sette Sale".                                    Fot 2959

1293  System of intercommunicating water-chambers of the "Settle Sale".        Fot 2956

TRIBUNAL AURELIUM. In addition to the podium, which was used by persons engaged in a trial, the Tribunal Aurelium was also provided with theatre-like accommodation for the public, the GRADUS AURELII. The tribunal was built either by C. Aurelius Cotta, the consul for 75 B. C., or by M. Aurelius Cotta in the following year. Cicero, who alone mentions either Tribunal or Gradus by name, states that the monument lay at the south-east end of the Forum, close to the Temple of Castor. In 1888, Richter noted a platform of tufa blocks on the north side of the Temple of Julius Caesar, lying at an angle of 8° 30′ to this subsequently-built temple, but parallel with the Temple of Castor. An extension of the same platform is found on the south side of the Temple of Caesar, beneath the north pier of the Arch of Augustus, which dates from 29 B. C. Other parts of the republican, tufa-built platform were also disclosed during the excavation of the Augustan monuments near the Temple of Caesar (see Arcus Augusti, Porticus Iulia, Porticus Gai et Luci, Puteal Libonis). With the help of data recovered during the excavations of 1952 and 1959, the outline of the monument is ascertainable, and its identification with the Tribunal and Gradus Aurelii is rendered probable.

F. M. NICHOLS, The Roman Forum, 1877, p. 81 f.; H. JORDAN, Top I, 2, p. 405; O. RICHTER, Antike Denkmäler I, 1888, p. 14, 1; Taf. 27, 28; id., JdI IV, 1889, p. 148 f.; C. J. O'CONNER, AJA IV, 1900, pp. 303–309; id., Bulletin of the Univ. of Wisconsin, 1904, pp. 178–182; H. THÉDENAT, FR, p. 148; E. DE RUGGIERO, p. 72 f.; E. B. VAN DEMAN, JRS XII, 1922, p. 26 f., plan I; N. W. DE WITT, ClPhil XXI, 1926, pp. 220–222; H. D. JOHNSON, The Roman Tribunal, 1927, pp. 54–64; P-A, p. 539 f.; C. GIOFFREDI, Studia et documenta historiae et iuris IX, 1943, pp. 272–274; G. LUGLI, Centro, p. 99 f.; id., MonMin, pp. 74–76; M. E. BLAKE I, p. 146; E. WELIN, SFR, pp. 104–110; G. ROMANELLI, Gnomon XXVI, 1954, p. 259; B. ANDREAE, AA, 1957, p. 156 f.; G. CARETTONI, JRS L, 1960, p. 195.

1294 Tufa blocks of the podium of the Tribunal Aurelium, seen underneath the north pier of the Arch of Augustus (s. plan I, 98, 4).
                                                                                                    Fot 2944

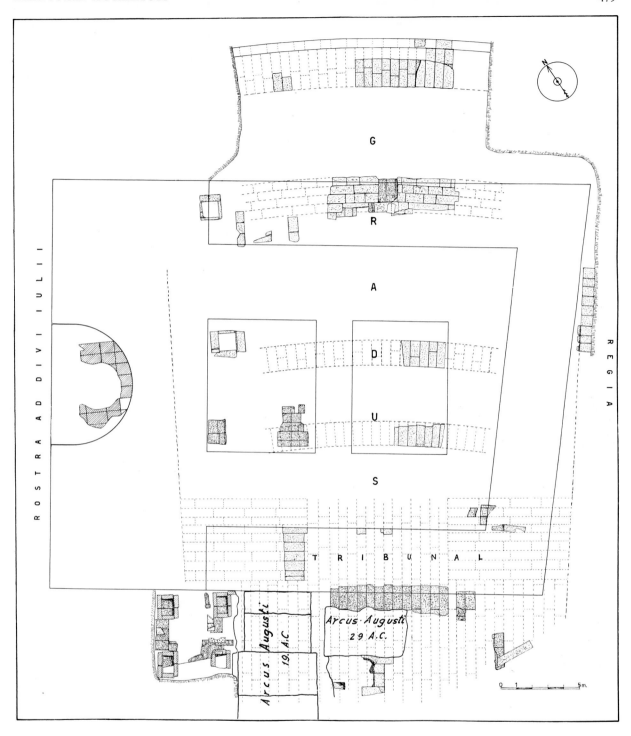

1295 Plan of the Tribunal Aurelium and Gradus Aurelii (R. Gamberini Mongenet 1961).

1296  Tufa blocks of the Gradus Aurelii beneath the pronaos of the Temple of Caesar. To the right, remains of a road
which was built after the demolition of the tribunal.                                          Fot 5413

1297 The tufa blocks of the Gradus Aurelii on the north side of the Temple of Caesar. The blocks in the foreground were subsequently realigned for use in the foundations of the Porticus Iulia.                                        Fot 6609

Tribunal Praetorium. The place where the praetor urbanus administered justice was originally in the Comitium, beside the Puteal of Attus Navius, but it was subsequently transferred to the Puteal Libonis (q. v.) on the Forum. Numerous sources place it in the neighbourhood of the Fornix Fabianus and the Regia, between the temples of Castor and Vesta. Topographical references to the Tribunal Praetorium correspond with those for the Tribunal Aurelium (q. v.), and the two places cannot have been far apart. Moreover, Cicero states that the Tribunal Praetorium was "non longe a gradibus Aurelii" (pro Flacco 66). Perhaps, like many tribunals, it was no more than a wooden platform, and there is no conclusive evidence that this particular one was of stone. Its identification, by Lugli, with the monument which lies across the front of the Temple of Julius Caesar, therefore remains a hypothesis which is only partly supported by literary sources. A contrary opinion, based on the inscription of Surdinus (s. Ficus Olea Vitis I, p. 397), that the Tribunal Praetorium should be sought beside the Statue of Marsyas, is likely to be mistaken, since Surdinus was praetor inter cives et peregrinos (CIL VI, 1468), and not praetor urbanus.

Th. Mommsen, Jahrbücher des gem. deutschen Rechts VI, 1863, pp. 389–397 (Jur. Schriften III, 1907, pp. 319–326); H. Jordan, Top I, 1, p. 499 f.; I, 2, pp. 402–404; Ch. Hülsen, Die neuesten Ausgrabungen auf dem Forum Romanum, 1910, pp. 15–21; Hülsen–Carter, pp. 149–151; E. De Ruggiero, pp. 72–74; H. D. Johnson, The Roman Tribunal, 1927, pp. 48–53; P-A, p. 540 f.; C. Gioffredi, Studia et documenta historiae et iuris IX, 1943, pp. 262–268; G. Lugli, Centro, p. 99 f.; id., MonMin, p. 62 f.; E. Welin, SFR, pp. 60–73, 127 f.; S. Stucchi, Mon, p. 77 f.

1298 Steps beside the Temple of Castor, which may have led up to the "Tribunal Praetorium".                                                Fot 140

1299 The "Tribunal Praetorium" in front of the Rostra Aedis Divi Iuli.                    Fot 139

UMBILICUS ROMAE. The umbilicus, which was supposed to mark the centre of Rome, and of the Roman World, is known to us only from relatively late sources; the 4th century Regionary Catalogue (CodTop I, p. 174) and the 8th century Einsideln Intinerary (CodTop II, pp. 177, 191, 195). The former places it between the Temple of Concord and the Temple of Saturn, while the latter has it near the church of SS. Sergius and Bacchus. On the strength of these two indications, the Umbilicus Romae is identifiable with a three tiered brick cylinder, which stands at the northern end of the Hemicyclium of the Rostra. It is an early 4th century structure, but is later in date then the Tetrarchy monument of A. D. 303 (s. Basis Decennalia I, p. 198). The brick structure may have been crowned by a circular aedicula, dating from an earlier period, travertine fragments of which have been found in the immediate vicinity. The monument was discovered in 1803, during the isolation of the Arch of Septimius Severus.

C. BUNSEN, AnnInst, 1834, p. 11; id., Le Forum Romain, 1835, p. 14 f.; PLATNER–BUNSEN, Beschreibung III, 1, p. 73 f.; III, 2, p. 101 f.; L. CANINA, Esposizione del Foro Romano (2), 1845, p. 152; G. MONTIROLI, Osservazioni sulla topografia della parte meridionale del Foro Romano, 1859, p. 13; F. M. NICHOLS, The Roman Forum, 1877, p. 18 f.; id., Notizie dei Rostri, 1885, pp. 33–35, 45–50; H. JORDAN, AnnInst, 1883, p. 57 f.; id., Top I, 2, p. 245 f.; II, p. 454; J. H. MIDDLETON I, p. 263 f.; R. LANCIANI, Ruins, p. 280; E. B. VAN DEMAN, AJA XIII, 1909, p. 186; CH. HÜLSEN, FR, p. 76; H. THÉDENAT, FR, pp. 134, 233; E. DE RUGGIERO, p. 375 f.; W. SCHEEL, RM XLIII, 1928, pp. 202, 210, 217 f., 255; P-A, p. 544; G. LUGLI, Centro, p. 146 f.

1300 The top tier of the Umbilicus Romae with travertine base; a fragment of the entablature of the aedicula in the
        foreground.
                                                                                                         Fot 53

1301  The triple tiered cylinder of the Umbilicus, with the north wall of the Hemicyclium to the left.        Fot 5787

1302  The Umbilicus beside the Arch of Septimius Severus, and a column shaft from the Milliarium Aureum, which now
     lies below the Temple of Saturn (s. II, 751) – L. Rossini, Archi, tav. LII, 1835.                      Fot 6178

USTRINA ANTONINORUM. A podium, 13 m. square, surrounded by a double enclosure, was discovered on the south side of the Column of Antoninus Pius, when the latter was excavated in 1703 (s. Columna Antonini I, p. 270). The enclosure was entered from the north, on the side facing the column. Francesco Bianchini took part in the excavations, and produced a detailed account of them (RM IV, 1889, pp. 49–59). He identified the complex as the Ustrinum for the funeral pyres of Faustina and Antoninus Pius. It was surrounded by an inner wall, and an outer balustrade, both constructed in travertine. A similar edifice, with identical measurements, came to light during the construction of the new Parliament building, in 1907, between Piazza del Parlamento, Via della Missione and Via dell'Impresa. Marble blocks from the central podium, together with various architectural fragments, were removed to the Museo Nazionale Romano, while the monument itself, still not fully excavated, disappeared in the foundations of the new Chamber of Deputies. It is likely to be the Ustrinum of Marcus Aurelius.

CH. HÜLSEN, RM IV, 1889, pp. 48–64; H. JORDAN, Top I, 3, p. 604 f.; D. VAGLIERI, NSc, 1907, pp.525–528, 681; 1908, pp. 19, 46; A. PASQUI, NSc, 1909, pp. 10 f., 429 f.; G. GATTI, BCom XXXV, 1907, p. 326 f.; XXXVI, 1908, p. 86; XXXVII, 1909, p. 113; XXXVIII, 1910, p. 245; R. LANCIANI, RendLinc 5, XVII, 1908, p. 92; R. PARIBENI, BArte IV, 1910, pp. 315–317; G. MANCINI, StRom I, 1913, pp. 3–15; R. DELBRÜCK, AA, 1913, pp. 140–143; R. PARIBENI, OP II, pp. 32–35; id., MusNaz, p. 52, No. 5; P-A, p. 545; G. LUGLI, Mon III, pp. 249–252; B. GOETZE, Ein röm. Rundgrab in Falerii, 1939, pp. 14, 38; L. CREMA, ArchRom, p. 505.

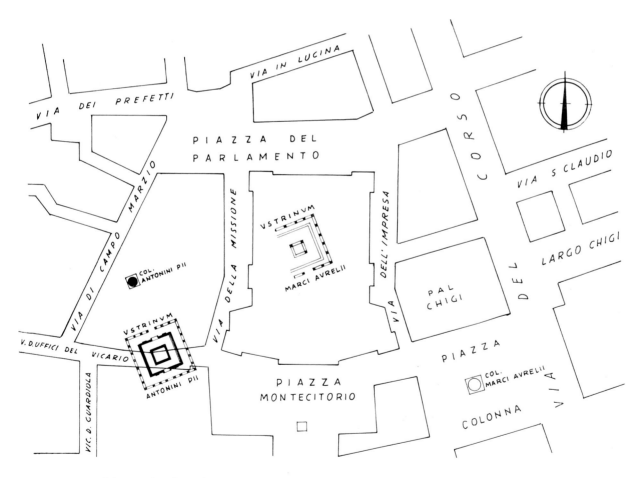

1303 Site-plan of the Ustrina Antoninorum.

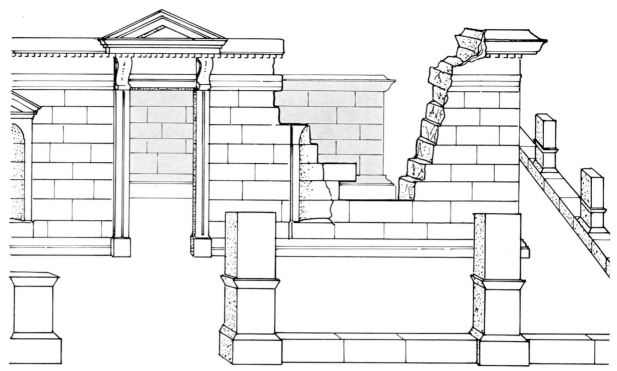

1304 Reconstruction of the remains of the Ustrinum of Antoninus Pius, from a drawing by Bianchini in Codex Veronese
356 (RM IV, 1889, p. 57).

1305 Acroteria and architectural fragments from the Ustrinum, found in 1907, on the site of the new Parliament building.
Fot 686

1306 Marble blocks from the Ustrinum of Piazza del Parlamento, now in the Museo Nazionale Romano.     Fot 685

1307 A marble dado and capping from the Ustrinum, now in the Museo Nazionale Romano.     Fot 684

VEIOVIS, TEMPLUM. The Temple of Veiovis stood behind the Tabularium, between the two summits of the Capitoline. In literature it was called "inter duos lucos" (Vitruvius IV, 8, 4) or "inter Arcum et Capitolium" (Gellius V, 12). When a subterranean corridor was built in 1939, to connect the three palaces on the Piazza del Campidoglio, the temple was discovered under the south-west corner of the Palazzo Senatorio. The remains date from a restoration of the temple, which coincides with the building of the Tabularium in 78 B. C. Archaeological probes under the podium of the excavated temple, establish the existence of an earlier temple of the middle of the 2nd century B. C., and also reveal traces of the first temple, which was vowed by the praetor L. Furius Purpurio in 196 B. C., and consecrated by Q. Marcius Ralla four years later.

H. JORDAN, Top I, 2, p. 115 f.; O. GILBERT, Rom II, pp. 99–101; W. H. ROSCHER VI, pp. 174–176; P-A, p. 548 f.; A. M. COLINI, BCom LXVII, 1939, p. 201; id., BCom LXX, 1942, pp. 5–56; A. MUÑOZ, Capitolium XV, 1940, p. 626 f.; G. MARCHETTI-LONGHI, ib., pp. 789–802; id., RM LVIII, 1943, pp. 32–42; H. FUHRMANN, AA, 1940, p. 457; C. PIETRANGELI, Arti Figurative I, 1945, p. 81; G. LUGLI, Centro, pp. 39–42; id., Tecnica II, Tav. LV, 2; CH. PICARD, RA 6, XXV, 1946, pp. 70–75; M. E. BLAKE I, p. 143; II, p. 102; L. CREMA, ArchRom, p. 47; K. LATTE, Römische Religionsgeschichte, 1960, pp. 81–83; E. GJERSTAD, ActaInstSueciae XVII, 3, 1960, pp. 207–209.

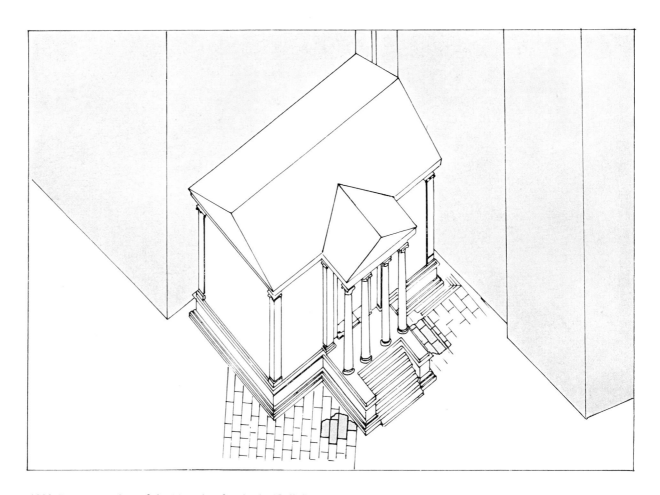

1308 Reconstruction of the Temple of Veiovis (Colini).

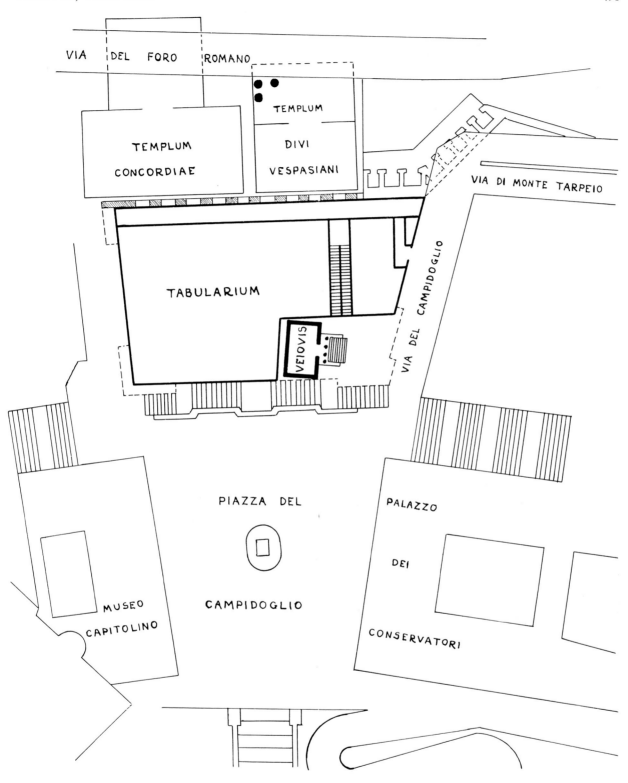

1309 Site-plan of the temple.

1310  The right side of the pronaos, with the cella on the right.                        Rip X  C/3960

1311  The north-east corner of the podium of the temple.                                    Inst Neg 41.1775

1312 The right side of the stairway.

Rip X C/4038

1313 The cult statue of Veiovis.
Inst Neg 54.120

VENUS ET ROMA, TEMPLUM. Hadrian built a temple on the Velia dedicated to Roma and to Venus, the legendary ancestress of the Roman people. It stood on the site of the vestibule of the Domus Aurea, where Nero had erected a colossal statue of himself (s. Colossus Neronis I, p. 268). The building was started on the 21st April 121 A. D., and consecrated either in 136 or 137 A. D. Maxentius rebuilt the temple after a fire in 307 A. D. Only the podium of the Hadrianic building remains; the whole of the upper structure, including the marble floor of the cellae, belongs to the rebuilding by Maxentius. The ruins of the temple were excavated in 1810/14 and 1827/29. The existing columns of the podium were re-erected in 1934/35.

A. PALLADIO, I Quattro Libri dell'Architettura, 1570, IV, pp. 36–38; G. ZORZI, Palladio, p. 77, figg. 168, 169; C. BUNSEN, BullInst, 1829, p. 32; A. NIBBY, Rom Ant II, pp. 723–740; PLATNER-BUNSEN, Beschreibung III, 1, pp. 299–308; F. REBER, Ruinen, pp. 400–405; V. LALOUX, Mél II, 1882, pp. 362-378; R. LANCIANI, Ruins, pp. 194–198; id., Storia I, pp. 40, 53, 57, 98; II, pp. 220–222; CH. HÜLSEN, FR, pp. 218–222; H. JORDAN, Top I, 3, pp. 17–20; E. DE RUGGIERO, pp. 185–190; G. CULTRERA, MemLinc 5, XVII, 1923, p. 525; G. T. RIVOIRA, RomArch, pp. 131 f., 215; H. MATTINGLY, JRS XV, 1925, p. 219 f.; P-A, pp. 552–554; C. Ricci, VdI, pp. 75–78; J. GAGÉ, Revue Études Latines XI, 1933, pp. 415, 418–421; id., Mélanges F. Cumont, 1936, pp. 151–187; P. L. STRACK, Untersuchungen z. röm. Reichsprägung II, 1933, pp. 102 f., 174–177; A. MUÑOZ, Capitolium XI, 1935, pp. 215–234; id., La sistemazione del Tempio di Venere e Roma, 1935; G. A. S. SNIJDER, JdI LV, 1940, pp. 1–11; D. F. BROWN, AN, pp. 241–248; G. LUGLI, Centro, pp. 234–240 (Bibl: p. 240); id., Tecnica II, Tavv. C, 2; CCIX, 3; H. BLOCH, Bolli, pp. 250–253; F. CASTAGNOLI, ArchStorPat LXX, 1947, pp. 163–169; D. E. STRONG, BSR XXI, 1953, pp. 122 f., 127-129; L. CREMA, ArchRom, pp. 382, 584.

1314  The Temple of Venus and Roma, seen from the east.                                    Fot 216

1315  The cella of Venus.                                                              Fot 214

498

VENUS ET ROMA, TEMPLUM

1316 A coin of Antoninus Pius with the Temple of Venus
and Roma (BMC, Emp IV, p. 206, Ni. 1284, 1285).
Fot 4705

1317 The podium of the Temple of Venus and Roma, with the columns which were re-erected in 1934/35.　　Fot 217

1318 The cella of Roma, with the marble floor of the time of Maxentius. Fot 4246

VERMINUS, ARA. In February 1876, an altar was discovered in a tower of the inner wall of the Agger Servianus (II, 808). It had been dedicated to the deity Verminus by a certain A. Postumius Albinus, described in the inscription as "duovir lege Plaetoria" (CIL VI, 3732, 31057). The same Postumius also renewed the altar in front of Temple C, in the Area Sacra del Largo Argentina. Verminus was apparently venerated as the protector of cattle against worm disease (verminatio), the name being derived from vermis. Hence it is probable that Postumius Albinus was the consul of the year 180 B. C., who erected an altar to Verminus during the pestilence of 175 and 174 B. C. (Livy XLI, 21).

G. HENZEN, BullInst, 1876, p. 85 f.; R. LANCIANI, BCom IV, 1876, pp. 24–29; F. STUDNICZKA, ÖJh VI, 1903, p. 142; CH. HÜLSEN, RM XX, 1905, p. 41 f.; W. HELBIG, Führer I, p. 595 f., No. 1043; H. C. BOWERMAN, Roman sacrificial altars, 1913, p. 10 f.; W. H. ROSCHER VI, p. 214 f.; P-A, p. 555 f.; G. SÄF-LUND, Eranos XXVIII, 1930, pp. 188–194; id., Mura, p. 157; G. LUGLI, Historia VII, 1933, pp. 27–30; G. MARCHETTI-LONGHI, BCom LXI, 1933, pp. 178– 190; LXXI, 1943/45, p. 58; F. MÜNZER, BCom LXVII, 1939, pp. 27–30; D. MUSTILLI, p. 8, No. 14 (Bibl: p. 8); M. E. BLAKE I, p. 137; G. DE SANCTIS, RivFil LXIII, 1935, p. 126; id., Storia dei Romani IV, II, 1, 1953, p. 305; A. DEGRASSI, Doxa II, 1949, p. 67 f.; id., Inscr. Lat. liberae rei publicae I, 1957, p. 162, No. 281; F. CASTAGNOLI, BCom LXXVII, 1959/60, p. 18.

1319 The altar of Verminus in the Museo Nuovo Capitolino.                                    Mus Cap C/14

VESPASIANUS, DIVUS, TEMPLUM. The Temple of Vespasian stands between the Temple of Concord and the Porticus Deorum Consentium. It was started by Titus and finished by Domitian, and is referred to in the Constantinian Regionary Catalogue as TEMPLUM VESPASIANI ET TITI (CodTop I, p. 115 f.), although the dedicatory inscription mentioned Divus Vespasianus Augustus alone (CIL VI, 938). This inscription was copied in the 8th century by the Anonymous Einsidlensis. The temple was restored by Septimius Severus and Caracalla. The three columns of the north-east corner are preserved. Until 1813, they were buried for about two thirds of their height and, when the surrounding earth was removed, the structure was found to have been so much weakened by stone robbers, that it was necessary to dismantle and re-erect the columns on strengthened foundations.

G. VALADIER, Racc. delle più insigne fabbriche di Roma antica V, 1818; C. BUNSEN, BullInst, 1829, p. 33; TOURNON, Études statistiques sur Rome II, 1831, pp. 245 f., 281 f., pls. 18–21; ST. PIALE, Degli antichi templi di Vespasiano e della Concordia, Dissertazioni II, 1833, XXIII; A. NIBBY, RomAnt I, pp. 541–545; L. CANINA, AnnInst, 1851, p. 276; F. REBER, Ruinen, pp. 81–86; H. JORDAN, Top I, 2, p. 192 f.; J. H. MIDDLETON I, pp. 338–340; R. LANCIANI, Ruins, pp. 288–291; CH. HÜLSEN, FR, pp. 84–86; H. THÉDENAT, FR, pp. 158 f., 361 f.; E. DE RUGGIERO, pp. 201–203; E. B. VAN DEMAN, AJA XVI, 1912, p. 410 f.; E. STRONG, SR I, p. 129; P-A, p. 556; P. H. VON BLANCKENHAGEN, FlArch, pp. 60–62; G. LUGLI, Centro, p. 114; id., Tecnica I, p. 333; M. E. BLAKE II, p. 97; L. CREMA, ArchRom, p. 283.

1320 The Temple of Vespasian; to the left, the columns of the pronaos, to the right, the rear wall of the cella against the Tabularium.                                                                 Fot 191

1321 The podium of the temple, with the pedestal on which the statues of the deified Vespasian and Titus stood. A built-up gate of the Tabularium is seen behind the rear wall of the cella (s. a. II, 1197).                          Fot 190

1322 The three columns of the north-east corner of the temple; the last letters of the dedicatory inscription (CIL VI, 938) appear on the entablature.                                                                                                                  Fot 189

1323 A fragment of the frieze of the Temple of Vespasian, decorated with implements of sacrifice and bulls' skulls; now in the Tabularium.                                                    Anderson 3240

VESTA, AEDES. The Temple of Vesta, which stood on the Sacra Via opposite the Regia, was excavated in 1883, and in 1899/1900. It was partly restored in 1930. According to legend, it was founded by Numa Pompilius, the second king of Rome, and it was destroyed by fire and rebuilt several times. The remains of the foundations and the podium date from the time of Augustus (14–12 B. C.), whereas most of the architectural fragments belong to a restoration by Iulia Domna, consort of Septimius Severus, at the beginning of the 3rd century A. D., after it had been burnt down in the reign of Commodus (191 A. D.).

R. LANCIANI, NSc, 1882, pp. 229–233; H. JORDAN, Top I, 2, pp. 290 f., 421–423; id., Der Tempel der Vesta u. d. Haus d. Vestalinnen, 1886, pp. 3–25; H. AUER, Der Tempel d. Vesta u. d. Haus der Vestalinnen, 1888, pp. 10–20 (217–226); H. DE GEYMÜLLER, Mél XI, 1891, p. 136, pl. I; CH. HÜLSEN, RM VII, 1892, pp. 284–287; VIII, 1893, p. 285 f.; R. LANCIANI, Ruins, pp. 221–224 (Bibl: p. 224); G. BONI, NSc, 1900, pp. 159–191; id., AttiScStor, pp. 525–530; D. VAGLIERI, BCom XXVIII, 1900, pp. 281–285; XXXI 1903, pp. 57–69; TH. ASHBY, CR XIII, 1899, p. 184 f.; XV, 1901, p. 139; H. DRESSEL, Zeitschrift f. Numismatik XXII, 1900, pp. 20–31; CH. HÜLSEN, RM XVII, 1902, pp. 88–92; id., FR, pp. 175–181; R. LANCIANI, Storia II, p. 203 f.; W. ALTMANN, Rundbauten, pp. 51–60; E. B. VAN DEMAN, AJA, XVI,

1324 The Temple of Vesta in the Forum, the podium.                                    Fot 256

1912, pp. 393, 413, 426; H. Thédenat, FR, pp. 84–91, 312–314; E. De Ruggiero, pp. 126–137; Capitolium II, 1926/27, pp. 219–224; G. Cozzo, Boll. dell'Assoz. Archeol. Romana, N. S. I, 1929, pp. 16–19; P-A, pp. 557–559, 59; W. Technau, AA, 1930, p. 359 f.; A. Bartoli, BCom LXI, 1933, p. 259 f.; id., RendPontAcc 3, XXI, 1945/46, p. 5 f.; id., MALinc XLV, 1959, pp. 2–143; D. F. Brown, AN, pp. 260–272; H. Bloch, Bolli, p. 84 f.; G. Lugli, Centro, pp. 202–208 (Bibl: p. 212); id., Tecnica I, p. 430, 441; II, Tav. XCIX, 1; M. E. Blake I, p. 120; II, p. 89; G. A. Mansuelli, Galleria degli Uffizi, le sculture I, 1958, p. 168, No. 143; S. Stucchi, Mon, pp. 89–95; G. Carettoni, JRS L, 1960, p. 193 f.; E. Gjerstad, ActaInstSueciae XVII, 3, 1960, pp. 310–320, 359–374; L. Crema, ArchRom, pp. 48, 522.

1325  The Temple of Vesta with the exterior partly reconstructed in 1930.                                            Fot 255

1326 A coin of Iulia Domna, showing the Temple of Vesta which had been restored by her (BMC, Emp. V, p. 169, No. 97).

Fot 3242

1327 The relief, showing the Temple of Vesta, in the Uffizi in Florence before it was restored in 1783, when it was sent from Rome to Florence.                    Fot 3004

1328 The relief after restoration; the new capital of the right pilaster behind the temple is obviously wrongly restored.
Alinari 45942

1329  The aedicula Vestae, for the image of the goddess; it dates from the time of Hadrian, and has capitals similar to
those on the relief in Florence.                                                                             Fot 257

VESTA IN DOMO PALATINA. On March 6th in the year 12 B. C., Augustus became Pontifex Maximus, and handed the official residence, the Domus Publica (s. I, p. 362), over to the Vestal Virgins. On April 28th in the same year, he dedicated a shrine to the goddess Vesta, in his own house on the Palatine. The Fasti Praenestini (CIL I², p. 236) call this sanctuary "signum et ara"*, while in the Fasti Caeretani (CIL I², p. 213) it is only "signum". The Vestal sanctuary of the Palatine may be recognized on the Pedestal of Augustus, in the Museum at Sorrento, and also on a coin of Tiberius, struck in memory of "Divus Augustus Pater". If so, it was a circular Ionic temple, having, on pillars in front of it, a bull and a ram. The same arrangement appears in a relief, depicting a sacrifice to Vesta, in the Palermo Museum; although the Ionic columns of different heights, in the background of this relief, can scarcely represent a temple.

R. LANCIANI, BCom XI, 1883, pp. 198–202; E. SAMTER, RM IX, 1894, pp. 125–133; CH. HÜLSEN, ib., pp. 238–245; id., RM X, 1895, pp. 28–37; W. ALTMANN, Rundbauten, p. 72; H. JORDAN, Top I, 3, p. 75 f.; A. BARTOLI, NSc, 1929, pp. 26–28; P-A, p. 557; G. E. RIZZO, BCom LX, 1932, pp. 25–50; G. LUGLI, Centro, p. 441 f.; id., Atti Acc. di S. Luca, N. S. I, 1951/52, pp. 49–51; A. DEGRASSI, Actes du II congrès intern. d'épigraphie grecque et latine, 1953, p. 99 f.; id., RM LXII, 1955, pp. 144–154; I. SCOTT RYBERG, Rites, pp. 48–53; S. STUCCHI, Mon, pp. 7–10 et passim.

* Degrassis' new reading of Fast. Praen. as "signum et ara" in place of the former reading "aedicula et ara", is not by itself an argument against the existence of a Temple of Vesta on the Palatine. It rather supports the theory that the relief and the coin depict a temple of "Vesta in Domo Palatina", since the building shown is a circular temple, and not an aedicula.

1330 A relief in the Palermo Museum, showing the goddess Vesta, Vestal Virgins, and the Pontifex Maximus, together with a bull and a ram on pedestals, an altar and an architectural background.

1331 Coin of Tiberius, depicting a round temple, with a bull and a ram on pedestals.                    MCR B/750

1332 Marble pedestal in the Museum at Sorrento, showing the goddess Vesta in the foreground, with an Ionic rotunda behind, and a bull and a ram on pedestals.                                                                 Fot 3033

VICUS IUGARIUS. From earliest times, a trade route led through the Sabine territory, from Praeneste and Tibur to the Roman river crossing. It followed the line where, later, the Clivus Suburanus and the Argiletum lay; and the part which lay nearest to the Tiber became the Vicus Iugarius, passing from the Forum to the Porta Carmentalis of the Servian Wall. In 1882, the part of the Vicus Iugarius, between the Temple of Saturn and the Basilica Iulia, was excavated down to its ancient level; while the man-high cloaca, which lies beneath it, was explored as far as the apse of S. Maria della Consolazione. At the point where the Vicus Iugarius enters the Forum, it was spanned by an arch (ianus). The brick and travertine of this arch are still visible, beside the north-west portico of the Basilica Iulia, and beside the podium of the Temple of Saturn.

R. LANCIANI, NSc, 1883, pp. 14, 47 f.; H. JORDAN, Top I, 1, pp. 515–517; I, 2, p. 468; O. GILBERT, Rom I, pp. 257–263; III, p. 416 f.; B. LUINI, BCom XXVII, 1899, pp. 248–250; CH. HÜLSEN, RM XVII, 1902, p. 9 f.; TH. ASHBY, CR XVI, 1902, p. 94; H. THÉDENAT, FR, pp. 175, 225 f.; E. DE RUGGIERO, pp. 510–512; E. B. VAN DEMAN, JRS XII, 1922, p. 17 f.; P-A, p. 574 f.; G. SÄFLUND, Mura, p. 180 f.; G. COZZO, Il luogo primitivo di Roma, 1935, p. 121 f.; G. LUGLI, Atti 3 CStR I, p. 257; A. MUÑOZ, L'isolamento del Colle Capitolino, 1943, p. 39 f.; G. MARCHETTI-LONGHI, RendPontAcc 3, XX, 1943/44, pp. 14–21, 48–52; G. LUGLI, Centro, pp. 78, 531–533; M. E. BLAKE I, p. 160; E. NASH, AC XI, 1959, p. 232.

1333 The Vicus Iugarius, between the Temple of Saturn and the Basilica Iulia. To the right, a brick pier of the street-arch (ianus), marking the entry to the Forum.

Fot 117

VICUS TUSCUS. The street, whose name implies that there was a quarter in the city inhabited by Etruscans, entered the Sacra Via between the Temple of Castor and the Basilica Iulia. It connected the Forum Romanum with the Forum Boarium and the Circus Maximus. During the excavation of the Temple of Castor, in 1871, the part of the Vicus Tuscus along its north-west side, was explored. Under the polygonal paving of the imperial period, an older street of small cubes of brick was discovered, which is earlier than the Tiberian rebuilding of the Temple of Castor. Behind the temple, stood the statue of the Etruscan god VORTUMNUS, the base of which was found in 1549. Its inscription (CIL VI, 804) refers to a restoration by Diocletian and Maximinian, at the beginning of the 4th century.

TH. MOMMSEN, Gesammelte Schriften V, 1908, p. 56 (Archäol. Zeitung IV, 1846, p. 227); A. PELLEGRINI, BullInst, 1871, p. 130; P. ROSA, Relazione, pp. 53, 55; H. JORDAN, Top I, 1, pp. 273 f., 517 f.; I, 2, pp. 468–470; O. GILBERT, Rom II, pp. 101–118; III, p. 416; R. LANCIANI, Ruins, p. 119; id., Storia II, p. 204 f.; G. GATTI, BCom XXVII, 1899, p. 253; TH. ASHBY, CR XIII, 1899, p. 466; CH. HÜLSEN, FR, p. 144; H. THÉDENAT, FR, pp. 145, 174, 213 f.; E. DE RUGGIERO, p. 509 f.; E.B. VAN DEMAN, JRS XII, 1922, p. 16 f.; P-A, pp. 579 f., 489; G. COZZO, Il luogo primitivo di Roma, 1935, pp. 105–110; G. MARCHETTI-LONGHI, RendPontAcc 3, XX, 1943/44, pp. 14–17; G. LUGLI, Centro, p. 78 f.

1334 The Vicus Tuscus, between the Basilica Iulia and the Temple of Castor.                    Fot 119

VIVARIUM. Wild animals destined for the amphitheatre were kept in an enclosure called the Vivarium (Gellius II, 20). At Rome, it lay immediately outside the Porta Praenestina, between the Via Labicana (now Casilina) and those arches of the Aqua Claudia (q. v. I, 30) which were built into the Aurelian Wall. According to Procopius' description of the unsuccessful Gothic attack, in the year 537 A. D. (Bell. Got. I, 22, 23), it consisted of a low, unfortified wall, running parallel with the Claudian aqueduct, until it joined the city wall close to the Porta Praenestina. A gate led into the enclosure from the side of the city. In an inscription of 241 A. D. (CIL VI, 130), we hear also of a CUSTOS VIVARI. The arches of the aqueduct, which had been walled up since the time of Aurelian, and constituted the southern wall of the Vivarium, were reopened in 1955, to ease the flow of modern traffic. In mediaeval literature, the name Vivarium is applied to the Praetorian Camp, while an adjacent building is sometimes called Vivariolum; obviously erroneous identifications, considering Procopius' explicit description. Even in recent times, some topographers have perpetuated the mistake.

NARDINI–NIBBY II, p. 17 f.; A. NIBBY, RomAnt I, pp. 385–387; L. CANINA, AnnInst, 1838, p. 207 f.; R. LANCIANI, BCom IV, 1876, p. 188; L. BRUZZA, ib. V, 1877, p. 93; P. ADINOLFI II, p. 267 f.; R. LANCIANI, Ruins, p. 383 f.; id., Storia II, pp. 247–249; H. JORDAN, Top I, 3, pp. 365–367, 391 f.; P-A, p. 582 f.; I. A. RICHMOND, Wall, p. 184; U. Gnoli, Topografia e Toponomastica di Roma medioevale e moderna, 1939, p. 348; G. LUGLI, Mon II, p. 188; III, p. 484; A. M. COLINI, Celio, p. 117.

1335 The site of the Vivarium, outside the Porta Maggiore.                                    Fot 648

VOLCANAL. Since, by ancient tradition, sanctuaries of Vulcan, the fire god, have to be built outside the city, it follows that the Volcanal, at the base of the Capitoline, must go back to the period when the Forum was still outside the inhabited area of the two primitive villages; that of the Latins on the Palatine, and that of the Sabines on the Quirinal Hill. The AREA VOLCANI lay above the Comitium, and in the time of the Kings and in the early Republic, it was used as a platform from which to address the people, who were assembled in the Comitium. Originally, the sacred enclosure of Vulcan extended from the place where the Temple of Concord now stands, to the Rostra and the Arch of Septimius Severus. To embrace differences in level of some 5 m. between these extremes, it must have been terraced in steps. An altar was discovered in 1901 and, at the same time, a tufa pavement with a drainage channel, which appears to mark the south-east boundary of the sanctuary. Although only 6 m. apart, the difference in level between the two features is 1.43 m. (BCom XXX, 1902, Tav. IV; RM XX, 1905, Taf. I). The Temple of Concord and the Rostra encroached so far on the Area Volcani, that there remained only a small space around the altar, which itself measured 3.95 × 2.80 m. Even so, the cult continued into imperial times, as an inscription dedicated to Vulcan by Augustus in 9 B. C. attests (CIL VI, 457).

O. GILBERT, Rom I, pp. 248–257; H. JORDAN, Top I, 2, pp. 339–341; CH. HÜLSEN, RM VIII, 1893, p. 87[1] f.; TH. ASHBY, CR XV, 1901, p. 89; XVI, 1902, p. 94; D. VAGLIERI, BCom XXX, 1902, p. 25 f.; XXXI, 1903, pp. 159–162; R. LANCIANI, BCom XXX, 1902, pp. 125–133, Tav. IV; id., Storia II, p. 187; CH. HÜLSEN, RM XVII, 1902, p. 10 f.; XX, 1905, pp. 7–9, Taf. I; id., FR, pp. 76–78; O. RICHTER, Beiträge IV, p. 16 f.; H. THÉDENAT, FR, pp. 69–71; E. DE RUGGIERO, pp. 229–233; T. FRANK, Buildings, p. 59; F. VON DUHN, Italische Gräberkunde I, 1924, pp. 414–417; P–A, p. 583 f.; G. LUGLI, Centro, p. 147 f.; K. LATTE, Römische Religionsgeschichte, 1960, p. 129 f.

1336 The rock hewn altar of Vulcan, immediately to the west of the Umbilicus Urbis Romae.
Fot 65

1337  A drainage channel, with tufa pavement to the right and a step to the left; part of the south-east boundary of the
      Volcanal.                                                                                              Fot 5758

VOLCANAL                                                                                  519

1338  Tufa pavement, drainage channel and step, seen from the Umbilicus.                    Fot 5760

# GENERAL INDEX

# INSCRIPTIONS

APOLLO PALATINUS I, p. 31, Bibl: H. A. CAHN, Museum Helveticum I, 1944, pp. 203–208; id., Numismatica XII, 1946, pp. 49–53

APPIADES I, p. 33, Bibl. col. 2, line 2: for Prasiteles read Pasiteles

ARA PACIS AUGUSTAE I, p. 63, Bibl: L. BUDDE, Forschungen u. Fortschritte XXIV, 1948, pp. 32–34; A. WOTSCHITZKY, ÖJh XLII, 1955, pp. 42–53; J. M. C. TOYNBEE, JRS LI, 1961, pp. 153–156

ARCUS AUGUSTI I, p. 93: plan fig. 94, incorrectly assembled in certain copies of the first printing, to be corrected as shown herewith

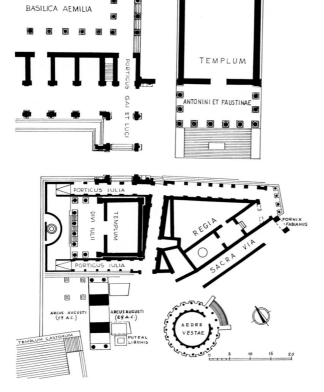

ARCUS CONSTANTINI I, p. 104, Bibl: I. MAULL, ÖJh XLII, 1955, pp. 53–67; F. SANGUINETTI, Palladio N. S. X, 1960, pp. 84–89

ARCUS DOLABELLAE ET SILANI I, p. 113, line 2: for C. Julius Silanus read C. Junius Silanus

ATRIUM VESTAE I, p. 154, Bibl: E. WELIN, SFR, pp. 207–214

BASILICA IULIA I, p. 186, Bibl: G. CARETTONI–L. FABBRINI, RendLinc 8, XVI, 1961, pp. 53–60

BASILICA NEPTUNI I, p. 196, Bibl: P-A, pp. 81, 519 f.; L. RESPIGHI, RendPontAcc 3, IX, 1933, pp. 119–123; G. GATTI, BCom LXII, 1934, p. 172

CARCER MAMERTINUS I, p. 206, line 5 f.: C. Vibius Rufinus and M. Cocceius Nerva who are mentioned in the inscription held the office of consul between 39 and 41 A. D. and not in 22, when another M. Cocceius Nerva was consul (A. Degressi, I Fasti Consolari dell'Impero Romano, 1952, pp. 8, 11; id., Epigraphica VIII, 1946, p. 37 f.; F. W. Adams, AJA LV, 1951, p. 240; M. E. Blake II, p. 19)

CERES LIBER LIBERAQUE I, p. 227, Bibl: A. ALFÖLDI, Studi e materiali di storia delle religioni XXXII, 1961, pp. 30–39

CHALCIDICUM I, p. 230, Bibl. col. 2, line 4: G. LUGLI, Centro, for p. 182 read 132

COLOSSUS NERONIS I, p. 268, Bibl. col. 1, line 3 f.: F. PRÉCHAC, Mél XXXVII, 1918/19, pp. 285–296 instead of 1913, p. 133 f.

COLUMNA TRAIANA I, p. 283, Bibl: H. St. JONES, BSR V, 1910, pp. 435–459; M. TURCAN DÉLÉANI, Mél LXX, 1958, pp. 149–176; S. STUCCHI, RendAccNapoli XXXII, 1957, pp. 149–164; id., Contributo alla conoscenza della topografia dell'arte e della storia nella Colonna Traiana (Atti dell'Accademia di Udine 7, I, 1957/60)

CONCORDIA, TEMPLUM I, p. 292, Bibl: O. L. RICHMOND, Essays and studies pres. to W. Ridgeway, 1913, pp. 198–203; M. BERNHART, Deutsches Jahrbuch f. Numismatik I, 1938, p. 146 f.; C. C. VERMEULE, JHS LXXVII, 1957, p. 284 f.; for A. NIBBY, RomAnt II read RomAnt I, pp. 531–541

DOLIOLA I, p. 305, Bibl: C. BÉMONT, Mél LXXII, 1960, p. 140

DOMUS AUGUSTIANA I, p. 316 f., Bibl: G. CARETTONI, Studi Romani IX, 1961, pp. 508–516

HERCULES CUBANS I, p. 462, Bibl: S. STUCCHI, Il ritratto bronzeo di Costantino nel museo di Cividale (estratto Studi Goriziani XIII, 1950), pp. 28–36

IANUS GEMINUS I, p. 502, Bibl: L. A. HOLLAND, Janus and the bridge, 1961, pp. 198–203

IUPPITER O. M. CAPITOLINUS I, p. 530, Bibl: H. JUCKER, Jahrbuch des Bernischen Historischen Museums, XXXIX–XL, 1959/60, pp. 289–295

IUPPITER ULTOR I, p. 537, Bibl: G. CARETTONI, Studi Romani IX, 1961, p. 516 f.

OBELISCUS VATICANUS II, p. 161, Bibl: M. Floriani Squarciapino, Studi Romani X, 1962, pp. 167–170